FATHER LACOMBE

The Black-Robe Voyageur

BY

KATHERINE HUGHES

McCLELLAND & STEWART
PUBLISHERS - - TORONTO

Printing Statement:

Due to the very old age and scarcity of this book,
many of the pages may be hard to read due to the
blurring of the original text, possible missing pages,
missing text, dark backgrounds and other issues
beyond our control.

Because this is such an important and rare work, we
believe it is best to reproduce this book regardless of
its original condition.

Thank you for your understanding.

TO
THE FAITH AND GRIT
OF THE UNWRITTEN HEROES
IN THE OLD GUARD OF OBLATES
IN WESTERN CANADA

"Send me men girt for the combat,
    Men who are grit to the core. . . .
Send me the best of your breeding,
    Lend me your chosen ones;
Them will I take to my bosom,
    Them will I call my sons. . .
And I will not be won by weaklings,
    Subtile, suave and mild,
But by men with the hearts of Vikings,
    And the simple faith of a child."

Service.

PREFACE

NEAR the Lake of the Woods at sunrise one morning in 1882 I saw a priest standing on a flat rock, his crucifix in his right hand and his broad hat in the other, silhouetted against the rising sun, which made a golden halo about him, talking to a group of Indians—men, women and papooses—who were listening with reverent attention. It was a scene never to be forgotten, and the noble and saintly countenance of the priest brought it to me that this must be Father Lacombe of whom I had heard so much; and it was.

My acquaintance with him, begun that morning, has been full of charm to me, and my only regret is that in these later years the pleasure of meeting him has come at lengthening intervals. His life, devoted and self-sacrificing, has been like peaceful moonlight —commonplace to some, but to others full of quiet splendour, serenity, mystery and of much more for which there are no words.

We who know him love him because of his goodness and we feel that he is great; but we may not say he is great because of this or of that. His life has been hidden from the world in far-away Indian encampments and it is there we must look for accounts of his good works and great deeds.

The noble and elevating example of devotion and

self-sacrifice that has been given us by Father Lacombe in his more than sixty years of work among the
Indians of Western Canada should not be lost, for
he would be stony-hearted indeed who would not be
softened and humanized by such an example, which
must bring even to the irreligious a feeling of profound respect for the faith which inspired and sustained this good man.

It is fortunate, therefore, that Miss Hughes who
is so well fitted in every way and especially by her
intimate knowledge of the country in which Father
Lacombe has laboured so long and with the conditions
surrounding him, should have undertaken a record
of his life, with a reverent love of her subject to guide
her pen; and I regard it as a very great honour that
she has asked me to write a Preface for her book.

W. C. VAN HORNE.

Montreal, 21st April, 1910.

FOREWORD

FATHER LACOMBE's peculiarly vivid intellect—which even yet seizes upon every detail in events and people that touch on his life—holds the Past as in a mirror. To avail myself of this knowledge in securing quite accurate pictures of early Western periods and incidents I have for some years submitted this venerable man month after month to what he laughingly termed "inquisitions."

Some others of the few real Old-Timers remaining have likewise submitted to my "inquisitions," and generously contributed to my knowledge of details. Their names occur in the narrative; I desire to thank them here for their valuable assistance.

I would also acknowledge my indebtedness to my friends—Bishop Legal, who opened to me the Archives of St. Albert and his letters from Father Lacombe, the Hon. Alexander Rutherford, who gave me access to his library of rare Canadiana, and others.

K. H.

FOREWORD TO NEW EDITION

In adding a final chapter to this Life—after the passing of Père Lacombe—I desire to state for those who have not had the happiness of a personal acquaintance with him that there is no inaccuracy in the variety of tongues in which he seems to speak in this narrative of his life.

On occasions—and perhaps this is not always sufficiently indicated in the text—I simply translate into English what he, speaking in French, has said to me or to others; and the same is true of extracts from his writing in French.

But on every possible occasion I have preserved what he said to me in his own inimitable and picturesque English. The result may be to represent him as speaking broken and picturesque English at one time—and more usual English at another. But I feel that readers will understand the seeming variance.

I would also state—with regard to some of the early reviews written outside of Canada—that where I repeat conversations in Père Lacombe's Life I am not making magnificent guesses at what these people likely would have said. I am repeating from the lips of participants what actually was said—or what I myself heard.

This record is History—picturesque western History caught for posterity before it had passed out of memory—and while many of its makers still walked with us.

K. H.

CONTENTS

PART ONE

I

IN OLD QUEBEC

1839–1849

II

THE WEST BECKONS

1849

III

HIS *WANDERJAHR* AT PEMBINA

1849–1850

CONTENTS

X

A CRUSADER OF THE PLAINS

1865

XI

BATTLE BETWEEN BLACKFEET AND CREES

1865

XII

COURSING THE WIDE PLAINS

1865–1867

XIII

A HUNTING GROUND FOR SOULS

1867–1868

CONTENTS

II

OTTAWA POLITICS AND RED RIVER COLONIZING
1873–1876

III

THE PLAINS INDIANS ARE CORALLED
1876–1880

IV

CHAPLAIN ON FIRST TRANSCONTINENTAL
1880–1882

V

THE VANISHING WILDERNESS
1882–1883

CONTENTS

VI

CANADIAN PACIFIC MARKS EPOCH

1883

VII

FOUNDATION OF INDIAN SCHOOLS

1883–1884

VIII

METIS REBELLION OF 1885

1885

IX

TOURS THE EAST WITH CROWFOOT

1885–1888

X

A NEW WEST EMERGES

1882–1892

XI

MANITOBA SCHOOL QUESTION LOOMS UP

1892–1894

XII

KEEPING STEP WITH PROGRESS

1894–1896

CONTENTS

XX

EXIT

1916

PART I

FATHER LACOMBE

THE ENTRANCE

" All the world's a stage. . . .
And one man in his time plays many parts,
His Acts being seven Ages."

THE first half of the nineteenth century was drawing to a close: Canada was in the throes of national
birth. Montreal—having looked on at its Parliament Buildings destroyed by fire, and authority's
symbol, the Mace, tossed about on the shoulders of a
mob—lay in the grim shadow of a cholera epidemic.

Meanwhile—out over the beckoning trails of the
green West a stripling of twenty was making his way
into the wonderland of the *voyageurs*—the mysterious and little-known *Pays d'en Haut*. He brought
with him little more than the staff and scrip of the
medieval pilgrim—this *Monias,* but he was of the type
that trader and dusky trapper alike welcomed.

They found him at first moulded in the courtliness
and restraint of manner characteristic of the men who
tutored him in the quiet old Palace at Montreal, but
there soon sprang up in him what the eagle-eyes of
the boy had always denoted—a fearlessness, a force
and a primitive dignity that more than matched the
best material of the strong new country before him.

1

It is sixty years since then—at this time of writing
—and through all that formative period of the West
the figure of this stripling—rounding into maturity,
or bending to a venerable old age—stands silhouetted,
in imperious lines or again with tender charm, against
the pages of western history.

At the outset he appears as a knight-errant on
the western Plains—a picturesque figure with the
Red Cross of his flag floating above him, here, there
and everywhere along the prairies between the Red
River and the Mountains of the Setting Sun . . .
now sharing the tepees of the nomad tribes; now
making a stand at some mission-place—with axe and
plough guiding the Metis and Indian to the ways of
the white man . . . leading them out from the
blanket and tepee to the school and homestead.

As time passes, on some of his endless journeyings
to and fro across the Continent he appears on the
plains again—a peaceful Clovis leading his countrymen from a land outgrown to new fields of promise.
And when a young civilization of many needs, spiritual and material, emerges from the prairies—the
knight-errant of Western priesthood is found again
and again measuring the gray corridors of Canada's
Parliament Buildings or suppliant for others in the
cold magnificence of European courts.

. . . .

Then fell the evening of Life. The vigorous form
grew bent and the erstwhile shoulders narrowed.
. . . Now there remains in his Hermitage among

the foothills an old Christian medicine-man with only the warmth and light of his wonderful eyes undimmed by Time: relit perhaps with the radiance of the light that shines across the Great Divide.

I

THE character of the race from which Albert Lacombe sprang is most subtly revealed in Quebec's old legend of the *Chasse-Galerie.*

It is an exquisite mosaic of racial and domestic feeling, instinct with the warmth and daring and insouciance of the *Canadien habitant*—misty with the pathos of the *Canadien errant.*

It grew up imperceptibly in the days of the Old Regime, when the reckless *voyageurs* pushed farther and farther west in the wake of Le Verandrye's canoe, and the hearts of their womenfolk followed after.

It mirrored the dare-devil hearts of the *coureurs de bois* drawn home on New Year's Eve from far-off Athabasca and Saskatchewan to the glowing hearths of their kinsfolk on the banks of the St. Lawrence.

On that one night their souls sickened of the stern, coarse life in far-off trading posts, of stag dances in the Bachelors' Hall and the ungraceful shuffle of blanketed squaws. Their ghostly canoes—so the legend runs—rode down the winter storm with spirit-cargoes.

Their wraiths, invading the cheery homes of Quebec, embraced the old people and stole kisses from the girls in the dances—then, *mon Dieu,* were whisked up again into the canoes; and pallid with regrets borne back to the wilderness.

In this legend of the *Chasse Galerie* there is embodied the spiritual essence of French-Canada and its people—the tinge of mysticism that hints of the poet-heart, the fine daring, the warm sympathies, the quick forgetfulness, the love of home, the joy of life. And this is the land and these the people that produced Father Lacombe.

Whether or not the *Chasse Galerie* came home for the fireside feast in 1839, the chimes in the gray tower of Saint Sulpice rang out a heartening welcome to the New Year. Twenty miles across the snow the gay *carillon* was answered with peals from the churches of Montreal; and in the home of Albert Lacombe, worthy *habitant* of Saint Sulpice, there was a glad confusion.

The household was making ready for the ancient ceremony of paternal blessing that ushers in the New Year in a French-Canadian home. The father, consciously fine in his best suit of homespun and his finest linen woven by the deft hands of his goodwife, seated himself in the old *fauteuil* that had belonged to his father.

His wife—carrying herself with loving pride "like the queen of the home, doing its honours," her son recalls—stood near him, watching tenderly the mobile trusting faces of their seven little

ones as they knelt about their father's knees, resting
their baby hands on his strong limbs.

Albert the eldest voiced prettily, as his mother
had taught him, their New Year's wishes for their
father, closing with a request for a blessing upon
themselves. Then suddenly, prompted by his own
exceedingly warm heart, he broke through the usual
forms of ceremony to cry to his mother:

"And, *Maman,* you know how we love you!"

In the raftered kitchen, whose brown wooden walls
and primitive furnishings were mellowed by the early
morning firelight this vivid tableau of *habitant* life
defined the starting-place of history in the life of
Father Lacombe, who was born in this *"gentille pa-
roisse"* of St. Sulpice on February 28, 1827.

Albert Lacombe was a quietly genial, industrious
man neither rich nor poor, attached to his home and
farmwork, with a desire to see his sons follow in his
own footsteps. He and his wife had never received
any adequate education as books go, but they were
versed in all the arts that made up the round of their
simple pleasant life in the leisurely parish.

Albert, *pere,* and Albert, *fils,* each spring went back
into a cabin in the maple woods and made sugar and
syrup to supply the household for the entire year.
The father enjoyed his pipe, his jokes and tricks—
for he was full of a quaint humour—his old *camarades*
and his occasional *coup* of *boisson blanc*—the mint-
julep of the north. But he was not a hunter: he did

not even keep a gun in his house, and during the Papineau Rising of 1837 he remained unexcited, placidly loyal.

Like the majority of the Quebec *habitants* he drew an exceeding delight from his pipe and home-grown tobacco; yet each year before midnight of *Mardi Gras*, the eve of Lent, he would place his pipe with all the solemnity of a rite upon the mantel, "where it remained sleeping," says his son, "without tobacco, smoke or fire until the feast of Easter. The pipe, too, kept the fast."

Madame Agathe Lacombe, like her husband, was of a cheerful domestic nature, pious, thrifty and industrious. She was a brunette of trim, strong physique and very active. Her son, however, resembled his father in face and form rather than her.

Albert when not at school was kept closely at work on the farm, and his boyish spirit chafed at the monotonous round. Picking stones on new land, feeding the pigs, driving the plough! This, when the boy's heart in him was burning to leave the farm, to go to college—to be a great man, a priest maybe like the old *curé*, Monsieur de Viau; or perhaps to leave books altogether and like his grand-uncle, Joseph Lacombe, to go far into the *Pays d'en Haut* with the fur-company and be the most daring *voyageur* of them all. Either career seemed blissful to the boy, for these two men were the heroes of his childhood.

The kindly old *curé* grew attached to the boy. *"Mon petit sauvage"* (my little Indian), he used to call him—not only because his skin and eyes were flashing dark, but because his mother, Agathe Duhamel *dite Sans-Facon,* was the descendant of that Duhamel maiden carried into captivity over a hundred years earlier by an Ojibway chief. The French girl bore him two sons before her *voyageur* uncle stole her and the boys from a camp at Sault Ste. Marie, and restored her to the Duhamels of Saint Sulpice. One of these boys was an ancestor of Madame Lacombe.

One Sunday afternoon in the summer of 1840 Albert Lacombe with his wife and children sat sunning themselves by the doorway of their home, when the *curé* drove up to them in an old vehicle drawn by a fat old horse. He seated himself for a short intimate chat as a father might with his son.

He enquired about the crops, the farmwork, all the good *habitant's* plans; then turning suddenly toward the boy Albert he said:

"My little Indian, what are you going to do?"

The child's brain throbbed in confusion. He knew; but how could he tell *Monsieur le curé?* He looked desperately up to his father.

"Monsieur le curé," the father said, "Albert would go to the big college; but I have no means to send him. And besides I need him here to help me."

"My lad," said the old *curé* directing all his attention to the boy, "do you want very much to go to college?"

Albert, always emotional, could make no reply in

words; but his hand grasped the extended hand of the priest and the tears that shone in the dark eyes were eloquent.

"Eh, bien," said the *curé* turning to the father. "You will send him to the college, and I will pay his way. Who knows? . . . Some day our little Indian may be a priest and work for the Indians!"

In this way, thanks to M. Viau, another bright young mind was added to the regiment of talented boys without means who were then and still are being provided for in Quebec colleges by the parish priests or by religious communities.

Robust, active and ambitious as a student at L'Assomption College, the little Indian worked hard, played hard, and stood well in his classes.

The rector of the college, made aware of Albert's desire for the priesthood, placed him at the conclusion of his classics in charge of a junior class in the college, investing him at the same time with the cassock as a mark of his purpose.

In 1847 he was called to the bishop's Palace in Montreal to continue his theological studies there. Bishop Bourget assigned to him the duties of under-secretary as assistant to Canon Pare, while his theological course was pursued under the direction of Monsignor Prince, the coadjutor bishop.

These studies were shared by Edouard Fabre (afterward Archbishop of Montreal). A lifelong friendship sprang up between the young men. They discovered that they had the same birthday; and each

year when Madame Fabre—a *grande dame* of the old
school—celebrated her son's birthday she made it clear
that the fête was equally Albert's and her son's.

Life at the Palace was pleasant, yet the *voyageur*
spirit in Albert Lacombe regarded it only as a means
to an end.   Sixty years later he said:

"There at the house of the Bishop, my good protector, my dear friend, I was very happy.   They were
good to me—*le petit sauvage,* they called me.   The
Canons loved me and were kind; I cannot tell you
how kind.   I had not too much work to fatigue me.
I was well. . . .   The *curés,* the parish priests
from many parts of the country, would come there—
Oh! hundreds of them came there, one or two at a
time and camped there for three or four nights.

"They were fine pleasant men—I liked to meet
them.   They lived in comfortable houses, they were
liked by their people.   They did good work. . . .
But I would look at them and say to myself, 'No,
that is not for me.   I would not live quiet like that
for all the world.   I must go out and work—I must
save my soul in my own way.' "

In the winter of 1848 Father George Belcourt,
a missionary from the far Pembina district, sought
hospitality from the venerable bishop and alms for
his missions from the Catholics of Quebec.   He was
a powerful, big man with a rugged face and great
force of personality.   No country *curé* with delicious
morsels of talk about this or that quaint parishioner;
with preferences for this viand or that—but a man

whose tales were of the wild rush of the buffalo hunt, of the wily Saulteaux and Metis or murderous Sioux to whom he ministered; of the splendid struggle for human souls in a primitive land.

Albert Lacombe hung on the stranger's words, in the community hall, at table, everywhere he went: and when one Sunday night Father Belcourt preached in the old cathedral of St. Jacques, at least one young man in the Sanctuary listened enraptured to the tales he told and the rousing appeal he made for help.

"Sunday night, when the cathedral was filled," he has written in his letters, "the missionary went up into the pulpit and painted in an eloquent way the life and work of his missions. . . . I was struck to the heart. An interior voice called to me—'*Quem mittem?* (Whom shall I send?) and I said in reply, '*Ecce ego, mitte me*' (Behold, I am here; send me)."

The following morning he opened his mind to the bishop. And Age counselled Youth, testing its metal.

"Wait and reflect; and above all pray that you may come to know God's will in the matter. Is that the work for which the Creator has destined you?"

The young man's heart thumped in acclaim of this as his destiny, but perceiving the bishop's tender thought for himself he bided his time as patiently as he might. His early patron—the venerable Abbe Viau—who was now an invalid in a hospice nearby, counselled delay. Canon Pare and Canon Mercier

to whom he owed so much instruction, advised him to
give up the idea.

"You are happy with us; you are too young to go
so far. Stay," they said. The young man could not
argue against such affectionate opposition as this.
He went his way in silence, with his mind unchanged.

"I knew I wanted to be a priest, but failing this
mission-life, if I had to be a *curé,* I would have decided to return to the world. I wanted to make every
sacrifice, or none. That was my nature," he has said.

As spring came again the candidate's restless desire for the missions became more than ever apparent.
The bishop sent for him and after questioning him
closely to ascertain the genuineness of his vocation,
told him to prepare for ordination: he might leave
for the West the following summer. Albert was exultant, although he went about his preparation with
a tinge of sadness.

On June 13th in St. Hyacinthe on the occasion of
the annual retreat at the old college, he was raised to
the priesthood. Hundreds witnessed the ceremony,
and at the imposition of hands sixty priests in turn
approached the young Levite to place a hand on his
handsome dark head and salute him as brother.

Father Lacombe returned joyfully to Montreal,
only to have his joy dashed at the very threshold.
. . . The servant who admitted him announced
that the Abbe Viau had died suddenly that forenoon.

The young priest could not believe the news in his
first grief; only the evening before he had talked

long with his venerable patron, who seemed in the best of spirits and kissing his little Indian paternally, blessed him in leave-taking, with these words:

"*Mon cher Albert,* I shall pray to-morrow that you will always be a good and holy priest."

And now the Abbe Viau was dead. At the very hour his protege's ordination had taken place the old priest had given up his soul to his Master. "Whilst I wept beside his inanimate body," Father Lacombe wrote years later, "he seemed to say to me: '*Cursum consummavi* . . . (I have finished the course .). Take my place as priest, for I have helped to make you what you are to-day.' "

The plague of cholera now fell with blighting force on Montreal. The entire energies of the Bishop's household were directed to combatting the dread disease. Canon Mercier, a man of much charm and intellect warmly loved by Father Lacombe, was weakened by his untiring ministry and succumbed to the plague.

It was not until seven weeks after his ordination that Father Lacombe could leave for the West. His departure, marked by a most striking scene, was described at length in the *Melanges Religieux,* a church paper published in Montreal at that period. From this and other sources an account of this scene has been compiled.

Its significance—like that of the Mass that prefaced the voyages of Columbus and Cartier and Champlain, or the prayers of the departing Pilgrim

Fathers—is that great deeds of venture and self-sacrifice have always been undertaken by the believing heart, the man to whom a supernatural world is a reality. The mocker criticises from the comfortable depths of an armchair at his Club.

II

It was past sunset on the evening of July 31, 1849. In gray old Montreal, whose early history is inwoven with churchmen and church influences, in the chapel of the Bishop's Palace there was enacted that evening a religious drama which fits in well with the story of a metropolis founded by the knightly de Maisonneuve.

A young man—dark, vivid, strongly-built and black-gowned—stood on the steps before the altar, his hands almost clenched in an effort to hide the emotion that flooded him—his head upraised as in mental distress shutting out from his vision a long row of ecclesiastics, while one by one the venerable Bishop, the Canons and Abbes approached him and bent to kiss his feet.

He knew this was only the old custom taken from the Seminary of Foreign Missions at Paris, and suggested by the Biblical verse:

"How beautiful upon the mountains are the feet of him that bringeth good tidings and that preacheth peace. . . ."

He knew this, but his whole soul was in protest against it now. Once he had thought the custom strangely poetic and symbolic—but now, submitted to it himself? . . . The priest's sturdy, clear-

eyed young manhood rebelled against such tribute
from men he knew to be stronger, holier, more
worldly-wise and more intellectual than himself.   But
as they came—and came, bending silently to his feet,
the young man was seized on a moment with the awe
of a new, almost *terrible* knowledge. . . .

Hah! It was not then himself, Albert Lacombe,
the pet of the Bishop's House, the newly-ordained,
whom they saluted thus: it was instead the fulfilment
in him of the ages-old command that the Peace and
Good Will of the Christ should be carried by Christians to the bourne of the visible world! He, *"le
petit sauvage,"* the village boy of Saint Sulpice, was
now to be an ambassador of Christ—and as such these
old men honoured him.

His head sank in humility.   Protest died before
the higher thought, and the ceremony became a fresh
consecration of himself then—and for his lifetime, a
memory that did at critical moments gird him in
honour and duty and right.

"My heart was almost suffocated with emotions,"
writes Father Lacombe himself of this occasion in
his Memoirs, "when, the prayer for travellers being
said, His Lordship called me to the altar and leaving
me stand there before the tabernacle this venerable
bishop lowered himself to my feet to kiss them.
Then his coadjutor, and one after another all the
priests of the Palace. . . . Ah! . . . The
ceremony was finished, but for me its memory will
endure forever.   Still to-day in my difficulties and

hardships I think with new courage of that solemn
moment and I see again those men, long since disappeared from the world, but who watch from above,
praying for me in Heaven."

The bishop in a voice heavy with feeling added a
brief parting word.   He reminded him, says the *Melanges Religieux,* of the immensity of the sacrifice he
had imposed upon himself and of the dangers he
would incur.   .   .   .   "My dear friend, my brother,"
he continued feelingly, "we cannot go with you on
your journey, but you will be accompanied by our
prayers and our hearts' best wishes.   .   .   .

"Go where the Spirit of God has called you.   Go
to those nations still seated in darkness and ignorance.
Go to console them and make them children of God.
May the holy angels accompany you.   Go, in fine,
with all our dearest wishes and represent there the
diocese of Montreal."   Then bending toward the
young priest, he concluded solemnly:

"My son, never forget your holy and precious calling.   .   .   .   *If God is with you, who can be against
you?*"

The following morning Father Lacombe left La-
chine, still the point of embarkation for the *Pays d'en
Haut* as it had been ten years earlier when the bri-
gades of canoes set out amid cheers and the songs of
the *voyageurs.*

As the primitive steamboat pushed away from the
dock the youthful passenger sought his cabin and
fought the pain of leave-taking like a man.   He was

glad to land at Buffalo, for neither captain nor crew
had been considerate of the shy young priest who
spoke very little English. The crew, of a rough class
and unsympathetic to his race and creed, did not
trouble to hide their jeers at his long cassock—his
"petticoat," as they termed it.

From Buffalo through to Dubuque the journey
was made by boat and by stage alternately. Occasionally his fellow-passengers made themselves as
objectionable as the boat's crew had been. In all his
love-sheltered days—among the child-hearted, courteous folk of Saint Sulpice and with the refined and
gentle men of L'Assomption and the Palace—he had
seen nothing of the rougher side of life. He consequently chronicles that journey as one of the most
triste experiences of his life.

It was arranged that he should go first to Dubuque
in Iowa where Bishop Loras resided; for the mission
of Pembina on the Red River, whither he was bound,
was then in the diocesan limits of Dubuque. He
was received with wondering kindness by the venerable bishop and his vicar, Father Cretin. Both
marvelled at his air of extreme youth. On Sunday
he took part in the celebration of the Feast of the
Assumption, the patronal feast of the Church in the
United States, and preached his first sermon.

He spoke in French, for Dubuque was peopled
largely with French-Canadians. The bishop, who
formally assigned Father Lacombe to his new field,
was a cultured and pious priest from old France—

"with the mind of a statesman and the heart of a saint." He had worked in Alabama for many years and was then busily encouraging settlers to come to the rich prairies of Iowa.

The stay with Bishop Loras at Dubuque refreshed the young traveller, and he resumed his journey with new courage. On the bishop's advice he did not wear the soutane that had subjected him to such rudeness on the way from Canada, but the precaution was unnecessary. The captain and crew of the boat bound for St. Paul, with typical western tolerance, treated him very kindly and even helped him in his efforts to learn English.

For twelve days the boat puffed its slow way up the current, passing occasional encampments of Indians on the green banks. Here in the stillness and free airs of the wilderness the spirit of the great West first came to Father Lacombe. "I began to breathe freely at last; I felt myself a new man," he says of those delightful days on the Mississippi.

One day the boatmen called to him that St. Paul was at hand. He hurried forward to look on the scattered settlement of log-houses, whose occupants were hurrying down to the riverside to meet the boat. As Father Lacombe found his way up the hill along a path destined to widen into one of the main streets of St. Paul the metropolis, Father Ravoux came hurrying down to greet him.

St. Paul, which had dropped its disreputable old name of Pig's Eye to adopt the name of Abbe Galtier's mission, consisted of about thirty primitive log buildings built near the church and inhabited by French-Canadians, Metis and a few American traders. The house in which Father Ravoux entertained his young guest and on whose site a large newspaper office now stands was of logs and about eighteen feet square. It had been built by Abbe Galtier in 1841, serving as chapel and residence, and two years after Father Lacombe's visit the new Bishop Cretin took possession of it as his first episcopal palace.

Father Ravoux brought the Canadian into this bare little dwelling and asked him to consider himself master there while he waited for the Red River brigade to come. "For my part," he continued, "I must return to my headquarters at Fort Snelling this afternoon. You will officiate here to-morrow."

"But where am I to sleep?" the newcomer asked.

"Why, here," said the older priest, pointing to a long narrow box. "That box has blankets inside. Just open it up."

"But that's a coffin!" Father Lacombe cried, shuddering as his sensitive nature recoiled at the thought.

"Yes," the other agreed in the most matter of fact way. "A half-breed died in the woods the other day and I helped to make his coffin. It was too short, and we had to make another. I kept this one. It is very useful; I only had blankets before."

Studying English, listening to the yarns of the trappers and traders sunning themselves on the gossip-benches of the little village, Father Lacombe waited one month for the arrival of Father Belcourt's brigade. This was a new experience and his heart rose to it as he watched the train of clumsy carts come creaking down the trail. They were drawn by oxen, and the brigade was manned by a couple of Canadian freemen,[1] a Metis [2] and an Indian.

They loaded up the carts with supplies for the mission; then one day late in September they set out for Pembina, with Father Ravoux and the whole village looking on. They called out cheery adieux; the drivers snapped their long whips and the slow-breathing animals plodded along the trail aglow now with autumn tints.

The Pembina men announced early to the newcomer that the trails were bad through the woods, where they were obliged to travel for fear of the roving Indians. But nothing they said prepared him for the muddy roads, the marshes and creeks swollen by recent rain. At times their oxen and carts sank deep in a swamp, and the entire party was obliged to get into harness to draw them out, after they had carried most of the provisions on their backs to firm ground.

When in the neighborhood of Lac Rouge, in the country of a band of Saulteaux called the Plunderers, a fairly large party of these Indians suddenly came upon them.

---

[1] Former servants of the Hudson's Bay Company whose term of contract had expired.

[2] *Metis*—A person of mixed blood, and consequently a more correct term than "half-breeds" for natives who were in part Indians.

They exacted a tribute of food. It was not their intention to make war on a Blackrobe and Metis, but they proposed to exercise their right as master of that bit of territory. Probably, too, they were hungry. In any case the lordly braves went through the carts, took out what they wanted of provisions and articles intended for the mission. Then reducing the brigade's men to a proper state of subjection by threats the high-handed knights of the road went off in great good-humour.

The little party lightened their carts by caching some of their freight, then pushed on. They had about sickened of the trip as well as exhausted their pemmican when they met another caravan by which Father Belcourt had sent provisions. They pushed on with fresh spirit.

When one nightfall the young missionary's caravan made its way to the end of the trail, the first snowfall of the year was enveloping them in a ghostly mist, through which the lights of the rude mission-place set down in the wilderness shone as a goal of delights.

Father Belcourt came bustling out to meet him and drew him into the grateful light of the hearth. He was another sort of man than Loras or Ravoux—less fine-fibred, but splendidly strong and able to cope with any band of Indians or any western emergency. He held sway like an Emperor in this woodland kingdom, by force of his personality as well as by his office.

III

HERE in the forest-mission of Pembina, Father Lacombe was to serve the apprenticeship to his life-work, his *wanderjahre* between youth and the serious battlefield of life.

The mission had been established in 1818 by Rev. Severe Dumoulin, who with Father Provencher had answered Lord Selkirk's request for priests. A number of French freemen once employed by the North-West Company had settled with their Metis families about Pembina. In 1824 many of these settlers founded a new home on the White Horse Plains across the border. Pembina, however, remained a mission-headquarters for the wandering Saulteaux, and when Father Lacombe arrived was a village of some size composed of American half-breeds and Indians.

He at once bent himself to the study of Saulteau, one of the Algonquin dialects. He did not find the task difficult, for then and throughout his life Indian languages had a strong fascination for him. He had the further advantage of using a dictionary and grammar composed by Father Belcourt.

In December the two men went to St. Boniface to pay their respects to Bishop Provencher. On their return home Father Lacombe again applied himself

to his studies, taking spiritual charge as well of the
mission, while his intrepid superior spent the winter
journeying by dog-sleighs and on foot hundreds of
miles though the forest.

The young missionary was not dissatisfied with his
first season at Pembina. That is perhaps the best
that can be said of it. He found his small flock devout and attentive to their religious exercises during
the long quiet winter. He did not lack food of a
rough order, nor did he have any hardship to endure.
But the lack of congenial company and the comparative inactivity weighed on him. He found
vent for his restless energies only in his Indian studies.
These he devoured and consequently made notable
advance.

Spring came with warm breaths from the South-
land, pushing the anemones and bloodroot up like little friends to greet the lonely young priest. It
sounded, too, a reveille to the languid Metis. One day
a band of them came down the river in canoes from
their winter camp. Almost daily others followed by
the river or across the plains, for Pembina was a
famous rendezvous of the buffalo-hunters.

At last all the Metis of that region had gathered
there. The Mission grew in a few days to the pro-
portions of a town, and the woodland was dotted with
tents. The Pembina Metis had sowed and planted
their gardens, and were now ready with the keenest
anticipation for the yearly excursion to the prairies.

This was the Golden Age of the Indian and Metis,

when the bison still roamed the great plains in unnumbered thousands. The tender buffalo flesh, dried, fresh or pounded, made a food both appetizing and nutritious; the buffalo skin made robes for garments and bedding, hide for tepees and canoes; while on the unwooded plains the sun-dried manure served the purpose of fuel.

The buffalo in fine was the chief factor of life in the West; its pursuit the chief joy of the native. From the first the missionaries had learned to look on the time of this buffalo-hunt as most favourable for teaching Christian doctrines to the Indians. They were then most comfortable and correspondingly amiable, and in the long evenings or longer days when they sat sunning themselves while the women prepared the meat of the last kill the Indian warrior smoked his pipe happily and listened with pleasure to the old story of the Redemption.

It fell to Father Lacombe's lot to be the chaplain of the great Hunt in 1850. He was alive to the pleasures and novelty of his new assignment, for all about him the preparations of his people were tinged with joyousness and excitement. He took a hand in the preparations, but unfortunately as he was squaring a board to mend his mission-cart the broad-axe slipped and cut his right foot badly.

To his intense regret Father Belcourt decided he should remain at the Mission, but the sympathetic Metis perceiving his disappointment and anxious for his company begged his superior to let the young priest—the *Monias*—come. They promised to take every care of him, and Father Belcourt yielded.

On the great eve Father Lacombe called the band together. In the open air they recited with him the evening prayers and startled the forest-echoes with their lusty rendering of the hymns Father Belcourt had translated into Indian.

"No order," says Father Lacombe, "had been observed up to this in their mode of arrival or their preparations, but *Voila!* how the scene changes . . . !" The women and children withdrew after prayers to their lodges, and the fine discipline of a military camp suddenly pervaded the assembly. The hunters held a council to select, by a majority of votes, a Chief and ten captains, who in turn selected ten or fifteen others to act as scouts. Then they drew up anew the laws of the hunt, which were as the laws of the Medes and Persians—incontestable by the most independent once they were accepted.

The half-breed hunter Wilkie, who had been elected Chief, rose at the close of the council and asked for the hunters' acceptance of these laws as a whole. This being done by a majority of voices the Chief declared solemnly:

"If any among you do not approve of these laws, let him leave our camp and come not with us, for once we have set out together from this encampment no one will be free to separate from us."

No man left the assembly; they silently approved of its laws. These related to the time and mode of chasing buffalo, to the patrol of the camp by the guards and to the penalties fixed for the infringement of any of these laws.

The scene of departure next morning is given in detail by Father Lacombe:

"After an early Mass next morning the signal of departure was given by the guide of the day with a little flag. In an instant a great commotion ran through the whole camp. The lodges of skin and the tents were pulled down, the horses were brought into a corral from the prairie and the women made haste to pack into the carts their small household goods. Then the women and children took seats in the carts—the hunters mounted their buffalo-runners . . . and the camp set out on its march."

This remarkable procession, like some patriarchal exodus in the days of Jacob, moved slowly out over the dewy prairie shining a green-gold in the level sunlight. Propped up as comfortably as might be in a Red River cart Father Lacombe, watchful of his bandaged foot, was now off on the first of his many buffalo-hunts. He estimates there were from 800 to 1,000 carts in the camp that year and over 1,000 men, women and children, as well as hundreds of fine ponies for buffalo runners, cart horses, oxen and innumerable dogs.

Close on to the sixth day out, as the prairie air lay drenched in the mellow gold of the afternoon sun— and the slow-moving cavalcade began to throw long shadows across the tender grass, the Metis' long disorderly lines drew near to the Turtle Mountains. Scouts pushing on ahead saw in the distance an immense herd of buffalo, and thrilled with delight they hurried to the nearest hill and signalled the good news to their party.

The information flashed back by the flags was intoxicating. Joy like an infectious laugh ran through the whole regiment of marching Metis, and the buffalo-ponies, keen for the hunt as their masters were, understood the sudden commotion and halt. In a trice the women, children and old men dragged out the lodge poles and skins and erected the camp. The hunting-ponies were led aside, swiftly mounted —and presto! in a flash men and horses hurled themselves against the herd.

In full gallop, Father Lacombe with them, they flashed along the prairie and in less time than an onlooker could credit it the bluff, on which the scouts had paused, was covered with this cavalry of the plains. . . . U-la-la! On the green rolling prairies stretching before them to the horizon buffalo were grazing—thousands of them, forming a billowy black lake on the prairie.

"Our captains," writes Father Lacombe, "gave the word, and the hunters instantly fell into place forming one immense line of attack. It was all done with the least possible noise or commotion, so that the unsuspecting animals might not be aroused. For while their vision is short, their hearing and power of smell are very acute. Our ponies lined up without direction from their masters, pawing up the short herbage and dust—as ardent for the chase as the riders they carried."

Father Lacombe recited an Act of Contrition to which the hunters responded with bent heads. They raised their eyes, took a long glad survey from the bluff—then—

"*En avant!*" the leader cried, and men and horses as one flew forward with whirlwind velocity—and the poor stupid buffalo pitilessly trapped broke into confused flight.

The stillness of the plains was broken with the heavy thunder of stampeded bison, the shrillings of the Metis and the tumult of the rushing ponies blended with the animals' mad bellowing.

"What a scene! What confusion!" writes Father Lacombe in reminiscence. "The story of combats of Spanish bulls furious at their adversaries conveys a feeble picture compared to this magnificent attack. . . . of the men of the prairie attacking, defying, maddening the great beast of the plains. The buffalo, naturally timid and fearful, grows enraged at his pursuers, and from the moment he is wounded he becomes terrible and dangerous."

The Cossack and his marvels of horsemanship, the cowboy and his feats of broncho-riding have had their praises sung the world over—but the Metis buffalo-hunter of the Canadian plains has never yet had his due. These hunts, as described by Father Lacombe, were always filled with marvels of horsemanship.

. . . The hunter's daring as he urged his pony in
and out labyrinth paths among the doomed buffalo, was fiendish: he was exposing himself momenta-
rily to be thrown from his horse and trampled into
the earth under a hundred cruel insentient hoofs, or
to become a human plaything tossed again and again
into the air from the horns of an enraged animal.

As the hunters pressed on to harry the buffaloes,
they dropped the reins, guiding their ponies by the
pressure of their limbs only, or bending their half-
naked supple bodies now to this side, then to that—
while the trained pony responded with an obedience
that made rider and pony one. Each hunter carried a powder-horn at his belt and bullets in his
mouth; and discharging and reloading their short
flint-lock muskets with incredible dexterity, they
aimed at vital parts of the huge blundering beasts
beside them.

Sometimes in their driving haste a bullet slipped
down in the barrel of the gun and the charge ex-
ploded, lacerating the unfortunate Indian or Metis—
and the end was a tragedy! . . . Again borne
along in the exaltation of the chase, guiding the pony
with his body and repeatedly discharging his gun,
the hunter wounded several buffalo in what seemed
but one flash. And the joy and lust of the slaughter
entered into him, driving him on to new feats.

The attack was short, terrible and altogether de-
cisive. The melee of man and beast, the industrious,
designed work of carnage that day near the Turtle

Mountain lasted about twenty minutes; by which time the immense herd of buffalo was utterly put to rout. Hundreds of wounded animals strewed the plains: but on this occasion to Father Lacombe's anxious delight there were no accidents. No hunter, but lately exultant, lay moaning in the brief hour of pain that bridges the glory of the hunt—and Stillness.

Far out over the plains the scattered herd drew together again, and from some fruitless pursuit or successful skirmish the exhausted men and their ponies gathered in about the scene of combat. The hunters went out to look for the animals each had killed. The wounded buffalo groaned on every side. Some infuriated beasts, although mortally wounded, maintained themselves standing, vomiting blood yet stubbornly fighting against Death. They were incarnate Furies making a last stand on their own battleground.

The turmoil of the hunt was scarcely over before the stillness of the plains was broken by a new, lighter clamour. . . . Delighted women and children were hastening from the camp with carts drawn by old ponies, useless for running but well able to haul back the spoils.

Close on to 800 buffalo had been killed.

The hunters sought out their own spoils among the carcasses. They killed the wounded animals, employing their knives with a marvellous dexterity. "The head, feet and entrails of the buffalo remained on the field and became the portion of the wolves who scented the slaughter from afar off," Father Lacombe

writes, "and came by hundreds over the plains to
throw themselves on the reeking *débris* after the hunters had gone."

In picturesque disorder the party made its way
back through the cool evening airs to the fires of the
camp by Turtle Mountains. The meat had been
piled on the creaking carts by the women and hunters,
and the latter with their labours concluded walked
beside their tired mounts or rode them at a gentle
lope over the prairie, preceding the carts and the
womenfolk.

It was a triumphal procession of the primitive man.

At the camp the ponies were turned free. The
hunters sat about the fires, smoking and living the
brief wild hunt over again. Meanwhile the women
picked out the choicest bits of fresh meat and cooked
a savoury meal for their lords.

The following day the Metis in hundreds climbed
with Father Lacombe to the top of Turtle Mountain
and planted there a large wooden cross. The camp remained at this point for several days while the women
after the centuries-old fashion of their sex dressed
the buffalo skins and dried the meat. Father Lacombe watched their work with the interested eyes
of the newcomer. They first cut up the meat in very
long strips which they stretched to dry on scaffolds
made of young trees. After two or three days' exposure to the sun the meat was sufficiently dry for the
women to fold it into packages tightly bound with
sinew, each bundle weighing from 60 to 70 pounds.

Then with their stone mallets they pounded dried meat to powder in wooden bowls, mixing hot grease and dried berries with it, packing the whole into large sacks of buffalo-hide, called by the Metis—*tau-reaux.* . . . This was *pimik-kan,* the manna of the Canadian prairies.

On these hunting-trips the chaplain's post was not one of sweet doing-nothing. He was the father of the party, the physician, counsellor and arbiter of quarrels. Every morning at early dawn mass was said in his tent, and while Father Lacombe knelt after Mass in the customary thanksgiving there was perfect stillness in the camp, for the Indians and Metis alike respected the prayers and meditations of the Praying-man. During the day there were catechism classes for the children, and instruction for the women and aged people left in the camp while the men hunted.

Some days when the hunters were at home resting while the women did their share of the community-work, they brought themselves and their pipes around the priest's tent and listened to him or helped him in his study of Saulteau. And in the evening when all the camp was quiet; when the little coppery babies had fallen asleep and the dogs sank into slumber in gorged content, Father Lacombe would ring his bell and gather the whole camp about his tent.

There they sang hymns and prayed, until the priest said good-night to them, and the moccasined congregation withdrew quietly to their tepees and repose.

. . . The horses were hobbled within the circle of tents; the night-sentinels kept sleepless vigil—and the silence of the wide prairie fell upon the camp, upon the young Praying-man and his docile flock.

"You can never publish and I can never express how good these Metis children of the prairies were," Father Lacombe has observed. "In that Golden Age when they hunted buffalo and practised our Christianity—with the fervour of the first Christians— their lives were blameless. They were a beautiful race then—those children of the prairies."

For three months this pleasant, primitive existence continued, with long days of sunny quiet following upon the exciting moments of the chase. The hunts were many, and before the camp turned home toward Pembina each family had made ample provision for the next winter. They had stores of dried meat and pemmican for their own food as well as many bales of leather and meat and grease to exchange with the traders.

Moreover—"Each one had laid on a goodly supply of fat," says Father Lacombe, "which would serve him as a fine blanket to withstand the cold season."

Day by day as the winding cavalcade of laden carts and hunters neared Pembina little bands of hunters dropped out of the ranks and made their way to Fort Garry or other points. The power and authority of President Wilkie ceased to exist, and every man was free to direct his steps wherever he wished.

IV

WHEN Father Lacombe's cart stopped before the mission-house and his superior came out to greet him —warmly, but with the quizzical smile of the experienced—the younger man suddenly became conscious of the figure he made. He was unmistakably a returned chaplain of the hunt; his face was burnt to copper by the ardent sun; his soutane was soiled and frayed, even ragged in places. He remembered that the altar-linen and small ornaments of his portable chapel were in sad disarray and odorous of wood-smoke.

"But what of all that?" he asks. "Did I not come back happy of the good I had been permitted to do?" Souls kept reconciled to their Maker, sins prevented by the presence of the priest in the camp—what did the ragged soutane or the smoky linen matter?

For another winter Father Lacombe was left in charge of the Pembina mission. The ministerial duties of the young missionary were not heavy; his flock was small. He applied himself as assiduously as before to master the language. Perhaps some of the charm of novelty had worn away for a spirit naturally restless. In any case he found this winter a hard one.

While sensitive and impressionable—almost poetic

34

—in temperament he was assuredly, too, of a nature born to rule. But there was nothing here to dominate —no opposition to overcome! There seemed no outlet for his energies. He knew that all about him in this storied *Pays d'en Haut,* land of adventure and freedom, men were living out their lives as they would. The reckless blood of many an ancestor who had known his brief day of glory and freedom among the *voyageurs* stirred in him at the thought. He was restless and moody.

Did the man hear the spirit of the wild calling? If he did, the priest throttled the response, and with the subtler heroism that wins no acclaim carried out the round of each day's duties. He would have infinitely preferred the hardships and wanderings of Father Belcourt, his combat with the elements and the indifference of some of the tribes. But here he was left . . . like an old woman about the fire, because he was young and green and could not speak Indian fluently! At this thought he would set himself with fierce ardour to master the dialect.

Often, too, in his inner vision of Montreal's gray streets two thousand miles away he saw again that dim chapel in the Bishop's Palace—with the softened voices of children at play outside; with the good French-Canadian homes about and his brother-priests praying beside and for him; and above it all he always heard the gravely sweet accents of his beloved old guardian:

"Go, my son, and never forget your holy and

precious calling. . . . *If God is with you, who can be against you?"*

There was the rock on which the tidal forces of Nature broke. It was his priesthood alone that kept Albert Lacombe that winter from faring out over the forests and prairies—a *voyageur,* an Indian.

Spring came and Father Belcourt with it, and soon after the hunters re-assembled for the summer hunt. Father Lacombe went with them again as chaplain, but on their return, when the small harvest of their fields and gardens was gathered in, and even the long insistent singing of the grasshoppers had failed—the young priest saw the ghost of another such winter as the last approach—and he simply told himself he could not meet it. Discretion undoubtedly is at times the better part of valour.

He decided to go back to Montreal, until he could arrange to return to the western missions in another capacity. He planned, though vaguely, to join some religious order—perhaps the Oblates, a new order from France of which he had heard Bishop Provencher speak highly.

The rules of a religious order, he knew, in the stationing of its men and in periodical reunions, made special provision for the spiritual as well as material well-being of a man. Realizing the conflict of his years and his *voyageur* blood with the consecration of his life he decided he must have the sustaining influence of the Order's discipline and the assistance of brethren.

Father Belcourt agreed it was best for the young priest to follow his own counsel.

From St. Paul he retraced his voyage of 1849 to Montreal. After a brief visit to his parents he went to pass the winter with the venerable *curé* of Berthier, Abbe Gagnon, whom he assisted in his duties.

In March of the following year, 1852, the new coadjutor bishop of St. Boniface passed through Quebec. Father Lacombe decided this was his opportunity and hurried to offer the bishop his services for the Red River missions.

This was a notable meeting. The two young missionaries, twenty-five and twenty-eight years old respectively, offered excellent types of the two classes of the French-Canadian—the aristocrat and the *habitant*. Each was strong of physique though far from tall. Both had vivid dark faces lit by keen eyes; both were full of magnetism and energy, blessed with a playful humour and sympathetic to a remarkable degree.

The bishop was a man of scholarly tastes; the other a man of action and piety. The bishop's manner was graceful, easy and dignified, while behind the shyness and humility of the younger man was the dormant sense of power which was to develop into such native imperiousness. In each was the blood of daring men and enduring pioneer women, although of different classes.

Bishop Tache had no Indian ancestry and no insouciant *voyageur* behind him, but besides several generations of military men and statesmen there were among his mother's ancestors the name of Joliet the explorer, the Bouchers and Varennes de la Verandrye, the first and dauntless explorer of the Canadian West.

Two hours after they met, Father Lacombe began preparations for returning to the West! His land of Destiny was still beckoning to him.

.   .   .   .

Arriving at St. Boniface in 1852 with Bishop Tache and Father Grollier, Father Lacombe found the village in gloom. This was the year of the great floods along the Red River: houses and barns had been swept away, cattle drowned. The cathedral and palace being built of stone had become public warehouses and places of retreat.

The gloomy outlook for the winter season was as disheartening to Bishop Provencher as to his Metis, but fresh courage came to the venerable prelate with the arrival of the three energetic young men.

Father Lacombe's unexpected coming seemed to him entirely providential. It had been decided that Father Lacombe should make his novitiate at St. Boniface and acquaint himself with the constitution and discipline of the Oblate Order before taking up active missionary work. These plans were speedily upset on his arrival.

Father Thibault, who had gone up the Saskatchewan in 1841, had just arrived from Fort Edmonton by the spring brigade, utterly worn out with his labours. Father Bourassa, left there in charge, intended to return in the following spring. Bishop Provencher was at his wits' end to find a successor for these men—when Bishop Tache arrived with his unannounced companion.

As the old Bishop's eyes fell upon the robust young missionary he felt that there was the man for whom he looked. Providence had been obviously kind. When he talked with his coadjutor the difficulty of the novitiate arose. Still the very night the party arrived Bishop Provencher called Father Lacombe to his room and taking the young man's hands in his own, he appealed to him to renounce his year of novitiate and to go at once into the mission-field. At the close of his plea Father Lacombe recalling his Pembina experience urged his need of belonging to a religious Order.

"But what is to become of the mission to these people? Would you see it abandoned?" the bishop still pleaded. "I pray you grant me what I ask," he insisted humbly but powerfully.

The knowledge of this old man's sacrifice in 1818 when Lord Selkirk's appeal first brought him West lent force to his plea; while the intensity and humility of the enfeebled prelate moved Father Lacombe to the quick. He asked to be given the night to consider what he should do. The next morning he came to the bishop and slipping to his knees at the feet of the old man, yielded his own wishes. "My Lord, I cannot resist any longer. I consent to do what you

desire and will leave it all in the hands of your coadjutor, my superior."

In this way Father Lacombe came to be assigned
to the Edmonton district, and with Father Grollier, a
recent volunteer from France, he soon left for his
post.   Early in July, with the cathedral chimes ringing a parting salute, the party for the North took
leave of St. Boniface.   They parted on the banks of
the Red River with the noble Provencher, who was in
a few months to pass into Eternity.

At Cumberland House Father Lacombe continued
west in company with Chief Factor Rowand, who
ruled as governor over a district that ran from Cumberland House to the Rockies.   This man, who was
the most notable of the Company's officials on the
plains then, was an Irishman, a little man with eyes
of blue steel, an incomparable temper and a spirit
that did not know what fear was.   He was intellec-
tually bright, the master of several Indian dialects
and could terrorize an Indian in any of them.

The journey was made all day long in the open,
in the superb weather of the western summer with
crystal clear airs and radiant sunshine.   There were
no mosquitoes, and no serious sickness among the men,
of whom there were about eighty engaged in hauling
the ten York boats up the river.

At night the boatmen camped *à la belle etoile,* but
with no eyes for the beauty of the night after their
slavish toil in the leather harness all day.   Daylight

lingers long on the Saskatchewan, and it was used to the full for these trips.

The young priest's heart ached for the boatmen. . . . This then was the reality of life for the dashing *voyageurs* who had left Quebec parishes with such fine hopes of western freedom! The canoes had been done away with, the drudgery of these stout capacious boats was their lot—"Faugh! it was to be as the slaves in Africa," he said to himself; and even after fifty years had passed Father Lacombe spoke of the "tracking" of the mid-century days as a painful memory.

The men lived on pounded meat, pemmican, and water; they rarely knew the luxury of tea. Father Lacombe, however, ate his meals with John Rowand and his clerks and they had better fare—with tea and sugar and the finer pemmican made for the Gentlemen, together with choice bits of whatever game was killed along the way. All day they sat at their ease or walked leisurely along the banks before the plodding trackmen, and at night they slept under tents if they desired.

Of the boatmen's toil, Father Lacombe has written: "Imagine, if you please, after resting a few hours on the bare earth, to hear at three o'clock the cry, '*Leve! Leve!*' *Et puis,* hurrah—to pull and pull on the lines drawing the heavy boat up against the current, walking in the mud, the rocks, the swamp, along cliffs and sometimes in water to their arm pits

—and this under a burning sun or beating rain from early morning until darkness fell about nine o'clock. Without having seen it one can form no idea of the hardships, the cruel fatigues of these boatmen."

One of the men became sick during the trip. Father Lacombe [1] pitying him as he stumbled along in the tracking-harness went to Rowand and asked leave for this man to rest a few days as well as to share the food of their table.

The Chief Factor was equally astonished at the young missionary's interference with any system of the Company and at the boatmen's daring to confess illness. But Father Lacombe was insistent, and for a wonder Rowand gave way somewhat.

"Give him some of your food if you must," he said, "but he needs no rest. Any man who is not dead with three days' illness is not sick at all."

Father Lacombe grieved inwardly, and the incident made a strong impression on him; so strong that when they had arrived at Edmonton House and Rowand came showing him a very painful felon on his finger, Father Lacombe did what he could for him, but told him pointedly: "You are not suffering, Rowand!"

Three days later while the Chief Factor still suffered Father Lacombe went to him with a purpose.

"I had to say what was in my mind," he says, "though I feared trouble might come of it. I had to

---

[1] John Norris of Edmonton, who was one of the 1852 brigade, could recall for me almost sixty years later the pleasant ways and sympathy of the new missionary with the crew.

touch that man of Iron. I went to him and said—not that I was sorry, but—'You will understand what I mean, my friend, when I tell you that *you are not sick*. Three days have passed now, and you are not dead. So of course you are not sick; it is all imagination.'

"His face took on an awful cloud. If I had not been his friend and a priest, I believe he would have struck me. Hah! he was like a can of powder—that little man!"

On September 19th, as the boatmen sprang up from their earth-beds and blankets at dawn everyone was conscious of a new spirit abroad in the camp. The boatmen appeared newly resplendent in red-woolen shirts with fresh kerchiefs binding their heads and knotted tartanwise over their left shoulder. They had reached the home-lap; they felt the atmosphere, and fatigue was forgotten, while they pulled up past the unsuspected bar of gold-bearing sand that would lay hidden until Tom Clover should come over the mountains with his grizzly and gold-pan; past the shrubby flats and up between the high green banks to the landing below the Fort.

Against the clear autumn sky there furled and unfurled there the conquering flag of England with the magic letters—"H. B. C."—long ago interpreted by some wit in the service as "Here before Christ." Above the timber palisade on the hilltop the deep-sloping roof of the Big House marked the woodland court of this fiery little Governor.

For days a keen look-out had been kept for the packet and now at the first sight of the boats swinging around the green headland to the east the news was trumpeted through the courtyard and ran from house to house. The steward hastened to run the ensign up; another made the cannons ready for the salute, and the inhabitants of the Fort flocked down the winding path to the river, for this was the greatest event of the year at Edmonton House.

The shore was soon lined with people: Harriot the trader who had married Nancy Rowand, Sophy and Peggy and Adelaide Rowand eager to welcome their father home, clerks from the trading-shop, women and children from the men's quarters and Indians from neighbouring tepees.

On the *barge allege* (*Ogimaw-osie*) in which Rowand and Father Lacombe sat the pennant of the Company flew at the prow, and behind this came the other boats racing to be first, as with gay halloos and snatches of Canadian songs each man strove in the eyes of his home-folk to be the first to leap ashore. *"En roulant ma boule. . . . Hon!—hon!—hon!"* the snatches of Canadian boat-songs rose, with through them the wildly sweet chant of the ancient Algonquin canoe-song of the *voyageurs:*

> *"Moniang nind onjiba*
> *Mondaminek niji kasowin. . . ."*

The cannons in the bastions thundered a welcome when the Chief Factor stepped ashore, and the echoes

were multiplied by the quick fire of the Indians' musketry.   Rowand was pleasantly assailed with greeting as he passed up the steep hill-path through the
crowd, for however peppery and dominating their
"Governor" was at times he had a very warm heart,
loved and was loved by his people.

The young missionary walking beside him felt himself an object of vivid curiosity on the part of the
crowd, which in turn he scanned with interest as he
returned their hearty hand-clasps.   The boatmen,
promptly seized upon by their relatives and friends,
retailed the news of the distant forts while with the
mellowed radiance of the evening sun a great serenity
fell upon the woodland community.

For each white man there was hope of some home-
message in the packet of mail being sorted at the Big
House, and for all there was the knowledge that these
boats drawn up on the shore had arrived safely with
tobacco and ammunition and goods for another year.

V

Now at Fort Edmonton, the most important post west of Norway House, Father Lacombe found himself fully embarked upon his life work, master of his own actions, thrown on his own resources and initiative as he desired to be.

After journeying to Lac Ste. Anne to greet Father Bourassa, he set about finding a home for himself for the winter. The Chief Factor came to his assistance by lending him one of the buildings within the palisades, situated directly east of the river-gateway. It served him for both chapel and residence.

The Fort itself was at first a daily source of wonder and interest to the newcomer. It was like some rude baronial stronghold in the feudal ages of the Old World, with the liege's hall and retainers' cottages all safely enclosed within high palisades surmounted by guns. The palisade, twenty feet in height, was of stout trees split in halves and driven into the ground —the whole strengthened by binding timbers. Around this, compassing the entire Fort the sentinel's gallery ran, and at the four corners the peaked roofs of bastions rose, with the iron mouths of cannons filling the port-holes.

Massive riveted gates to which the steward alone held the keys gave entrance on each side to the courtyard which Palliser estimated as three hundred feet long by two hundred and ten wide. In the middle of the palisaded enclosure the Big House stood, and on the grassy plot in front of it two small brass cannons mounted guard. This official residence of the Chief Factor was a massive building of squared timber, about seventy feet deep and sixty wide, three stories high and with a gallery opening from the second story in front and rear.

From this front gallery a high stairway led down to the grassy courtyard, about which the Bachelors' Hall or Gentlemen's quarters, the Indian Hall, the men's quarters and warehouses were ranged. Within the Big House this stairway opened upon a wide hall, on either side of which lay two immense rooms, the Gentlemen's mess-room and the ball-room. Behind these were the living-rooms of Rowand's family. Below stairs were the steward's office, the armory, storerooms, and cellars; above, were offices and bed-rooms.

This was Rowand's Folly, as the Gentlemen Adventurers were wont to call the most pretentious house of the Company west of York Factory. It had already stood about thirty years, being built by Chief Factor Rowand after the Union, when he was given control of the united trading-posts of the Beaver district.

Fort Edmonton, established first in 1795, had already become the chief point of the Company's occupation on the plains, and in a few years when the Portage la Loche route was abandoned it was to

eclipse utterly the glories of old Fort Chipewyan in
the North and become the most important post west
of Fort Garry.

The resident population of the post in that winter
of 1852 was close to 150—for the boatmen had come
in to winter-quarters at the Post, where already were
the Gentlemen, the stewart, the interpreter, boat-
builders, coopers, carpenters, hunters, blacksmiths
and their families.   The boatmen were now variously
employed as labourers, cutting and hauling firewood
of which immense quantities were used in the wide
earthen fireplaces; searching for hemlock or spruce
bark to recover the roofs of their dwellings; repairing
roofs and sills; rechinking log walls and securing
further provisions of buffalo-meat and fish.

A post of such importance was consequently a
rather pleasant place for a new missionary to find
himself quartered.   Its palisaded quadrangle was a
woodland principality which held intensified cheer
from the very isolation of its environments.

The winters were cold but the fireplaces were deep,
the piles of spruce and aspen high and the log-houses
warm.   There were seasons each year when provisions
ran so low that even with lessened rations there was
no certainty of to-morrow's fast being broken, but
equally there were the seasons of plenty, and with the
exception of a couple of years when a colony of ob-
streperous Norwegian boatmen were brought in (and
had to be packed back to their native shores), the
Orkneymen, French-Canadians, and Metis who filled

the post were a harmonious, if rugged group of men.

Father Lacombe was to experience hardships and some starvation in years close at hand—to live as Father Thibault did first at Lac Ste. Anne, without bread, milk, sugar, salt and sometimes without tea. He was to learn what it meant to struggle against repugnance and to conquer "false delicacy of appetite"—forcing himself to eat unsavoury and indescribable morsels served on a piece of bark or in his fingers, that he might not wound the Indians' feelings or lose their confidence. In his own words:

"Conquered by Hunger, we could learn to consume these victuals without much repugnance, for under the empire of this cruel stepmother the world becomes savage."

But for this first year on the Saskatchewan he fared well, physically and mentally. He dined always at the mess-room in the Big House, where according to the semi-military discipline of the Gentlemen no women ate, and the meals served by Robidoux, a chef from Montreal, were excellent.

Before settling down for the winter Father Lacombe paid a visit to Lac la Biche, an Indian centre 150 miles northeast of the Fort. This point had been visited by Father Thibault but as yet had no permanent mission. The trip was made in the pleasant autumn weather when the men were coming in from the plains and from the lakes with flat-sleighs laden with dried meat and fish and ducks.

Alexis Cardinal, a half-breed who was to share many perilous trips with the young missionary, went with him as guide.   The two travelled happily all day in the golden autumn weather by hills and plain and woodland.   Pitching their camp at night they enjoyed a supper of game, for Alexis was already a famous hunter and dog-runner—then before dropping off to sleep under the stars they sat about the fire and silently enjoyed a pipe "of particularly fine flavour smoked *à longues touches*."

Fifteen days were passed at the Lake in teaching the Indians, but the priest found himself so handicapped by his slim knowledge of Cree that he returned to Edmonton resolved anew to master Cree— "or to blow my head off," as he picturesquely phrases his determination.   Before leaving the mission, however, he put on his white surplice and stole and mounting his pony rode along the shore of the lake blessing the site of the present mission and dedicating it to the Blessed Virgin, the liege-lady of these black-robed knights of Christ.

On his return to Edmonton he easily fitted his ministry into the life of the post.   The inhabitants of the Fort from Rowand down to the youngest dog-runner were mostly Catholic, and he busied himself instructing young and old daily.   On Sunday he tried to impress the Sabbath feeling by making the Mass as solemn as possible, and to this end taught the French-Canadians to sing the liturgy of the Mass.   Several hours each day were given to the study of Cree, which he describes as a delightful occupation.

His master was an amiable Scotch clerk who had recently come in from Jasper House, where in 1845 his wife had been baptized by Father de Smet. This man, Colin Fraser, had been the piper of Governor Simpson on the latter's princely tour of the West, and it is told of him with as much grim truth as humour, that when stationed at the lonely post of Jasper he used to take down his pipes at night and dance to their wild skirl before his own shadow on the wall.

Fraser enjoyed his work of tutoring the vivid mind of the younger man night after night, for Father Lacombe made marvellous progress. He ended each day by jotting down in an improvised notebook all the Cree words and rules of grammar he had learned. This became later the backbone of his dictionary.

The days passed as pleasantly as profitably, for while Father Lacombe instructed his people and felt himself advancing daily in Cree, he was also enjoying the good company of the Gentlemen in the Company's service. Many stories were told him by the men in the Fort that winter—wild tales of the days of rivalry and plunder between rival fur-companies and exciting stories of the hunt.

As is the case with all discerning missionaries, Father Lacombe directed his efforts mainly to instructing the younger members of his flock. But he brought some adults into the Christian faith even in his first season, and in one instance the conversion made a stir.

The bully of Fort Edmonton at that period was a Metis named Paulet Paul, a huge, wild, dark fellow noted as a fighter. On Father Lacombe's arrival Paulet treated the young priest with vaunted indifference, something, too, of the Indian contempt for a youth who had not yet won a name or recognition. But by degrees he condescended to smoke a pipe with him and other rugged Metis who visited the missionary.

At the beginning of Lent he dropped into Father Lacombe's little house suddenly one evening and asked to be made a Christian. Every day then for weeks he received especial instruction preparatory to his reception. A week before the feast he told Father Lacombe he was going to fast until Easter, but as he was working hard daily and absolutely the only food the men had then was dried meat and fish, Father Lacombe advised him not to limit his rations. But the converted bully persisted.

On Good Friday he looked so weak that Father Lacombe protested he was making himself ill. His sympathy was brushed aside by Paulet:

"No, I only fast; I will not eat nor drink until Sunday."

This was the penance Paulet had imposed upon himself for past sins; no sacrifice of an extra bite or special dainty, but a fast as entire as that of a man lost in a desert. He maintained this until Sunday. On that day Paulet was given a seat alone near the altar. Chief Factor Rowand and his daughter Adelaide sat near him and were his sponsors in baptism.

Paulet as a Christian was an improvement upon Paulet the bully, and the Factor noted it. Consequently toward the close of the following winter when Rowand sent a small party of men with dog-trains of goods out to meet an Indian band on the plains to trade for dried meat and furs Paulet was for once permitted to go in charge: as he very much desired.

Father Lacombe, then established at Ste. Anne, happened to be at the Fort on the day of their return. Paulet's companions came in without him, and one explained eagerly to the priest that his protege had made a fool of himself.

"Paulet," said this Metis, "has made lots of mischief out there with the Indians. The Indians said he put too much water into the rum, but he gave big presents of goods. He made a great man of Paulet at last—but he got poor bargains for the Company."

"*Hein*," thought Father Lacombe, "there is trouble ahead." He knew Rowand.

This is what he tells of the outcome in his own picturesque "English of the Nor'-West."

"By and bye I met Rowand, and he say to me blustering—'Well, that man of yours, that Paulet you baptize last year and recommend to me as a good man, he made a damfool of himself.'

"I answer nothing: I do not know what to say. But I watch out by the river until I see Paulet come with his toboggan and dog.

"'Hey, Paulet,' I say, 'what have you done? Rowand will make trouble for you.'

"He speak bravely—'Ha! that is all humbug that the men say. You will see.'

"But the big fellow look afraid. Then—quick! an idea came to me.

"'Paulet,' I say, 'I know what to do. You will go to Rowand and right at once you will ask him for his blessing as a god-father. (That is a fashion of the Metis on great occasions.) Go!'

"And I laugh as I remember what Rowand said, and I hurried to be with him when Paulet comes. By-and-by while I was walking up and down with him in the great Hall of the Big House, we hear somebody at the door. Suddenly Paulet came in and at once fell on his knees to Rowand.

"'My god-father,' he pray, 'give me your blessing.'

"Now Rowand was look surprise and shy, for though he consent when I coax him to be Paulet's god-father, he was not a very religious man. . . . At last he say, 'Here is the Father; ask his blessing.'

"I was trying not to laugh, but I get voice to say,

"'No, no; this is not my affair. It is yours. He is not my god-child—give him your blessing.'

"Now, John Rowand had a good heart behind his temper, and he could enjoy Paulet's finesse. . . . So he made some kind of a blessing—and he finish it off by going to the cupboard to get a drink of rum for Paulet!"

Father Lacombe to his latest years loved to dwell upon the memory of this man—"He was not big; in fac' he was very short, but he was brave, that little man, you know—brave like a lion. He feared no man; not even a whole tribe of Indians could make him afraid."

"Ah! he was a grand little man."

The camp-fires of the Saskatchewan still hear the echoes of that tribute.

Just once his anger fell on Father Lacombe, and the latter found it less easy than in Paulet's case to turn off the wrath of this little Napoleon of the North. The first winter he spent at Ste. Anne he found a couple of muskrat skins at the mission left by an Indian, as they had been trapped out of season and were consequently of little value as fur for trading. For this reason Father Lacombe felt their use would be no infringement upon the Company's rigid command that no employe or other white man allowed in the country should trap furs or get them in trade for any other purpose than the Company's benefit.

Father Lacombe took the skins to the wife of the half-breed servant at the Mission and had her dress the skin and sew strips of it on the collar and cuffs of his overcoat to protect him from the cold. One day, entering the Big House at Edmonton, he went at once to greet his friend the Chief Factor in his office.

Rowand, at the first glimpse of the priest and his fur-trimmed coat, grew furious. Without replying to the genial greeting he bellowed at him,

"What! you priest, you! You say you have come here to teach what is right. . . . And this is the way you give the example! Who gave you the right to wear that fur?"

He had given the astonished young priest no chance to make explanations; the latter gave him no time to withdraw his hasty speech.

"I tore off those miserable skins from my wrists," he says, "and I flung them in his face."

Then he wheeled about and left the room . . . but not before he had learned what Rowand meant when he said, "It is true we know only two powers— God and the Company!" One only marvels at the facility with which they made the laws of God conform to those of the Company.

"This incident," wrote Father Lacombe in his Memoirs, "like many others our missionaries experienced, evidences the spirit of the Company—noble, loved, liberal and kind to us, just in as far as the question of fur-trading did not enter into the game. So for the sake of our missionary work we had to be very prudent and watchful to do nothing that would compromise our interests.

"We had to suffer with patience and endure for the moment what we could not prevent, however unjust the affair might appear. The first missionaries were exceedingly poor and had little assistance from

their superiors, who for their part had few resources
at their disposition.   The Society of the Propagation
of the Faith was far from being able to assist us then
as it did later; moreover our means of transport were
practically nil.   We depended entirely upon the
good-will of this good Company to go from one post
to another and to convey thither our small luggage.

"The chief officers, few of whom were Catholic,
sometimes looked on our arrival and our work with a
jealous eye.   In addition to this they felt that their
policy was being interfered with—that policy of pre-
venting the entrance of civilization and of retaining
the *ancien regime.*   We were received and tolerated,
but it was because they could not do otherwise.

"Still," he writes, summing up the memory of those
years, "considering our position, the conditions of the
country and the ideas and principles of this Company
—I venture to say that we have been honorably and
charitably treated by the Company."

And elsewhere he writes: "I repeat what I have
said many times, that if we had not had the aid and
the hospitality of the Hudson's Bay Company, we
could not have for a long time begun or carried out
the establishment of the young Church of the Northwest."   He makes particular reference to the debt
of gratitude he personally owes to his first friend in
the Company, John Rowand, to William Christie
and Richard Hardisty.

From this it will be seen that Father Lacombe and
his fellow-workers understood clearly the terms on

which they were privileged to enter the country by
its masters, the Gentlemen Adventurers. They were
welcomed—sometimes only tolerated—because they
did not go in as money-makers, but as ministers of
the Gospel, intent upon laying the first foundations
of a moral civilization. Nor did they dare discuss the
ethics of the fur-trade or the attitude of the traders
to the Indians. This last, however, was ordinarily
very kind.

Father Lacombe had an instance of this as his first
winter in Edmonton House drew to a close. An
Indian woman hailing from the plains with her people came to him mourning that her husband had died
during the winter-hunt, that she had little or no fur
and her husband owed a large debt to the Company.
She had only a few ponies to meet this debt and she
asked Father Lacombe to speak for herself and her
children to the Chief Factor.

He went to Rowand and the latter turned over his
books. The debt was close on to 3,000 skins—beaver-
skins, not dollars or pounds sterling, being the currency of this fur-trader's land.

"Now, who will pay that?" demanded Rowand of
the priest with mock fierceness. *"Bien,* hurrah!
. . ." and he ran his quill pen through the account.

The honourable Company of the Gentlemen Adventurers of England trading into the Hudson's Bay
could not hold a mortgage upon the future of a poor
widow and her children!

VI

MARCH blew a reveille over the bleak hills, waking the rivers to music and stirring the myriad forces of the woods. The Indians began to come in from the winter-hunt, Father Lacombe looking on with lively interest at this newest phase of life in the Far West.

The Strongwood and Plains Crees traded at Edmonton House all the year round, but once or twice a year in spring or autumn the Blackfeet and their Blood and Piegan allies came to trade in large numbers: they rarely travelled in small bands in their enemies' country.

When they came riding up to the Fort their barbaric cavalcades were always picturesque. Half-naked supple bronze warriors rode by startlingly painted, bearing skin shields on their arms, full quivers at their sides, and eagle-feathers in their hair. Rugged squaws with trains of lively children kept ward over the primitive lodge-equipment tied by thongs to the travoix behind their ponies. Iron kettles jangled and the mongrel half-fed dogs made a running, yelping accompaniment to the whole.

This they were when near at hand and analyzed, but seen winding down the bridle-trail in the ravine on the south bank, with the sun glittering on their brass ornaments and the small flags of the chiefs flut-

tering peace signals in the van—the Blackfeet coming to trade at Fort Edmonton offered the most
picturesque panorama of human life in the west.

While the warriors turned their ponies loose on the
meadows about the Fort and strode about among their
brethren, and their chiefs brought gifts and parleyed
with the Chief Factor, their dusky womenkind were
at work—and a town of smoky lodges was springing
up magically on the hill and meadows near the Fort.
Then trading began. In those days the Company
still employed rum in their trading, and they surrounded their dealings with precautions sprung from
the experience of savages inflamed with liquor.

So although the chiefs and their gifts of robes and
pemmican were received in the Indian Hall by Row-
and, the trading was accomplished through a grating
between the Indian Hall and the trading-shop. On
the shelves but little goods were displayed—on the
principle that the Indian would not want what he
could not see. All the gates of the Fort were closed,
except one to the Indian Hall. At times even
this was closed and the trading done through a grating in the gate.

First the Indians demanded rum, and it was given
to them—rum of the first quality carefully diluted
with water. The Blackfeet being fiercer than the
Crees received a weaker cup or keg, for the standard
of mixing in those days defined seven parts of water
to one of rum for Blackfeet and only three parts
water to one of rum for the Crees.

After a goodly exchange of peltry for liquor the orgies began, as described in earlier days by Father Thibault. In 1852 they had in no way altered, and Father Lacombe was the witness of frightful scenes "which I deplored but could in no way prevent." Meanwhile there were men stationed with loaded muskets in the sentinel's gallery that surrounded the palisade, and the cannon in the bastions stood ready for action. These precautions were rigidly preserved when the Blackfeet came to trade, for they had burned down the Old Bow Fort in John Rowand's time and killed white men on several occasions.

When the snow had quite disappeared and the renewed delights of spring tempted him afield, Father Lacombe took many long walks through the valley. On one of these excursions he came upon the cross that had been planted there with so much solemnity by Father Demers and Father Blanchet in 1838.[1] The cross lay on the top of the hill close to the Fort. Father Lacombe lifted it up from the ground and replanted it firmly, so that for some years it again lifted its arms of appeal.

He decided now to make his headquarters at Lac Ste. Anne, as his predecessors had done; meanwhile arranging for frequent visits to Edmonton.

Lac Ste. Anne, fifty miles northwest of Edmonton, was the first permanent mission for Crees and

[1] The new Parliament Buildings at Edmonton are built directly over the site of the old Cross erected here by Father Demers and his companion on their way to the Pacific in 1838.

Cree-Metis established by Father Thibault on the Upper Saskatchewan. He had selected this place in 1842 because the soil and fishing were good and there was an abundance of fuel. Being remote from the Blackfoot trail to the Fort, there was a further advantage in security from these traditional enemies of the Crees.

Early in the autumn word came that another Oblate, Père Remas, had been assigned to the mission at Lac la Biche. Father Lacombe set out on horseback with Alexis to visit the newcomer. The lake was almost 200 miles away across country, but the riding-trails were good, and this journey through the woods was only a delight for him.

At Lac la Biche he found the Indians were absent hunting while Father Remas was altogether miserable. He had arrived too late to make a garden, and was consequently in an impoverished state. Father Lacombe, distressed at his condition, insisted that he should return home with him and await the promised pastoral visit of Bishop Tache.

The latter set out from his episcopal hut at Ile a la Crosse in February, 1854. The ceremonial reception Rowand planned for him at Edmonton was prevented by his arrival very late at night on March 22, but the next morning he was aroused by the cannons' thunder of welcome.

This was the first visit of a Bishop to Edmonton House, and during the week of the visitor's stay the Fort was in as nearly holiday mood as a strong-hearted disciplinarian like Rowand would permit. Personally the Chief Factor and his daughters showered kind attentions upon the young prelate.

Then he was escorted in his dog-cariole to Ste. Anne, where for three weeks Father Lacombe played the part of host—a role that always came happily to his generous nature. At Ste. Anne the three Oblates, dwelling upon the Bishop's recent experiences at Fort Pitt, where he was desolated at the debauchery of the Indians and Metis with drink, found a great deal of consolation in the conduct of the excellent colony at Ste. Anne.

Yet fifteen years earlier these Metis had been like those of Pitt. The contrast made the Bishop resolve firmly not only to find more missionaries for permanent missions, but to use with the various Chief Factors and the Governor at Fort Garry every effort possible to prevent the trading of liquor to the Indians. This soon became the cry of every missionary in Rupert's Land, but it was only six years later that their campaign had effect.

During the Bishop's visit to Ste. Anne he confirmed 98 Indians and baptized 22 adults, already instructed by Father Lacombe, and who gave every evidence of a sincere desire to live in accordance with the missionary's teachings. On Easter Monday the Bishop took his leave accompanied by the two missionaries.

Father Lacombe, loth to part with his brethren, rode on beside them far past the Fort. When he said adieu it was with heavy hearts they saw the boyish figure turn his cayuse on the woodland path, and take his solitary way back to Ste. Anne.

While Father Lacombe returned to his own post Bishop Tache journeyed on to Father Remas' log-shack. It was a miserable abode, twelve feet square and six high, where he had spent several miserable weeks alone in 1853 before Father Lacombe had come riding like a Fairy Benevolent and carried him off to Ste. Anne.

The seats of the mission were made of stumps of trees; its other meagre fittings were in accordance. Its cupboard was painfully slim. But here, with one year's experience of the west and with a plentiful supply of seed for a garden, Father Remas was re-installed, and the Bishop rode on.

.　　.　　.　　.　　.　　.　　.　　.　　.

In the summer of 1855 a stir was made in the Saskatchewan mission-field by the arrival of new workers with consequent changes of position. One of the newcomers was Vital Grandin, a handsome young Breton priest, a delicate, fair-haired youth who was to become an intimate friend of Father Lacombe in later years as well as one of the most striking figures among the pioneer missionaries of the west.

In the late summer of 1855, Father Lacombe made his first visit to the Peace River, as Father Bourassa had done in 1845 and Father Thibault still earlier. He went on horseback to the Athabasca near the old Fort Assinaboine and then proceeded in a small row-

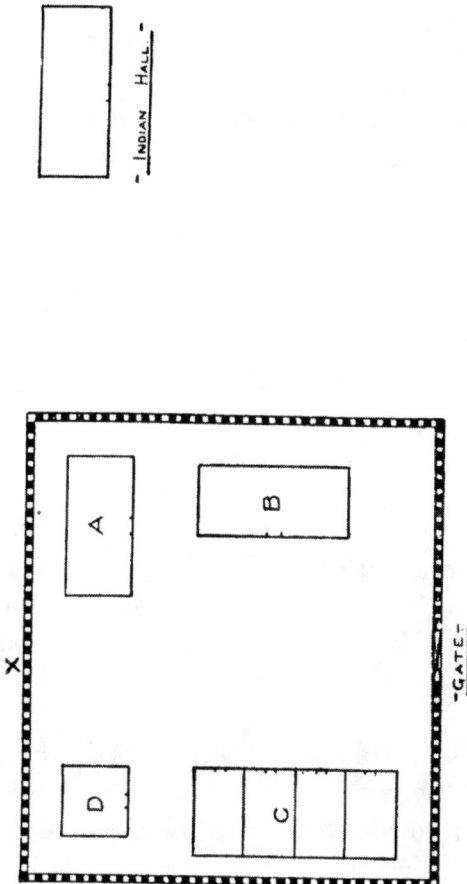

— Indian Hall —

A

B

X

D

C

— Gate —

"A" - Trader's House
"B" - Shop & Store-room.
"C" - Men's Quarters.
"D" - Stables.
"X" - Stockade.

— Plan of Trading-Post at Lesser Slave Lake in the Fifties. —

boat down that river to the Little Slave and up this to Lesser Slave Lake.

Along the south shore of the lake he came upon a large encampment of Crees, drawn there at that season doubtless by the hosts of ducks and wavies that haunt the lake. Father Lacombe spent several days among them before pushing on to the post, where he was warmly welcomed by his former teacher, Colin Fraser, now in charge of the Company's post here.

The post was built on the hillside that slopes gently up from the lake, with the Indian Hall outside the stockade and some distance east of it.

Colin Fraser supplied his friend with ponies and guide to ride to Fort Dunvegan, the Company's headquarters on the Peace. It was over 160 miles away, along the trappers' trail through the pleasant autumn woods. Bourassa, the officer in charge, received Father Lacombe very kindly and every opportunity was given him to minister to the employes, who, as at Edmonton, were largely French-Canadian and Catholic.

On his return to Ste. Anne he at once entered upon his deferred novitiate.

When the prescribed year of religious seclusion and prayer was concluded, he pronounced his vows of poverty, chastity and obedience, as a member of the Oblates of Mary Immaculate.

In September he visited the Indians of Jasper House,[1] the most interesting of these being a band

---

[1] Jasper House, which was named after Jasper Hawes, an English

of Iroquois, descendants of old canoemen from Caughnawaga.

Father Lacombe set out with two pack-horses carrying his portable chapel and provisions, and saddle-ponies for himself and his Metis guide, Michel Nipissing. Fallen timber, creeks and swamps tried the horses' strength and the travellers' patience.

The second afternoon on the trail, as they made their way through a haze of smoke, the wind rose and there came a crackling like thunder. The guide knew what it meant: a forest fire was racing to meet them, licking up and snapping the dry spruce and fallen timber like so much tinder.

While they groped their way painfully in search of a river the smoke settled down on them like a pall.

"It is only to die!" Michel cried. Michel was not brave as was the redoubtable Alexis. But Father Lacombe cried back to him:

"*Akai!* Courage! The river is near. *Akame-yimo!*"

They reached its banks, made the horses jump in and leaped after them. They threw water over the trembling animals and themselves as the flames approached and rushed past them. For almost two days men and horses stayed in a dugout in the bank, while the bush glowed with hot embers of the fire.

officer in the Hudson's Bay Company who established it early in the nineteenth century, was situated on the Athabasca River where it emerges from the Rockies. It was visited by Père de Smet on his heroic trip as Peacemaker in 1845–46, and a summit, six miles west of the Fort, was named for him.

After two days more of painful travelling, the young priest, overcome by fatigue and fever, declared he could go no further. They camped on the bank of a small stream that evening, and when Father Lacombe refused to eat, Michel became greatly distressed. His fears were varied and he came to the broken man with a quaint plea:

"My father," he said, "I am afraid you will die here—then what will become of me? People will say I have ill-treated you—perhaps killed you. Give me a piece of paper that I can show Père Remas to let him know that I have been good to you."

Father Lacombe gave him the note he wanted, and then in turn, frightened by the man's fear, he asked Michel in case of his death to bury him under a butte of sand near by and go at once to Father Remas with the news. Perhaps because in all his healthy young life before Father Lacombe had known no illness, he was unnecessarily afraid of this. However, it was to his own intense surprise that he was able in a couple of days to mount his pony and continue the journey. After two weeks of ministry with the Indians he returned home, the Indians following him as he rode out of their camp, firing their guns in salute and crying out their farewells.

That winter an urgent call came to him from the Blackfoot nation. These men were absolute pagans, whose country was considered wild and unsafe but the proud race was now terribly afflicted, their children dying off like flies with a mysterious sickness. Some few of them had met Father Lacombe at Fort Edmonton and in their extremity they begged him to come to them.

This was well into February, 1857.

Across the river [1] from Edmonton, Father Lacombe came upon a sickening spectacle—three mangled bodies of Blackfeet, whose feet and hands were cut off and hung on trees.

He sent Alexis back to the Fort for men to bury the bodies; then the two resumed their journey, sturdily trudging over the snowy plain toward the Buffalo Lake.

[1] On the site of Strathcona's business-centre to-day.

VII

At dusk the teepees of a Cree encampment rose before them near the southern extremity of a small lake, and the travellers were taken in and fed. Many of the Indians in this camp were catechumens of Father Lacombe and warmly attached to him. When they heard he was bound for the Blackfoot camp, they urged him in every possible way not to go. They said the Blackfeet would blame their disease on the whites and would either refuse to receive him or might kill him.

Father Lacombe reminded them that he had received a prayer for help, and he was not going to turn back when fellow-creatures in trouble needed him. He and Alexis pushed on, losing their way for a while in a snowstorm, but at the end of a couple of days they came upon the encampment of the Blackfeet. Mindful of the character of these Indians, he signalled to them from a short distance.

"Soon a crowd came around me," he writes of this in his Memoirs. "What a scene! Imagine these men, women and children—half-naked, although it was quite cold weather and their bodies reddened with the fever which devoured them. For some minutes I did not know what was going to happen. They swarmed about me, disputing for my person. Some caught my hands; others my soutane. One tried to lift me up toward the sky crying out some prayer to the Master of Life for pity."

The unfortunate savages were crazed with fever and fear, and they looked to him, the friend of Ninna-stakow, as some great medicine-man to relieve them. He released himself from the crowd and entering a near-by lodge found a stoically silent man, who held out to him the dead body of his child. It was the last of his family to die. Three other bodies lay inside the lodge, and the despairing father weakened with disease would not for the moment separate himself from this last child.

There were about sixty tents in all, and from every side the priest's ears were stricken with low moans or lamentations. The epidemic he found to be scarlet fever of a severe type. It was carrying off scores of their people and the Indians were terrified out of their habitual bravery by the unseen foe which stalked so ruthlessly through the camp.

The poor young Blackrobe with his small box of remedies did everything he could to stem the disease. Night and day he passed through their tents, consoling and tending them, but at the thought of how little he could do, his warm young nature was in a torment of rebellion only second to their own.

There were several camps to visit, all a few miles apart on the snowy plains, and he had spent twenty tireless days among them, when he was himself stricken with the disease.

His remedies were gone and he felt himself consumed with the fever. He reconciled himself to this inglorious end of the years of work planned for himself, but in a few days, to his own and Alexis' great joy, he began to recover.

The epidemic had now about spent itself, and on his recovery he arranged for the burial of all the dead Indians. Because of the frozen ground, the Indians could not dig graves, as he would have preferred them to do, nor did the exhausted warriors build their usual burial platforms and expose the bodies to the pure elements. They simply gathered the dead bodies together in skin lodges—ten or fifteen in each lodge—and then covered the remains with stones and snow.

The work of Father Lacombe's mission in 1858 and 1859 has been concisely pictured in this sentence from Bishop Tache's "Twenty Years of Missions". . . . "At Lac Ste. Anne Father Remas and Father Lacombe multiplied themselves to advance the reign of Christ."

Their days were divided between work in the fields and their ministry to the Metis and Indians in and about the mission. It was a peaceful, uneventful period, in which from day to day the simple-hearted, affectionate children of the forest gathered about the priests for instruction, or less willingly exerted themselves with shovel and hoe to work under direction in the barley and turnip or potato fields about their homes.

One evening early in January, 1858, when the

little woodland settlement of about forty-five houses was intent upon its evening meal and the ruddy fire-glow just tinted the opaqueness of its parchment windows a Metis came on foot to the mission from the Fort. In answer to the inevitable greeting—"What news?"—he replied that a strange white man, a Doctor, had arrived at the Fort a couple of days before the New Year.

The Doctor, he said, was one of a large party sent by the great Queen Mother across the sea to report on the west and her children there.

The half-breed had other gossip of the Fort, but the first news overshadowed all the rest. For the poor young Father Frain, who had arrived from France a few months before, had been ailing continually since his arrival, and the opportunity of consulting a physician seemed providential. Next morning Father Lacombe got out his toboggan-cariole and dogs to take him to the Fort.

Father Frain was well wrapped in buffalo robes and then with a *"Marche; Hourrah!"* from their robust, leather-clad master the dogs made off. It was fifty miles to the Fort through the woods. That evening after dusk had fallen and the big gates of the Fort were closed the watchman heard a vigorous pounding on the main gates—Father Lacombe and his invalid waited outside.

Dr. James Hector of the Palliser Expedition—for he was the newcomer—was called to attend the sick priest. Mr. Swanston hospitably assigned a

room to Father Frain. The Doctor did what he
could for him, but the improvement was slight. It
was the country and the diet that were killing the
young man. They decided to send him down to the
Red River—and thence to Louisiana in sunnier
climes.

About the middle of February Dr. Hector went
out to Ste. Anne to secure half-breeds there for the
Expedition's journey in the coming summer. He
spent Sunday with Father Lacombe, whom he char-
acterizes in his official reports as most genial and
hospitable. During this winter and in the following
year Father Lacombe met the Doctor (later Sir
James Hector of New Zealand) several times, and
his relations with him and the botanist, M. Bourgeau,
were very pleasant.

The latter whiled away some time during the
tedious winter days in carving wooden candlesticks
for the altar in the Fort chapel.

Judging from a portion of his report to the Government, Dr. Hector and his companions were impressed with the prowess of Father Lacombe's prized
dog-train and his man Alexis, for Hector wrote:

"M. Le Combe, the Roman Catholic priest, has
frequently been driven from Lac Ste. Anne to the
Fort in a dog-cariole—50 miles: after which his man
Alexis, one of the best runners in the country, loaded
the sled with 400 pounds of meat and returned to
the misison before next morning!"

Affairs, spiritual and temporal, prospered with

our pioneer in 1859. His regular ministry lay
largely with the freemen and Metis, but the Indians
came to him for direction in increasing numbers.
Their conduct was in general very good and in accordance with their new belief. Sometimes he found his
little chapel at Ste. Anne too small for the devout
Christians who gathered there, and on the whole the
mission at the Christianized Devil's Lake was satis-
fying.

A pleasant picture of life at Ste. Anne this year
is given by Lord Southesk in his book of western
travel. When he reached Fort Edmonton in August
he found the Company's servants at work harvesting
wheat on the eastern meadows below the fort. On
August 19 he set out with a pack-train bound for the
mountains. The following morning Father Lacombe,
busy at some repairs in his chapel, was called out
to welcome a stranger.

"A fine looking man—tall—a gentleman" was
Southesk, as Father Lacombe recalls him; while in
his book the English traveller says he met with a
most cordial reception here and had the pleasure of
dining with "Peres Lacombe and Le Frain at the
Roman Catholic mission-house."—"Agreeable men
and perfect gentlemen," he notes in his diary that
they are, and comments that Rome has an advantage
in the class of men she assigns to her missions, as she
always sends out "polished, highly-educated gentlemen."

"On the pressing invitation of my kind host,"

writes Lord Southesk, "I remained for the night at
the mission-house. Everything there is wonderfully
neat and flourishing: it is a true oasis in the desert—
the cows fat and fine, the horses the same, the dogs,
the very cats the same. A well-arranged and well-
kept garden, gay with many flowers (some of them
the commonest flowers of the woods and plains
brought to perfection by care and labour).

"The house beautifully clean: meals served up as
in a gentleman's dining-room. Excellent preserves
of service-berries and wild raspberries—everything
made use of and turned to account. Surrounded by
such comfort and refinement and in the society of
such agreeable entertainers I passed a most pleasant
evening, one that often recalled itself to my memory
amidst the experiences of later times."

He found the walls of the rooms decorated with
religious pictures, while the home-made book shelves
held a goodly library of books of a philosophical and
theological character. Southesk wanted to buy
horses for his journey in order to push on more
quickly and set his fancy on a black colt at the mission. Being a gift to Father Lacombe from some
Indians in return for special kindness shown them,
the priest would not part with it.

Still Pere Lacombe, he adds, was anxious to oblige
him, so he looked up two very good horses for which
Southesk paid £19 each. At the same time the missionary made his guest a present of a sack of pemmi-

can, a valuable gift in those days and particularly that year.

"I felt quite sorry to leave Ste. Anne," the courtly Southesk writes; "all was so kindly and pleasant at the mission. The good fathers loaded us with provisions—fish, potatoes, dried meat, etc. God bless them and prosper their mission."

From this it would seem that Père Lacombe at thirty-three was charming socially and as open-handed and impulsively generous as at eighty-three.

Lord Southesk did not forget his agreeable host. In New York, on the point of sailing for England, he despatched to the missionary a long letter and small brass lock for the home-made cabinet on which the Earl found the young priest at work on his arrival.

In his book Southesk makes no mention of Father Remas, for the latter was absent then at St. Boniface. He had gone with a brigade of carts to meet three Grey Nuns from Montreal, who were to open a home that would be at once a boarding-school, orphanage, hospital and refuge for the aged.

Father Lacombe's active mind seized upon a hundred details of work for the Indians which could be better accomplished by the nuns than by himself. So he was overjoyed to welcome them.

The pastoral visit of the Bishop shortly before Christmas was the outstanding event of 1860. The memory of these pastoral visits of Bishop Tache could warm Father Lacombe's heart decades afterward: it is readily understood that the pleasure at the moment was indescribable. For Bishop Tache—young, brilliant, and spiritually zealous—was like Father Lacombe himself a man of great heart and of strong social charm. He was a brilliant raconteur, and a warmly sympathetic friend.

An unexpected meeting with him one day on the road from Lac la Biche made the forest-trail a porch to Paradise for Father Lacombe. He promptly turned his dogs about and the three arrived at Ste. Anne at eight o'clock at night, as everyone was about to retire.

"Our arrival, quite unexpectedly, especially at that hour, turned everything upside down," writes Father Lacombe in the Memoirs. "They rushed to the chapel—everyone rushed there—the Fathers, the Sisters and the Christians living about us. They were so agitated and surprised that they sang everything that came into their heads. And Father Remas—ah, that dear old Father! only found himself as the *Te Deum* was being chanted, and so at the end joined his voice in the grand fête. What harmony!" he concludes with a touch of laughing sarcasm.

For days this little mission lost in the woods was like a dovecote in a flutter of delight. The three Grey Nuns were gladdened like children by the messages from their Sisters at St. Boniface and letters from the home-folk in Quebec. The priests rejoiced openly in the presence of their brilliant and humorous brother.

The Indian children of the school and the old people who had never beheld a bishop before, regarded him with awe; while the Metis couple, Michel and his wife, were more than ever important since they had a bishop to cook for.

To Father Lacombe fell the task of secretly contriving a crozier for the bishop, when it was found that he had brought none with him: it was not a convenient thing to pack in canoes or dog-carioles. With an Indian hunting-knife Father Lacombe fashioned one of greenwood and tinted it with yellow ochre.

The Bishop carried it with dignity at the midnight Mass, remarking that this was a pastoral staff as primitive as the shepherds carried on the Great Night! The motley congregation was impressed, and for years after the wondrously-tinted staff had a place over the rafters at Ste. Anne, where it was the subject of many tender and laughing reminiscences.

Before Bishop Tache went away a very important step was taken by him in conjunction with Father Lacombe. Lac Ste. Anne mission, as we have seen, was established by Father Thibault mainly for the Crees, because it was remote from the Blackfoot trail to Fort Edmonton.

But since the visit of Father Lacombe to the Blackfeet during the epidemic that race had been hankering for a share of the magnetic little man's attentions; while he felt the time had come when he should turn to this neglected people.

Consequently, one day at Lac Ste. Anne a Blackfoot chief, attired in savage splendour, sought an audience with the bishop. In the name of his tribe he asked that a priest should be sent among his people. The chief promised that the missionary would be unmolested, and that, while he was with them, they would not make war on their Cree enemies.

He wanted the priest to carry a white flag bearing a Red Cross as a sign easily recognized and to be respected by all. (This proviso is quite obviously the result of Father Lacombe's conferences with the chief and his people.) The interview caused the bishop to decide upon what Father Lacombe had been urging for some time—the foundation of another mission nearer the Fort, where the Blackfeet could be assembled from time to time.

There was still another reason influencing the bishop. Each year increasing numbers of Metis were abandoning their nomad-life to settle about the mission and learn to farm. Father Lacombe in his numerous excursions through the country had seen many places with better soil than that about the lake; where also there were no muskegs to trap unwary cattle in spring.

Consequently during the bishop's visit it was arranged the two should visit these points.

They made long trips into the country by dog-train and snowshoes. One day, they reached a fine hill overlooking the Sturgeon valley, where that pretty river winds on itself in many curves and Big Lake gleams in the distance. The prospect at once held the bishop's attention.

VIII

STANDING on this hill-top, where Father Lacombe had so often paused to rest his dog-train, the two pioneers made a halt. They surveyed the broad valley intently, refreshing themselves with a choice morsel of pemmican as they did so. The Bishop finally turned from his survey and said:

"*Mon Père,* the site is indeed magnificent. I choose it for the new mission, and I want it to be called St. Albert, in honour of your patron."

Father Lacombe acquiesced in this order, which was, he confesses, quite agreeable to him. Then the bishop planted his staff in the snow where they stood, saying:

"Here you will build the chapel!"

And on the exact spot where the staff had been planted, Father Lacombe a few months later erected the altar of the mission chapel.

Friends of Father Lacombe—aware of his intuitive knowledge of human nature and the subtle diplomacy hidden under his most naïve and simple plainsman's exterior—will gather from this incident, as on numerous other occasions with Indians and whites, that Father Lacombe had his companion do exactly what he wanted him to do. . . . And all the while the bishop felt he was the prime mover in it all!

It was now 1861, and Ste. Anne mission had arrived at a period where life meant a peaceful round of work. This was not what the ardent nature of Father Lacombe desired. He turned with eagerness in the springtime to the building of the new mission. Father Remas was preparing then to go up to Jasper House to hold missions for the Indians there. Father Caer, who had come in the previous summer to replace Father Frain, was to go to the prairies with the hunters for four months. Ste. Anne was almost deserted by pastors and flock.

The snow had melted from the face of *our good old Mother,* as some of his Indians called the Earth, when Father Lacombe got ponies, oxen and farm implements together, and with the devoted Normand couple for servants made his way to the big hill by the Sturgeon. They pitched their skin tents on the summit of *"la chère colline."* After Mass on the following morning Father Lacombe walked out over his new domain, showing its beauties to the appreciative Metis couple with all the delights of a landed proprietor.

Early on Monday morning Father Lacombe, Michel and two other Metis crossed the river to the spruce forest on the opposite hill and began to get out logs for the buildings. But before the first stroke was put in the trees, the four knelt, as Father

Lacombe directed, and asked the Great Master to bless their work.

Soon the forest rang with the strokes of their axes, and Rose—the wife of Michel—in her tent listened with delight to the echoes as she boiled the dried meat for their noonday meal.

For ten days the logging continued, one of the oxen being employed to haul the logs to the site. A saw-pit was made, and logs sawed under the young priest's instruction. Meanwhile two of the men were employed in clearing and breaking the soil.

There was only one plough: Father Lacombe was anxious to cultivate as great an area as possible; so he arranged that one man should plough part of the day with two oxen, while the other man with another yoke should plough late into the night. This was possible because of the long twilight of the Saskatchewan valley.

Very soon a number of the Ste. Anne Metis and freemen turned up at the new mission, preferring it to the summer hunt for a novelty. The men began to get timber for houses; the women were set to work on a large communal garden where carrots, onions, beets, cabbages, turnips and other vegetables were sown in abundance. But the ruling-spirit of all this activity; now in the saw-pit, now at work on the houses, again in the fields—was Father Lacombe, altogether happy in finding an adequate outlet for his energy.

All through the spring the work progressed. July

came and the fertile grainlands on the hilltop were
touched with the colour of the harvest. Father
Lacombe and his regiment of workers were enjoying
their own potatoes and vegetables. The houses which
had risen "by enchantment," as the Genius of the
place declared, would soon be ready for habitation.
They were quite seemly structures for the period and
the place, all being fitted with floors and doors and
windows, as well as shingles on the roofs made by
the Genius and his zealous helpers.

Autumn came—the incomparable golden autumn
of the western prairies, and the harvests were reaped
and stacked, golden tents on the stripped fields. The
vegetables were covered away in root-cellars on the
side of the hill. The grain that had not properly
matured was stacked for feed for the cattle and pigs,
while the rest was threshed and brought to the Company's grist-mill at Fort Edmonton.

Alexis and some noted hunters went out to the
plains for buffalo: others at the mission brought home
each night tempting stores of wild ducks from the
marshy ponds fringing the Lake. . . . *"Qu'il
etait delicieux pour les Métis comme pour l'Indien,
ce temps de l'Age d'Or, quand la chasse etait encore
abondante!"* Father Lacombe writes rapturously.
. . . "How full of delights for the Metis as for
the Indian, this Golden Age when the Hunt was still
abundant!"

By this time twenty Metis families had been
attracted to St. Albert, and were working on their

houses or lodges for the winter. . . . And with all this the heart of Father Lacombe was very glad.

In September a young traveller was carried into the mission terribly wounded by the accidental discharge of his gun. Father Lacombe put him in his own bed, where he and Michel did everything they could for him. They dressed his terrible wound, mitigating his numbed terror by their sympathy. He lingered a couple of weeks.

The unfortunate youth was from Hamilton, Ontario. Father Lacombe never enquired what his business in the west had been, and he has long ago forgotten his name, but at the time he wrote to the man's family and received a grateful response from them.

The following year, 1862, Father Lacombe says he opened—"with my axe in my hand"—at work on buildings for the new mission. In the spring he decided there must be a bridge across the Sturgeon at the foot of the hill. The river was greatly swollen this season and crossing doubly difficult, yet he held to his custom of attending the Fort on every alternate Sunday to celebrate Mass. The previous summer he had built a small scow or raft, which he used as a ferry, swimming his pony across.

"But I grew so tired of this," he told me once. "I say to myself one day—'I'll make a bridge.' Next Sunday after Mass I went outside and called aloud:

" 'My friends, I'm finished to cross that way in the

water walking in the mud on the bank and pushing the scow. I'll build me a bridge, and if any of you do not help me—that man will not cross on the bridge: he will go through the water. Yes, I will have a man there to watch.'

"Next morning that whole settlement came out with me. They brought axes, ropes, everything we need. I put an old *Canadien* freeman as supervisor, and in three days we had a solid bridge. While they worked I fed them all, with pemmican and tea."

For a long time this was known along the Saskatchewan as The Bridge. Lord Milton and Cheadle noted it as the only bridge they had seen in the Hudson's Bay Territory. To the inhabitants it was a marvel. Like children they crossed and re-crossed it scores of times at first simply for the delight and novelty of it.

The bridge built and the convent well advanced, Father Lacombe decided he should go over the prairies to St. Boniface to report to his bishop and bring back the yearly supplies of the missions from Outside. At that time it had become necessary to pay the Indians and Metis for work. A man's hire was one skin a day, which meant that he must be paid in goods to the value of one beaver-skin.

Anticipating the need of several workmen at the new mission, Father Lacombe decided to secure as large a supply of goods as possible. To avoid paying the high freight rates of the Company, he organized now a brigade of Red River carts—the historical wooden conveyance of western Canada, which has creaked its commonplace way into history as effectually as did Boadicea's more brilliant chariot.

This was the first brigade of carts to cross the prairies with freight between Fort Edmonton and the Red River.

The voyage across the prairies was made each way in one month, and on his return in August Father Lacombe brought with him an Oblate novice, Brother Scollen, to open a school for the children at Fort Edmonton. This school [1]—the first regular school to be opened west of Manitoba—was held in a loghouse within the Fort, and there were twenty pupils, the children of the Company's clerks and servants.

They were not scholars of a conventional type. Many of them wore deerskin garments and leggings, and carried lumps of pemmican or dried meat in their pockets as dainties. At the sound of the *voyageurs'* songs or cheers in autumn, they flew like arrows from their bows out to the bank to welcome the brigade home. When gunshot signals arose from the southern bank, they rushed to see what stranger would return in the boat sent across from the Fort. They were wild as hares.

This autumn in descending the ladder from a trap-

---

[1] It is worth recording that only forty-five years later over one hundred students of the new University of Alberta could look across the Saskatchewan at the deserted gray Fort, from which this school-house had long before vanished—and speak of the Fort and all pertaining to it as something connected with an age quite remote. . . . So quickly has this Age made progress in the West!

door in the storehouse loft, Father Lacombe missed his footing. The ladder slipped, his load of tools fell and instinctively grasping the floor above him, the heavy trapdoor crashed down on his hand. He called: no one came. . . .

He grew faint, and in his impatience fearing death would result, he fumbled in his pocket for his knife, planning to cut his hand off at the wrist. The knife was not there. . . . Rallying his strength for one desperate effort, he drew his body up, crashed on the door with his head and hand. . . . It moved slightly—he wrenched his hand out, and fell to the floor unconscious.

Michel and Rose, greatly distressed, found him there a little later, still unconscious, and for fifteen days his hand was so shockingly bruised he was unable to celebrate Mass.

By the end of this year—1862—St. Albert had assumed an air of pastoral permanence. The following year opened peacefully enough for the little colony. In the spring Father Lacombe sent Father Caer with some Metis to St. Boniface with the carts, while he remained at his post—an energizing spirit—putting in the grain crops, building a grist-mill and completing the shelter for the nuns, while work was begun on a larger house for them.

The past winter had been so hard that the Indians and some traders were in a state of semi-starvation for months. The Crees and Blackfeet made peace, because they needed all their energies for the hunt.

Fort Edmonton, in spite of its traditional stores, knew the nip of want toward the end of winter, but at St. Albert the little colony's store of dried meat was eked out with vegetables and grain from the mission-farm and fish dried in the autumn.

The Genius presiding there now became even more anxious to assure them a continual supply of food, and with this intention he set to work upon a flour-mill that he had ordered from St. Boniface with the last year's carts. His day-dreams already showed him grain-fields yellowed for the harvest and extending to all points of "this dear hillside." He gave small prizes to the Metis for putting in large crops on their own farms, and the system proved effective.

With the help of an American adventurer, who had sought the free hospitality of the mission during the winter, Father Lacombe set up the machinery of his little mill. It was a vexing task, for neither of the amateurs understood their work. With the machinery once placed, there was more trouble ahead taming the Indian ponies to furnish power.

More strenuously than their human prototypes these bronchos resisted the yoke of civilization, the drudgery of modern industry. Father Lacombe was determined, though. His will, that later proved a match for whole Indian tribes, was not to be overcome by bronchos. By degrees they were broken in, and on occasions when they were simply "furious," Father Lacombe resorted to the use of oxen, with a

Metis sitting near to touch them up when they lagged.

Like a verse out of the history of The-House-that-Jack-built is the passage written by Father Lacombe to a benefactor in Quebec concerning "the wild ponies that turn the big wheel that catches the cogs of a little wheel, that pulls round the band that sets the millstones in motion . . ." to grind the flour for the colony of St. Albert.

"Having neither blacksmiths, nor iron, nor implements the supply of power to our invention was often interrupted. . . . However, we at last made flour—to the great admiration of our people."

This was the first horse-power mill erected on the western plains, and it had a somewhat varied course not unattended by misfortune.

IX

In August of this year, Governor Dallas of the Hudson's Bay Company arrived at Fort Edmonton on a tour of inspection.

With Mr. Christie he went riding out to see the mission, which had become the one point of interest easily accessible to the Fort. Furthermore, Dallas, who had come not long before from Oregon, and had shared there in the Company's determined opposition to the entry of American settlers, was suspicious of Father Lacombe's little colony, where the freemen and Metis were giving all their time to farming instead of trapping furs as the Company's dividends demanded they should.

His irritation attained its height when he reached the Sturgeon. There stood The Bridge! The boast of the settlement it might be, but as surely plain evidence of the intrusion of the white man and his uninvited Progress. Tut! tut! this was enough to make any Company man of the old school grow hot. Could not the Gentlemen Adventurers have built bridges over every stream in the west if they had wanted to see them there? And here was this priest building one with its invitation to settlers—the thin edge of the wedge of civilization being thrust in.

"Have that bridge removed to-morrow," Dallas ordered Christie sternly, and the Chief Factor assented quietly. At the mission dinner-table, where he was regaled with the best of its cream and the choicest of its vegetables, the stalwart Governor grew hot again, but this time with a sort of admiration. Emphasizing his remarks with strokes of his heavy fist on the little table, he said to Christie:

"See the thrifty way in which these missioners make the most of everything, in spite of their poverty. See how with all our resources and our hundreds of servants, our Forts are falling to ruin, while these priests who come into the country with nothing but a little book under their arm"—referring to the Breviary which Father Lacombe had under his arm—"they are performing wonders.

"Their houses spring up from the ground like trees—growing bigger and better all the time; while our Forts are tumbling to ruin. Sir, things must be improved!"

Before long things were changed at Fort Edmonton, but when the old Governor—in whom the sterner traditions of the Company seemed embodied—had gone on his way again, no hand was lifted at Mr. Christie's order against The Bridge. The Factor had no intention of working such an injustice upon his friend.

In 1863 Lord Milton and his travelling companion, W. B. Cheadle, visited St. Albert. They had already spent one dreary winter in a log hut built by them-

selves in the vicinity of Fort Carleton. Like most
people on the plains that season they had known what
it was to feel hungry. At Fort Edmonton, where
Richard Hardisty was now in charge during
Christie's absence, the travellers had to spend some
time waiting for horses and guides to push on to the
mountains.

Meanwhile they visited St. Albert and relate in
their book of travels:

"At Lake St. Alban's, about nine miles north of
the Fort, a colony of freemen—i. e., half-breeds who
have left the service of the Company—have formed
a small settlement which is presided over by a Romish
priest. Some forty miles beyond is the ancient colony of Lake St. Ann's of similar character, but with
more numerous inhabitants.

"Soon after our arrival Mr. Hardisty informed us
that five grizzly bears had attacked a band of horses
belonging to the priest of St. Albans and afterwards
pursued two men who were on horseback—one of
whom, being very badly mounted, narrowly escaped
by the stratagem of throwing down his coat and cap,
which the bears stopped to tear to pieces. The priest
had arranged to have a grand hunt on the morrow
and we resolved to join in the sport.

"We carefully prepared guns and revolvers and at
daylight next morning drove over with Baptiste to
St. Alban's. We found a little colony of some
twenty houses built on the rising ground near a small
lake and river. A substantial wooden bridge spanned

the latter, the only structure of the kind we had seen in the Hudson's Bay territory.

"The priest's house was a pretty white building with garden around it and adjoining it the chapel, school and nunnery. The worthy Father, M. Lacombe, was standing in front of his dwelling as we came up, and we at once introduced ourselves and inquired about the projected bear-hunt. He welcomed us very cordially, and informed us that no day had yet been fixed, but that he intended to preach a crusade against the marauders on the following Sunday, when a time should be appointed for the half-breeds to assemble for the hunt."

"Père Lacombe was an exceedingly intelligent man, and we found his society very agreeable. Although a French-Canadian he spoke English very fluently and his knowledge of the Cree language was acknowledged by the half-breeds to be superior to their own. Gladly accepting his invitation to stay and dine, we followed him into his house, which contained only a single room with a sleeping loft above.

"The furniture consisted of a small table and a couple of rough chairs, and the walls were adorned with several coloured prints, amongst which were a portrait of His Holiness the Pope, another of the Bishop of Red River, and a picture representing some very substantial and stolid looking angels lifting very jolly saints out of the flames of purgatory.

"After a capital dinner of soup, fish and dried meat with delicious vegetables we strolled around the settlement in company with our host. He showed us several very respectable farms, with rich cornfields, large bands of horses and herds of cattle. He had devoted himself to improving the condition of his flock, had brought out at a great expense ploughs and other farming implements for their use, and was at the present completing a corn-mill to be worked by horse-power.

"He had built a chapel and established schools for the half-breed children. The substantial bridge we had crossed was the result of his exertions. Altogether this little settlement was the most flourishing community we had seen since leaving Red River, and it must be confessed that the Romish Priests far excel their Protestant brethren in missionary enterprise and influence.

"They have established stations at Isle a la Crosse, St. Alban's, St. Ann's, and other places, far out of the wilds, undeterred by danger or hardship, and gathering half-breeds and Indians around them, have taught with considerable success the elements of civilization as well as religion; while the latter remain inert enjoying the ease and comfort of the Red River settlement, or at most make an occasional summer's visit to some of the nearest Posts." [1]

[1] In this last statement the travellers were rather severe, for although the Catholic missionaries certainly had gone into the wilderness in vastly larger numbers than any other, and had worked in heroic fashion, there were at that time two missionaries of the Church of England in the Mackenzie district, where the first went in 1859; while on the Upper Saskatchewan the Rev. Mr. Woolsey, a Wesleyan preacher,

This year with St. Albert completely hewn out of the forest and all matters progressing favourably, Father Lacombe felt his old desire to go far out into the plains to meet the Blackfeet in their own country. Taking his Alexis and a half-breed Kootenai and Cree, named Francois, who spoke some Blackfoot, he rode forth with plenty of dried meat for provisions.

For the first time he carried with him his Red Cross flag—a small white pennon about two feet by one and a half, with a red Cross emblazoned on it. It was the signal agreed upon with the Blackfoot chief at Ste. Anne in 1860. The little party scoured the plains due south and southeast of Fort Edmonton, but Father Lacombe's time was so occupied with the bands of Crees he met first that he finally returned to the mission without meeting any but one small camp of Blackfeet.

It was during this journey to the prairies that Father Lacombe had his famous encounter with the Sorcerer and medicine-man, White-Eagle, the ruling spirit in a camp of over 300 hostile pagan Crees of the plains.

had succeeded his kindly little predecessor, Mr. Rundle, and had a mission at Pigeon Lake.

In this year, too, the Rev. George MacDougall of the Methodist Church came into the Edmonton country. The latter was a man to whose useful life and fine character Father Lacombe gladly testifies in fraternal charity. He came after Milton and Cheadle's visit, however, and they had naturally drawn their conclusions from what they saw; meeting zealous French priests at every post and none of any other race or creed.

For days the missionary camped with his Alexis within their circle of tepees—unwelcomed, while he and his religion were most subtly misrepresented and reviled by the medicine-man. To this Father Lacombe opposed a subtlety and determination that more than matched White Eagle, and a dower of the "faith that moves mountains." Mounting his pony at dawn one day he rode outside the circle of tents holding his crucifix high in one hand and his Red Cross flag in the other. He raised the Indian chant of Ho-ho-ye-hi; then called upon the Indians to rise and hear his story, for he would talk to them again.

The Indians gathered about him again, and this time White Eagle's arguments were so completely overturned that the indignant medicine-man left the camp and before long almost the entire camp became Christian.

Father Lacombe returned to St. Albert for the remainder of the year with occasional visits to Fort Edmonton, which under William Christie's sway had assumed an improved aspect.

A house and chapel built for Father Lacombe stood just west of the Big House. This was undoubtedly intended not only to please the priest who was a warm friend of Christie, but to provide the Fort as well with a lightning-rod against the wrath of the Blackfeet.

In the following spring—in 1864—for the first time in Father Lacombe's recollection the Blackfeet threatened the peace of Fort Edmonton.

A large party—over seven hundred in all—had come in to trade, and were camped for some days on the hill behind the Fort. The meadows were alive with ponies, dogs and people, until one day after the trading had been concluded the order for departure was cried through the encampment—much to the relief of the Gentlemen Traders.

The lodges were pulled down and bound with thongs: the party dropped easily into marching-order, a file of hunters winding down the steep path to the river which was then low and easily forded. They made a picturesque array—lusty strong-featured bronzed men and women with lithe half-naked bodies and faces streaked with vermilion. The leaders wore eagle-feathers in their hair: the men were for the most part naked but for a buffalo-robe caught around them: the women wore decorated tunics of antelope-skin or blue cloth and richly beaded gaiters. Men and women alike sat their sure-footed bronchos with the ease of the plainsman, their primitive chattels fastened to travoix dragged behind the ponies.

The band had already crossed the Saskatchewan and their straggling numbers were climbing the trail up the wooded banks on the south side—when the trouble began. A Sarcee had lingered behind the party, and standing by the Indian Gate near the southeast bastion was intent upon a horse deal with Flatboat McLaine. Joe McDonald and a man named Smith stood near helping McLaine in the barter. Smith was endeavouring to make a deal for a bundle of old clothes and a quantity of alcohol in an old painkiller bottle.

With vigorous pantomime he would first let the Indian smell the alcohol, then pointing to the bottle and the clothes—magnificently proffer the whole for the horse. The Indian dallied: he wanted more—for a pony in those days was worth fifty to sixty skins. . . . Suddenly a small party of Cree warriors slipped around the bastion from the south side: without warning Little Pine, their leader, emptied his rifle into the Sarcee's thighs.

The Sarcee brave fell forward, mortally wounded, blood gushing from mouth and nostrils. McLaine seizing the body dragged it to the southeastern gate while the Crees made off, firing wild as they went. The Sarcee's wife in dumb agony ran to throw her arms around the bleeding body: she was pulled into the courtyard by the men, and the gates speedily closed by the steward.[1]

Father Lacombe was seated writing in his quarters. Startled there by the cry that a Blackfoot had been killed he hurried out to find the unfortunate Sarcee drenched in blood on the floor of the Indian Hall. His squaw crouched beside him moaning piteously.

[1] Malcolm Groat, the son of Alexander Groat, a popular drill-sergeant in Wellington's army in the Peninsular War, was steward of Fort Edmonton for several years. He was born in Glasgow and is a descendant of that Jan Groote who came from Holland early in the eighteenth century, and for services rendered had bestowed on him by King James II those lands upon which John O'Groat's house came to be built. Malcolm Groat came to Edmonton House from Scotland by way of the Hudson's Bay in 1862.

The warrior was not dead, and when his wounds were dressed, he was put in the care of Steward Groat and carried to a bed of blankets in the latter's room.

His wife stayed with him, crouching beside him like a stricken animal, moaning softly with heart-breaking poignancy. Groat called on McLaine to keep him company through this vigil, and McLaine—a good-hearted rough fellow—essayed to explain to the woman by signs that if her husband needed any assistance through the night she was to call himself and Groat. The two men climbed therewith to their bunks.

The well-meant offer only roused the pair to alarm, and from soft moans their voices raised to weird death-chants and cries, alternating with calls for "Lacombe!" or "Brazeau!" Groat finally brought the interpreter Brazeau and after he had reassured the unfortunate pair that no harm was meant to either by McLaine, they kept stoically quiet for the rest of the night.

For a couple of days the warrior lingered—then died. His body was buried under the trees in the Fort burying-ground by the river, and the woman laden with gifts was sent back to her own people.

Some weeks later a war-party of Blackfeet returned to the Fort. They were met far outside the gates by Brazeau, who had enjoyed a reputation among them for fearlessness since his Missouri days. He conducted the chiefs to the Indian Hall, where

Christie and Father Lacombe smoked the calumet
with them and sent them home laden with gifts.

About July of this year Dr. Rae, the explorer,
passed through Fort Edmonton on his way to British
Columbia.   As all travellers did at the time, when
they had heard of the little Utopia north of the Fort,
he went out to see it and its founder.

"Ah, my crops were fine.   The place—it looked
—yes, heavenly!" Father Lacombe recalls with enthusiasm.   "And Dr. Rae, he was astonished, he say
to me, to see such grain.

"At this time Alexis, *mon fameux Alexis,* had some
growth on his hand, big as a bird's egg and soft, and
the pain burned him.   When Dr. Rae came out to us
—like a Providence—I had him look at it, but Alexis
said he was afraid to have anything done for it.   I
said to Rae, 'When I talk to Alexis and he is turn
from you—cut it quick with your lance!'—He did,
and it cured the hand.   My poor Alexis!"

The crops that year were particularly good, and
Father Lacombe, anticipating plenty of work for his
mill, tried to improve it.   With the Brother Bowes
he built a dam on the Sturgeon to provide power.   In
June a steady downpour of rain made the lake and
rivers rise; small creeks swelled to the size of young
rivers; the dam was threatened with destruction.

Fearing the worst Father Lacombe got on his
horse and galloped round the settlement calling on his
people to come and help him.   They hung lanterns
in the trees by the riverside and all night worked un-

der his direction digging a canal at the bend above the mill-dam. The water was diverted from its regular course, pressure on the dam was relieved and that precious bit of frontier workmanship saved.

A surprise was now in store for Father Lacombe. Shortly before the brigade returned from Norway House Richard Hardisty, the young trader at Rocky Mountain House, had been down to the Red River. He brought back word to Father Lacombe that a brother of his was coming up by boat. A few days later as the newcomer, a slim youth of eighteen, rode out to the mission the two met on the St. Albert trail.

Gaspard Lacombe was a straight, self-reliant youth, less emotional than the missionary, yet resembling him strangely in face and figure. The lure of the open trail, that in Albert Lacombe had been overcome by his studies and ambitions, had conquered Gaspard. Suddenly leaving school at fourteen he set out roaming with a young man down through Virginia and Kentucky and back again through Ohio to Ontario—working his way as he went.

He returned home. To please his family he held a clerkship in Montreal for eighteen months. The wanderlust again seized him and off he went to Albany. Here a letter came from his mother, enclosing one from Father Lacombe, in which he alluded to American miners who had made their first find of Saskatchewan gold.

Within five hours Gaspard was on board a train for St. Paul.

The next summer he surprised Richard Hardisty at Fort Garry by asking to be taken to Edmonton House.

"But, you little fellow," the Edmonton man protested, "your brother will be vexed if I take you away back there!"

Gaspard, not unlike his brother in his determination, finally had his way, and as we have seen arrived at St. Albert.

Shortly after his arrival Gaspard Lacombe accompanied his brother out to Beaver Hills, where a big encampment of Crees were driving buffalo into pounds to slaughter them.

"Ah learned then," says Gaspard in his soft Southern accent, "what the Sisters meant when they wahned me that Father Lacombe gave everything away. Ma dear! the first day he gave away ma red flannel shirt—the only one Ah had in ma sack—because he had nothing himself but what he wore. . . . Heu! the vermin and cold were so bad Ah only stayed three days in the camp; some half-breeds passed bound for St. Albert. I joined them—Ah'd have left sooner if I could!"

From Beaver Hills Father Lacombe went to Rocky Mountain House to instruct a party of Blackfeet. One morning outside the gates he was hailed by a weary party [1] of American miners, half-famished

1 Jimmy Gibbons, who recalled these details for me at Edmonton in

and footsore. They had lived on horseflesh from the Devil's Lake to the Red River, where the Blackfeet had stolen all the rest of their horses. A fresh travoix trail had providentially guided them in to the post.

Father Lacombe led them into the Fort entrusting them to the hospitality of Richard Hardisty, the trader in charge. Savoury rabbit-stew, the best the post could offer, was set before the hungry men and devoured with relish.

Through Idaho and Montana, at Buffalo Hump and Orafino, in Bitter-root Valley, at Bannock and Pike's Peak, then up in the Kootenays—the strangers had known miner's luck, until now, drawn by the pale lure of Saskatchewan gold they had come on this voyage of mischance.

＊ ＊ ＊ ＊ ＊ ＊ ＊

It was in December, 1864, that the Rev. Father Vandenburghe of France arrived at St. Albert with Bishop Tache on a tour of inspection. Before their departure on January 9, new posts were assigned to Father Lacombe and his colleagues. As fond parents do with their children at Christmas, the Superiors had tried to give each his heart's desire—and so there fell to the lot of Father Lacombe "the mission of coursing the prairies to try and reach the poor savage Crees and Blackfeet."

1909, was one of the party—himself a red-shirted miner in California for years before when there still were "deadfalls" in the saloons along the waterfront of 'Frisco, and when a man could spend at Placerville on Sunday most of the gold he had washed out of the rich gulches during the week.

Father Lacombe was frankly delighted with his lot; St. Albert was becoming *"trop civilise"* for him, and his happy experience in the plains-Cree camp had unsettled him for the mission-routine. "I was dismissed from the prefecture of St. Albert and given a free field to course after the Crees and Blackfeet on the prairies. Behold me in my element! *Laetatus sum in his quae dicta sunt mihi!"*

With all the ardours of his warm nature Father Lacombe burned to reach every tribe on the plains— group after group, to gather these poor nomads in fresh colonies to live there in pastoral contentment and certainty of food. As each settlement was formed it would be his aim to turn it over to some of his younger brethren, while he pushed on again into the wilds with his Red Cross flag and his plough to bring into Christian submission still other bands of savages.

X

FATHER LACOMBE was now to be the missionary free-lance of the plains—to come and go as he would. It is with difficulty we follow the red and white gleams of his flag during the next six years. It was constantly appearing at the most unexpected points on the prairie between the Bow River and the Peace, the foothills and the Saskatchewan Forks.

This was his immense hunting-ground for souls— an area inhabited by eight different tribes—and his fearlessness, energy and daring there so matched those qualities in the bravest of their chiefs that they came to regard him as a great Christian medicine-man.

Yet there must have been other qualities in him more noticeable. For the Indian, when he names a white man, tries to sum up in one phrase the most striking qualities of the man—and to the Crees Father Lacombe was always known in this period as *Ka-miyo-atchakwe* (The Man-of-the-Beautiful-Soul). To the various Blackfeet tribes he was *Arsous-kitsi-rarpi* (The Man-of-the-Good-Heart).

On January 17, 1865, he left St. Albert with his man Alexis and four good dogs hauling a toboggan-sleigh on which they had all the equipment necessary for several weeks—blankets and buffalo-robes for sleeping in, an axe, Alexis' gun and provisions of dried meat for both dogs and men . . . *"Et puis, nous voila en marche!"*

At Fort Edmonton Mr. Christie's hand was taken in greeting, as the friendly Factor wished them God-speed. They pushed on, breaking the trail for the dogs where it was necessary. The trip was made without hardship until the third morning out, when they woke to a heavy snow storm and cutting wind. The morning meal was eaten quickly, for they re-solved to reach the Cree camp near the Red Deer River that night.

"Marche, Pappillon! Marches, mes chiens!" the little missionary urged in encouragement, and his good dogs set off in the teeth of the wind, the travel-lers in turn breaking the way for them with snow-shoes. There was "a sweet zephyr blowing, and the temperature must have been forty degrees below zero," Father Lacombe recalls.

Men talk little on these trips: there was but an occasional, "Are you cold, Alexis?" and "Not yet— but you, *mon Père?"*—"Courage! I'm holding out well."

Nibbling at dried meat instead of pausing for a meal they pushed on and reached the Crees' camp at night.

"A person must have experienced a similar arrival to have any idea of this," Father Lacombe writes in his Memoirs. "The darkness, the deafening howls of the dogs, the yells of the Crees, the remains of butchered animals lying about—and then the cold which devours you!"

But a Christian chief—Abraham Kiyiwin—who recognized the priest at once drew him into his tent and made the two rest there after they had eaten a steaming dish of buffalo-meat. Even though the hour was late, some of the men came to talk with the Blackrobe, squatting about him on the robes near the fire. He quickly dismissed them however; he wanted "a pleasant smoke, a bit of prayer and then—to bed."

But not to sleep, with the dogs—"a band of thieves" —prowling around the tent half the night! In a dozing state he heard one gnaw at a bone close by— and he sleepily wonders if they would tear his own body with their strong white teeth. But he is too tired to continue the speculation—*"C'est egal: on dort"*—He drops to sleep.

For six weeks he laboured among these Crees, and here as always on the plains-mission his days passed in a regular routine. If he could get a good tepee, where there was no snow, or the smoke was not too thick he would set up a little portable chapel and begin the day with Mass. After his breakfast, eaten from a rude dish as he squatted on the ground, he assembled the women, teaching them catechism, prayers or hymns.

Fifty women with almost as many infants!—and when these last began to cry—"I assure you," says Father Lacombe, "it was interesting—something then to try your patience."

At noon he was accustomed to call the children, both boys and girls about him and spent the afternoon teaching them. At least with them, he says, he enjoyed peace and tranquillity. After the encampment had taken their evening meal his little bell was rung by Alexis passing up and down through the camp like a crier, inviting all the men to the priest's tent.

"Ah, this is something more serious and dignified," he recalls in his Memoirs. "They come with their pipes—sometimes we smoked a calumet, the ceremonial pipe. Then I take on an attitude more majestic, more reserved, for these are the warriors, and they love ceremony. After each one has taken his place according to his rank, I intone in my finest voice a hymn. Then the sermon.

"Then all to our knees—some squat ungratefully on their heels! We pray—we sing, and at the last we pass about the calumet, whose smoke like incense crowns the religious service."

In addition to these meetings the missionary visited the sick to be found in most camps, and when he could, he administered healing drugs to them. Other diplomatic visits were paid to pagans of the tribe, of whom there were usually some in each camp. The most interesting of the Cree pagans—*Wihaskokiseyin*—Chief Sweet Grass, head chief of the nation, was in this camp, but to Father Lacombe as to other priests he would only reply on religious matters:

"Leave me in peace. When my time comes I will tell you." Notwithstanding this withholding of his personal adherence he was one of the best friends the priest had on the plains.

Before his departure Father Lacombe held a council in which he outlined his new plan of action, inviting the councillors to help him select a place as a permanent mission for the Cree Indians. They decided upon *Kamaheskutewegak*—"The-prairie-which-comes-out-to-the-river," or as it was named by Father Lacombe,[1] St. Paul des Cris.

Shortly after his return to St. Albert at the end of February a deputation of Blackfeet came for him, begging him to go with them. Their tribe was again stricken with a mysterious disease. They were helpless and panic-stricken. Father Lacombe hurried out to their camp and found them down with typhoid. It was not serious, however. There were few deaths; and after a couple of weeks he could return to St. Albert.

Here another call to Rocky Mountain House awaited him. Other bands of Blackfeet were down with the same disease. He went, and ministered to them for some weeks.

Early in May he rafted down the Saskatchewan to the site of his new establishment,[2] one hundred and fifty miles east of Fort Edmonton. The Company

[1] This old Mission station is now named Brousseau.

[2] Father Lacombe has in his possession still the Journal of St. Paul de Cris, written on a sheaf of foolscap pages doubled to about four inches in width, with a tattered brown Manila cover. This, although not complete, keeps definite record of many of the goings and comings of Father Lacombe in those days—and fortunately so, for even

had objected to this site, claiming that it would draw away the Indians from Fort Pitt.

But the Crees favoured it. Likewise the soil was so fertile and so easily broken that Father Lacombe determined to locate there in the hope of getting some of the Metis and Indians to till the land as at St. Albert. He found a large encampment of Crees, faithful to their promise, awaiting him. They greeted him with enthusiasm, running into the water to pull his raft ashore.

On this he and Alexis had fifty bushels of potatoes, seed-grain, a plow and provisions. His brother Gaspard and one Noel Courtepatte had conveyed other provisions over-land in ox-carts. As the multitude of Crees looked on with the interest of prospective owners the raft was unloaded.

On the following day the eager young missionary started to plow. The women and children flocked behind him, crushing the earth with their hands into fine particles. A couple of days later when the ground was prepared it was the women again who dropped the potatoes and vegetable-seeds.

The men tacitly objected to taking any active part, and Father Lacombe soon found it was not Metis he was dealing with here. He put himself to work this spring quite as energetically as at St. Albert, but with less success and half-hearted assistance. En-

his own memory, so retentive ordinarily of details, has but an incomplete record of these days. His rapidity of movement confused even himself.

feebled perhaps by his unusual hardships and exertions of the past four months he fell ill. The third week in May he writes to Bishop Tache:

"The heat of spring has changed the malady of the winter to a form of dysentery which carries off all whom it attacks. After ten days I am almost overcome by it. All our work is stopped, and I can only minister to the sick. If this sickness carries me off, at least my sacrifice is made. I will die happy among my neophytes, ministering to them as long as I have strength."

But he gradually recovered. Then as the Crees went off to the prairies to hunt buffalo he returned to St. Albert to convalesce.

In June he returned, bringing his brother. Together they improved the "skeleton of a house" built the previous winter by Gaspard and Alexis. Gaspard returned to St. Albert. For Father Lacombe it was:

"Hurrah for the prairies! We all went. We traversed creek after creek, swollen now to torrents; but these were no obstacles to hungry Indians sighing for fresh feasts of buffalo-meat. . . . Hey! I am in my element. My cart, my three horses, my good Alexis, and our Blackfoot cook with whom I am studying the Blackfoot language, my tent, my chapel-case, my catechisms and objects of piety— behold, my church and presbytery!" he writes to the Forets.

"To tell the truth, I am as happy as a Prince of

the Church. My people, about half of whom are
Christian and men of great prestige as hunters—they
respect me, they love me. I feel like a king here, a
new Moses in the midst of this new camp of Israel.
It is not the manna of the desert with which
we are nourished, but it is the delicious buffalo-
meat of the prairie which the good Master gives
us."

When they had travelled three days toward the
great sea of the prairies the scouts ranging ahead
wheeled back to signal to them—a herd of buffalo was
ahead! On the moment came the order to pitch camp.
The women and old men hastened about this duty,
while the hunters saddled their ponies. Guns,
powder, balls, whip and lasso—they saw all were in
place. Soon they were ready for the command—
the Hunt began!

Apart from the buffalo-hunts, which soon lost their
novelty, the life on the plains was full of delight for
Father Lacombe. By day the wide green prairies
drenched in radiant sunshine were pleasing. At
night, when the fury of the hunt was passed and
darkness put an end to the toil of the women, the
scene was still beautiful, day lingering long above the
purple-black expanse of the plains. Then he tells
us:

"Seated on the fresh grass, with the vaulted skies
sown with stars for our House of adoration, silence
falls—the ravens and the little birds are asleep, but
man keeps watch. It is then our songs of good-night

are sung to the Great Spirit—and how beautiful seem these hymns of the children of the wilderness!

"And there amidst them, happy in his lot, see this man in a soutane. How eloquent and fine it seems to him to say to them in their own language—taught by these fierce warriors—'Go, and sleep tranquilly, my children. May the Great Spirit bless you. *Au revoir*—till morning.' "

. . . .

Father Lacombe, desirous of dividing his new ministry impartially between the Blackfoot nation and the Crees, directed his way south toward a large camp of the former in October. He stayed some time with the Piegans and Bloods in the vicinity of the Red Deer River after he left St. Albert on October 23: then moved on to the camp of Chief Natous near Three Ponds,[1] where he arrived at the close of November. He was unaccompanied by Alexis and by a mere chance his young brother Gaspard was not with him.

Father Lacombe had already undergone many hardships of the trail. He was now to realise the crowning hazard of Indian life—"a terrible accident, which," as Father Andre wrote in a letter[2] of October 26, 1866, to Father LeFloch, "came near removing one of the most courageous and intrepid of our missionaries . . . Pere Lacombe."

[1] The scene of this battle was near the Battle River, some miles east of the present town of Hobbema.

[2] This letter is published in Vol. IV of the *Quebec Rapports*, in that portion devoted to chronicles of St. Boniface diocese.

XI

Food having become scarce in the south, Natous with other Blackfoot chiefs had led his band to the extreme northern boundary of their hunting ground. Camped a short distance away were two other bands of his nation, which Father Lacombe planned to visit when he had concluded his mission to the band of Natous. The possibility of any warlike interruption to his plans did not occur to him. He was, however, to have his entire plans for the winter upset by a renewal of the war between the Crees and Blackfeet.

This battle took place on the night of December the fourth. Father Lacombe was quartered in the lodge of Chief Natous. He and his savage host slumbered soundly on buffalo robes, their feet to the fire. . . . Suddenly harsh sounds forced themselves to the chief's consciousness. Natous leaped to his feet.

"*Assinaw! Assinaw!*"—The Crees! The Crees!— he cried instantly. His old wife rushed with him from the tent, Natous hastily priming his musket. In the darkness outside a deadly round of musketry crackled, then thundered, while weird lights quivered through the inky blackness: the Crees had come prepared for slaughter. Father Lacombe was shocked into rigidity for an instant: outside the voice of

Natous rose rallying his warriors to the defense of their camp.

The firelit lodge of the chief made a clear target for the enemy. Suddenly two poles snapped with the impact of balls that whizzed past Father Lacombe. As one in a stupor he noted smoking gun-wads fall near him. The soutane he had removed for the night, he now hastily threw on over his deer skin garments; snatching up the surplice and stole, and reverently kissing the cross of his Order before putting it in his belt, he prepared to move.

In accordance with the discipline of religious Orders he paused to make a brief, generous offering of his life to his Maker, from whom death or life might come that night. Then he was himself again, alert and fearless. A small sack containing the holy oils he hung at his side. Taking up his Red Cross flag he went out of the tent. Outside, he found himself in a hell of darkness and uncertainty and lust for blood. Many of the young Blackfoot warriors were away hunting buffalo, but those who remained under Natous fought on recklessly.

Above the din rose the voice of Natous animating his followers and defying the enemy. Father Lacombe, incensed by the treacherous attack, shouted an indignant command to the Crees to withdraw. Some of them were Christian, he felt, and would obey him. . . .

His voice rang out from a chest strong and deep as a Viking's. In the hideous din of the carnage it was entirely lost. The old warriors were crying out encouragement and advice to the young men. Some of the braves had raised wild war-chants, and on both sides came the fiendish yells of unbridled passion. Father Lacombe abandoned his futile effort.

The women, feverishly trying with knives and hands to dig trenches wherein to hide their children and themselves, raised their voices from time to time in lamentation. Within the camp in the darkness the living fell over the dead, and the wounded pleaded for help.

To make the night more appalling, the frenzied barking of the dogs rose hideously, blended with the pitiful whinnies of frightened or dying horses. The night was profoundly dark, unlit by moon or stars. Only the sinister flash of the musketry lit the painful scene.

Father Lacombe traversed the camping-ground over and over again, inspiring the warriors to their bravest efforts. He sought out the wounded, when he could find them in the darkness. A woman standing near him at the door of her lodge fell pierced by a bullet; he baptized her and prayed with her till she died.

Next morning she was found scalped; a daring enemy had come into the lodge at some time through the night and carried off the coveted trophy. A thieving Assinaboine in the act of pillaging the chief's tent was pierced by a ball and fell across the pile of robes grasping Father Lacombe's breviary. Back and forward through the darkness an intermittent rain of balls fell. Father Lacombe, moving continually with words of encouragement to the warriors, seemed to bear a charmed life.

At last, drawn by the sound of the battle, the Blackfoot warriors of the other bands came to the rescue, though not before the enemy had practically completed sacking the camp.

One party of the rescuers was led by Crowfoot, a young man already for his wisdom and bravery made a chief among his people. In the darkness he came up to Father Lacombe. A flash from a gun lit up his face, showing it still and strong.

"Who are you?" the priest asked, for the face was new to him.

"Crowfoot," the warrior replied, and Father Lacombe, rejoicing in the arrival of the noted young warrior, urged him to do his best for the safety of his people.

Three times that night the Crees and their Assinaboine recruits were repulsed from the hillock behind which the Blackfeet had secured cover, but dawn still found them fighting. Before this, twenty-five lodges —about half of the camp—had been destroyed.

Grateful for returning day, the Man of Prayer, in stole and surplice dingy with the smoke of battle, raising his crucifix in one hand and the Red Cross flag in the other, now called on his Blackfoot hosts to cease firing. Astounded at his actions, they complied and watched him walk deliberately out from the broken circle of tents toward the enemy, holding his crucifix aloft and waving his white and red flag.

The Indian warriors, trained to ambush in battle, marvelled at his bravery. Their Man-of-the-Good-Heart had always been to them a great medicine-man. Now he seemed a god come to their defence as he moved slowly through the mist, advancing directly upon the concealed enemy. The heroism of the action was unconscious, characteristic, superb.

"Here! you Crees. *Kamiyo-atchakwe* speaks! . . ."

He called aloud again and again, but his Crees did not hear him; and a fog, heavy with low-lying battle-smoke, hung like a curtain shutting him out from their vision.

He called to the unseen enemy; he waved his flag, but his efforts were unavailing. The irregular fire continued, bullets whizzed past his head and ploughed in the ground beside him. The Blackfeet called out to him, begging him to return, when suddenly a ball, which had already touched the earth, rebounded to his shoulder and glancing off struck his forehead. The wound was a mere scratch, but the shock was so great he staggered and lost his footing.

The Blackfeet believed him wounded—and a new wave of anger swept over their hearts. . . . The Crees had killed their friend, *Arsous-kitsi-rarpi!*—the Man-of-the-Good-Heart—who had nursed them through the typhoid and who was a hundred times endeared to them now by his unique bravery.

"Hee-yi-ho!"—they raised their war-cry; and flung themselves out upon the Crees—no longer repulsing attacks but driving one home to the heart of the enemy. From tepee to bluff—to coulee, they slipped over the thin snow, the Crees advancing and retreating, pursuing the same tactics. The battle lingered while the fog lay on the land, and it was long after dawn before a Blackfoot warrior who lay near the enemy cried out to them with scorn in a lull of firing:

"You have wounded your Blackrobe, Dogs! Have you not done enough?"

When this startling word ran through the ranks of the Crees, the firing ceased. . . . Was it true that they had killed their father, the Man of Prayer, the friend of Rowand and of Christie, the big white chiefs?

The battle received a sudden check, and the Crees did not wait to meet their Blackrobe, but speedily withdrew in confusion.

The engagement had lasted seven or eight hours, for the greater part of the time a disorderly skirmish. Of the Blackfeet, Chief Natous was badly wounded, about twelve persons were killed, two children stolen, and fifteen men and women wounded, some fatally. The camp had been pillaged of meat and robes, and twenty-five lodges destroyed. Their enemies carried ten dead warriors away from the snowy battlefield, while fully fifteen others were wounded.

The following day, notwithstanding their fatigue and the ills of the wounded, the Chiefs ordered the camp moved; ponies, human beings and dogs were soon in line of march over the snowy trails to another and larger camp of their nation twenty miles away.

Father Lacombe, like many of his Blackfoot friends, had lost in the battle all but what was on his person and the rescued breviary. Fully two hundred horses had been killed or stolen by the Crees, among them the two owned by Father Lacombe. The Indians, who at least never lacked in hospitality or generosity, gave him robes to keep him warm and lent him a horse to continue his journey.

He stayed with Natous' band about ten days longer, consoling them and caring for the wounded. Then, with three Indians as companions, he set out for Rocky Mountain House, whither he had sent a courier in the autumn to make a rendezvous with the Indians for Christmas.

It was a journey of several days during severe weather and over bad trails. The food of the little party consisted of an occasional partridge or rabbit, a few leathery pieces of dried meat, gnawed at by day, and at night boiled in snow-water. The last day found them fasting.

When the little cavalcade finally drew up before the gates of the post, Father Lacombe emerged from his buffalo robe, disfigured with stains and dirt, and stepped from his horse fairly into the arms of his astonished friend, Richard Hardisty.[1]

---

[1] The late Richard Hardisty (later Chief Factor Hardisty) was a member of a family long connected with the service of the Company in

Shocked at finding Father Lacombe in this guise, the warm-hearted trader began to make queries in a startled voice—when the other, with his irrepressible humour bubbling up again, reassured him:

"Don't cry, don't cry, my frien'. I've been to war; but now—you see—I am back."

There was reason, however, for Mr. Hardisty's alarm. Father Lacombe was about at the end of his resources and his friend set about restoring them.

"Richard Hardisty treated me like a brother that day. I felt so sick and tired and hungry when I got to Mountain House that I was ready to lie down in the snow and die. But he took our miserable party in before his big fire, and warmed and fed us and clothed me, and I always feel since then that he saved my life," Father Lacombe recalls.

We will leave him there happily seated before the blazing chimney-fire of *Meekoostakwan* (the Man-with-the-Red-Hair). The glowing blaze, like a warm soul in a homely person, beautified the whole dingy interior of the post—the smoky dark rafters, the log walls and rude woodland furnishings.

the Southern district, and was for several years in charge of Edmonton district. He was a brother of Lady Strathcona.

XII

It was Christmas week at Fort Edmonton in the year 1865, and within the snowy quadrangle of the Fort preparations for the home-joys of Christmas were under way.

Outside the gates were some Cree teepees whose owners had brought a rumour of Father Lacombe being killed in a battle near Three Ponds. They even showed a *capot* like his taken out of his tent, they said, and with several bullet-holes in it. The rumour was too terrible to be given credence, however, and was set down as an Indian yarn.

At the Big House, straying half-breed children found the kitchen for the time converted to a Paradise of good dishes and savoury odours with Murdo MacKenzie, the cook from "bonny Stornaway," presiding. Elsewhere the steward—Malcolm Groat— saw to it that extra rations of fish and buffalo meat and grease were portioned out, and to this some grog added to drink the Factor's health. In her own quarters, Mrs. Christie, the granddaughter of fine old "Credo" Sinclair of York Factory, planned a Santa Claus for her little ones.

A dog-cariole drawn at a merry trot by good dogs and followed by two sleds with their drivers came through the valley across the river. It was too cold then for men to linger on the gossip-benches by the flagstaff outside the southern gate, but the dog-train was awaited with curiosity by those within the Fort.

Several traders had already arrived from the out-posts and no one else was likely to make the Fort for Christmas but Richard Hardisty of Mountain House.   One of the runners resembled him.   .   .   .   But who did he have comfortably wrapped in buf-falo-robes in the cariole?

"You never know what you will meet around the bend—" is a proverb of the *voyageur* by land or water trail; and "You never know who will turn up next" might well be the word of the masters of Hud-son's Bay posts.

When the dog-train drew up at the Fort and Father Lacombe stepped out of the robes and wrap-pings, there was boisterous delight in the greetings of his friends.   .   .   .   Was ever an arrival more timely?

Mr. Christie ushered the two arrivals into the Big House and the little knot of people dispersed to their quarters.   Darkness fell; the big gates were clanged to, and the bell was rung for the evening meal and issuing of rations.

.   .   .   .

That Christmas Eve the brown spaciousness of the mess-room quivered with interest, and the centre of it all—Murdo MacKenzie [1] relates—was the worn

---

[1] When I met him forty-five years after this Christmas Eve,—still out of the range of modern Progress, still a cook in the employ of the big Company in its Peace River district.

young priest in the ragged greasy soutane, who
looked as though he had known hardships in plenty
since he departed.

The Gentlemen's mess-room of the Big House,
where this dinner was given, was a fine room—noted
alike for spaciousness and hospitality. Every one
who visited Edmonton House from Paul Kane's time
onward recorded its rugged pretentiousness. There
was nothing finer in the west, except the old Coun-
cil-room of Norway House.

Time, for their isolated kingdom, was regulated
by the great clock which hung on the mess-room wall.
Pictures hung there, too, good pictures, and swords
from the Old Land, and buffalo-horns and moose-
heads from the plains and forest of the New. There
was a cavernous fireplace and heavy mantel, about
which for close on to fifty years the gentlemen of
Edmonton House had lingered in chat after dinner.

At one side was a table laden with the brass candlesticks Murdo MacKenzie kept in polished array to
light the dinner-table each night. Two immense
heaters brought from England by way of the Hudson
Bay were required to heat the room.

"Ah, it was a *grand* place altogether," Murdo
recalls.

On this Christmas Eve, while the Gentlemen
listened, Mr. Christie plied his friends with questions,
and Murdo lingered as he passed about the dishes.
He recalls Father Lacombe telling how a bullet
whizzed over his head as he bent to lift an object

from the floor of the camp, and showing where that reflected bullet struck his shoulder.

To most that night would have seemed a terrifying experience, yet as we read in his letter to his Superior-General, Monsignor Fabre, Father Lacombe could say:

"I was never less afraid than I was during this combat."

But even as he talked the Star of Peace and Good-will was on the hills with the old message the angels sang to the shepherds. . . . The story-telling and the dinner ended, and Father Lacombe and Father Andre made their way to the confessional, where the quick-tempered, child-hearted but now subdued, *voyageurs* waited to ease their minds and make their hearts ready for the coming of the Child.

At midnight the bell pealed Yuletide greetings, and almost every one in the Fort came together in the church. The congregation listened there to the story of the Child-King told in English, French and Cree. They were wholesome western men, vigorous creatures of strong passions and ready faith, and they accepted happily the mysterious union of weakness and omnipotence, the tale of Love stooping to earth to win it otherwise than by force.

    .   .   .   .

During the year 1866 work went on more or less steadily at St. Paul de Cris. Again a small crop was put in and the shelter thrown up in 1865 improved. The mission became a stopping-place for priests to and from their missions.

In the spring Gaspard Lacombe, who with the miners, Little and Piler, had tired of gold-mining on the Saskatchewan, bade good-bye to his brother, riding through St. Paul de Cris on his way to St. Boniface.

Father Lacombe asked him if he felt any desire to join him in mission work. The young fellow half laughed, half shuddered at the idea. To live day after day in garments infested with vermin; to exist for weeks on dry meat or pemmican without tea— nothing in the world, he felt, could tie him to it, and he had no supernatural impulse to impel him.

So away he went to resume a life of fruitless contented wandering from the Red River to Mexico, from the Mississippi to the coast.

Most of the year of 1866 was spent by Father Lacombe on the prairies with his Indians. With a few weeks of rest at St. Albert after his eventful trip to the Blackfeet, he set out by dog-train for St. Paul de Cris. His only companion was a quaint little Irish-American called Jimmy-from-Cork, who had drifted into Fort Edmonton and was now anxious to make his way to the Red River. This man— Jimmy McCarthy—who was to make himself conspicuous at Fort Garry in 1870—had even then a varied and sombre career behind him.

Sam Livingstone and Jimmy Gibbons, the Fortyniners, standing on the river-bank near Victoria, one day in January, 1866, as Father Lacombe came trotting behind his dog-train, were astounded to find that the little man snugly wrapped in robes in Father Lacombe's dog-cariole was Jimmy-from-Cork!

The hospitable miners called out an invitation to the travellers to share their mid-day meal with them. Father Lacombe—his clumsy soutane tucked up about his leather trousers, as it always was when he travelled behind dogs—busied himself first with food for the animals. But his genial little companion, Gibbons recalls, stepped out of the cariole and patting the priest on the shoulder, said airily to his hosts:

"We've had a good trip, boys. Father Lacombe is a damn good runner, and he knows that Jimmy-from-Cork's legs are too short to run."

Assuredly fraternal charity and the frontier brings strange bed-fellows together!

Jimmy was, however, but a ship-in-the-night in Father Lacombe's life—one never hailed again—and in this unlike his hosts who remained his friends for their lifetime. Livingstone interested him greatly as one of the most picturesque figures he had met in the west. The son of an Anglican rector in Ireland and born in the Vale of Avoca, he had drifted through the United States to the Saskatchewan.

He was a fine-looking man, brimful of Celtic fire, with grizzled white hair worn long, down on his shoulders after the fashion of his old friend, Dr. John McLoughlin, the ruler of Oregon. Leather trousers and red shirt, and a gay handkerchief knotted about his throat with another on his wide sombrero completed in Sam Livingstone a striking picture of the frontiersman.

In February of this year Father Lacombe, going out from St. Paul with Alexis, made a trip north to meet some bands of wood-Crees. Following the direction of moans that broke the quiet of their camp one night, they found an Indian woman who had fled from her husband's tent when he brought another wife there, and after wandering all night and day found herself again at the abandoned camp of her people.

Her forces were exhausted, her feet frozen. Misery and hardship had dried her breast, and when her infant hungered there his cries pierced her numbing senses, prompting her vain search for help. Disappointed, she had lain down by the ashes of a camp-fire with a prayer to the Master of Life to spare her child.

Her people had only changed camp that day, and by hard travelling on the following day Father Lacombe came up to them. The worthless husband refused to take his wife or child to his tent again, but he scurried there himself with the lash of the Black-robe's scorn shaming him before his people. The woman was taken in a dog-sleigh to St. Albert, where the Sisters took herself and child into their home.

This year again on the prairies in the camps of the Crees as in previous seasons Father Lacombe met with *Wihaskokiseyin* (Sweet-Grass), the interesting pagan Indian. Father Lacombe describes him at this period as being unusually short for an Indian warrior and hunter. His bronzed features were fine, his body agile, his manner pleasant and rather graceful and though not of the stature of a great warrior he carried himself as a man who was every inch a chief and leader of men.

Toward the close of this year an Indian courier from the North brought Father Lacombe a letter from Bishop Grandin, appointed coadjutor to Bishop Tache in 1857. The Bishop was about to come south and establish a See at St. Albert—leaving the Athabasca-Mackenzie vicariate to the newly-consecrated Bishop Faraud.

He asked Father Lacombe to meet him at Carlton. He was naturally anxious to see the most noted of the workers in his new charge. Father Lacombe, equally desirous to meet one of the apostles of the Arctic missions planned to combine business with pleasure. He proposed to secure for St. Paul de Cris an allocation as a mission, with a resident priest and an annual grant from the Propagation funds for the diocese—to make of it, in fact, another St. Albert.

Leaving his flocks on the plains in March he hired "a good tough Indian" as guide, and with his own dogs they made Fort Pitt in four days. Here he hired a new guide, the first pleading fatigue.

Some Indians at the Fort begged him to spend a day or two with them before they left for the prairies, and Father Lacombe could not refuse.

The morning after they left Pitt they woke to a

head wind and mild weather. The snow thawing
burdened their snowshoes and the sun, dazzling on
the white plains, hurt their eyes.

On the last day named by the Bishop for the meeting at Carlton, the post was still 65 miles away. In
turn each walked ahead of the dogs to beat the trail,
holding deerskin mitts to screen their aching eyes.
At night they made a fire to brew some tea, but they
could not bear to look on the fire, and Father Lacombe
went to sleep rolled in a blanket holding his eyebrows
away from his inflamed eyes in hope of relief.

The following day the light was cruelly dazzling
as before, and the snow mushy by noon. Nightfall
found the travellers approaching Fort Carlton. As
they dragged themselves up the Fort hill, they met
an old Indian who told them the Bishop had left that
morning! . . . At the post Father Lacombe
found a letter from him. It was in French, in the
fine vague scrawl decipherable only by those familiar
with His Lordship's writing. The trader could not
read it, and Father Lacombe's eyes were too sore to
puzzle over it.

This was surely the refined cruelty of Fate.

What is to be done about it?—the priest asked himself? Retrace his steps, and have endured the hardships of that trip for nothing! The thought came
only to be dismissed. . . . He would of course
follow the Bishop.

"How far away do you think their camp will be
to-night?" he asked the master of the Fort.

The latter calculated the hour of starting and the condition of the trails—"Only twenty miles, or less," he returned, with perhaps hidden encouragement for the plucky priest.

"Will you lend me fresh dogs?"

Eheu! the dogs were all out with the hunters and the clerks. Thirty miles that day was enough for even a good traveller and his dogs—but the Bishop was ahead on the trail, slipping over the white plains to the Red River. . . . The tired dog-train must push on further.

So it was that at nine o'clock Father Lacombe set out again. The network of his snowshoes, that had been wet all day and now was frozen, cut the tired muscles of his feet. His poor dogs lagged, though the track was lighter than during the sunlit day: the only fresh creature on the trail was the Metis who had replaced his Fort Pitt guide. . . . ("That Fort Pitt Metis had to rest at Carlton. He was the second man I knocked out on that big trip," Father Lacombe recalled forty years later with a smiling *moue* of conscious pride.)

He was now travelling mechanically—the mind keyed to reach the goal in front and the poor body dragged behind. He followed the trail mile after mile doggedly, until they reached a point where it touched the river. They confidently looked for the camp here. But no dogs barked as they approached: there was no debris of fallen boughs. . . . The trail wound back from the river—no camp there.

At this disappointment, coming when his eager soul
had been attuned to hear Bishop Grandin's surprised
greeting, Father Lacombe's fatigue suddenly over-
came him. He pitied his panting dogs, flung prone
on the snow for repose.

"It is enough," he said to his man. "Make a fire
here; we go back to-morrow."

It was now after midnight.

The Metis was sympathetic, as Metis guides have
it in their nature to be: but he had heard the young
Bishop lamenting that he had missed this other Man-
of-Prayer. So when they "spelled" he encouraged
Father Lacombe to make still another effort.

"Maybe they are not half a mile ahead," he ventured.

On again through the soft starlight across the plains
—a mile was passed, and nearly three—when in a
bluff by the river bank they came upon the camp!

The Bishop's northern dogs barked most wolfishly.
The wearied newcomers answered with fainter yelps,
as the two men slipped quietly into camp. Bishop
Grandin, throwing back his buffalo-skin coverings,
rose eagerly to meet them, crying with quick Gallic
gladness.

"Is this you, Father Lacombe? Is it possible!"

He took his tired confrere into his arms, embracing
him as men of the Latin races do, and the wornout
priest let his tears come as they would. They always
did come easily to his emotional temperament.

The sinking fire was piled high again, the teakettle

swung hospitably over it, and when the entire camp had shared in this luxury of the plains the men dropped off to sleep, while the two priests talked long by the fire.

The Bishop was pressing his companion to come on to St. Boniface at daybreak, and share with him the pleasure of meeting Bishop Tache—that charming prelate, who could be profound or stately as a Lord Chancellor and as irresistibly droll as a schoolboy. But Father Lacombe refused; neither his dogs nor himself had strength left for the trip, he pleaded.

XIII

Next morning the Bishop took matters into his own hands, exercising the privilege of bishops and friends. He sent the Metis back to Fort Pitt with the dogs and equipment, forwarding word also to St. Paul de Cris that Father Lacombe had gone to St. Boniface. . . . Though at St. Paul Father Lacombe, free-lance of the missions, was expected only when he arrived!

Starting for St. Boniface, Father Lacombe was invited to seat himself in the Bishop's cariole; the latter would travel on snowshoes. Father Lacombe protested against enjoying the comforts of the cariole, but he was commanded in obedience to his superior to stay there, and he did.

The pleasant motion of the cariole, as the dogs drew it swiftly over the trail, combined with his over-wrought muscles to produce a sleep so profound that all day he was unconscious of his voyage and companions. He slept through the noon-spell, when the men silently prepared a meal, and when he awoke at the night's camping-place to see Bishop Grandin coming up to the fire with some faggots on his shoulder, he saluted him:

"Heh! Haven't we started yet?"

Always quick to recuperate, he was as fresh as a chickadee next morning, and insisted upon yielding the cariole to its owner.

From St. Boniface the Bishop went on to France to secure fresh funds and workers for his missions. In June Father Lacombe returned from the Red River with Father Leduc and a party of five Grey Nuns for the Mackenzie district—"these pearls of the world, who came as a blessing to the poor women and children of our missions," Father Lacombe writes.

Father Leduc, the new travelling-companion of our missionary, was a shrewd humorous recruit to the mission-field from Brittany, and on this trip a life-long friendship between the two men took root.

On August 13 there appeared at St. Paul de Cris the first brigade of carts brought over the prairies from St. Boniface by the Company. There were eighty-two carts—a showing which quite eclipsed Father Lacombe's modest pioneer brigade of 1862, and two days were occupied by their passing. The big company was five years behind the missionaries in adopting this method of transportation, but like all strong and conservative forces when it made the change it did so with eclat.

Eighty-two carts! To the wide-eyed natives at St. Paul the sight was as awe-inspiring as the steam-horse and iron road were to be years later. And as though this were not in itself sufficiently wonderful—ten days later there came creaking and groaning up the trail a second brigade of thirty-two carts belonging to the Company!

Between the fading lines of this old entry in the Journal can be read much wonderment and much leisure on the part of sundry dusky braves, who joyed in counting the carts as they passed rumbling down the trail.

One evening in October when Father Lacombe was in a small camp of Crees he had a new experience. The night prayer was over, but about twenty old men lingered near the priest's tent smoking and talking with him.

The long twilight lying in a gold fringe of light over the prairies was a beautiful hour; to Father Lacombe sitting among his old warriors, smoking his pipe with long draughts, and imbibing the quaint wisdom of the primeval races, it was particularly beautiful.

Suddenly their pleasurable calm was broken into by a rude war-chant!

"Heh! Heh! Hi-yi-ho-ho-huh!"

A band of young warriors returning from a hunt came riding out upon the ridge of land to the west. They advanced with the haze of orange light behind them, their ponies darkly silhouetted against the sky, their voices rising and falling in wild triumph.

They dashed into the encampment on panting ponies. The old men looked up with interested enquiry; the women and children roused from their tents came eagerly out to greet them, while the returned warriors proudly exhibited a prisoner, a young woman of one of the southern tribes.

When she caught sight of the priest sitting among the old men, she slipped from her horse and threw herself at Father Lacombe's feet, crying softly to herself. She was clad in white deerskin tunic, and her long dark hair was hanging loose about her. As she lay there the young men described with enthusiasm a chance encounter with a small band of Sarcee hunters, in which this woman's husband and a couple of others were killed.

Father Lacombe tells the story.

"I heard their talk. When they finish,—'Bon,' I say. 'Who owns this woman?'

"'I do,' said one young warrior, a strong proud-looking man.

"'Well, I want you to sell her to me.'

"They all laughed. 'I thought,' that young man said, 'you Men-of-Prayer did not want women.'

"I was cross then, for if you let an Indian be rude or too familiar with you, he keeps on and you lose all control of him.

"'Ha, you are a brave man!' I said. 'You make a weak woman a prisoner: now you come and say a thing so *stupide* to me. You know well why I want to buy this woman.'

"'I know,' the man said then ashamed at my voice. 'But I do not want to sell her. I want her.'

"He looked at her, when he said that: she was a fine young woman, you know. 'I want a wife,' he said, 'and I have nothing to buy one.'

" 'Well, if you will sell this one now, I will give you a horse; and I will give you goods from the Fort —a new coat—and shirt—and leggings for yourself, and some tea and tobacco.'

"I speak this all slowly, and I add to it because he did not look willing at first; but when I had finish he said quickly:

" 'Ha! you may take her. You offer much for her.'

"He was so quick at the last I think maybe he was afraid I would change my mind about paying so much.

"Then I say to the young woman: 'You are my property now, you see'—and I put my hand on her head and speak severely: 'You must do what I tell you and go only where I tell you.' I was afraid she might take up with another young Cree warrior by-and-bye, and the two run away from the camp.

"And I had my mind made up already to take that girl back to her people: Oh, I was planning a grand coup.

"She told me she was a Sarcee girl and that she knew my face when she rode in to the camp. She had seen me once when I was down with the Blackfeet and her own people, who are of allied nations. She prayed me now to protect her.

"I gave her in charge of a good Christian family

until we brought her up to the Sisters at St. Albert."

The Sarcee girl had now reached a haven in the little log convent, where during the winter she learned a little English together with the white women's ways. Next spring we shall see her figuring again rather dramatically in Father Lacombe's history.

After leaving the girl at St. Albert Father Lacombe returned to St. Paul and evidently had a hard time for several weeks, because the journal—like old Hudson's Bay journals in northern posts—records little else but cold, sickness and trouble. There were few fish to be had; the wolves ate his horses; Indians about the mission fell ill, and the little house was turned into a hospital with as many as ten patients at once.

In November Alexis the famous was sent to St. Albert for horses. The Journal relates with obvious pathos that after being a very long time away from the mission, because of severe weather, Alexis returned with only one horse! And of what use was one horse for the new surprising enterprise which Father Lacombe planned?

During the past summer he had designed a house-tent and his heart was set upon celebrating Midnight Mass for his Indians in this ambulant chapel; but it was too heavy for the dogs to haul to the prairies. Father Lacombe finally succeeded in buying another horse from an Indian, and he and Alexis set out proudly for the plains. The Journal's meagre entry

for the rest of December was a note of severe cold
and snowstorms.

But the simply-worded and more lengthy entry for
January, 1868, is pitiful in what it conveys between
the lines. Like all the other items of this smoke-
stained Journal it is in French and reads:

"January, 1868.

"This voyage and mission of Père Lacombe have
been very trying, not because of so much work among
the Indians but chiefly for the great Fast which he
and his companions endured during twenty [1] days:
they having nothing but some mouthfuls of dirty and
disgusting nourishment to eat, and that only at night
after having tramped all day in snow, sometimes
above the knees.

"Notwithstanding these adversities the Father was
able to visit and see all the Christians of this mission.
They were found scattered at different points of the
prairie in the hope of falling in with buffalo—and
these were not numerous this year. . . . It was
opposite the Nose Hill that the Father made this mission. . . .

"The house-tent went well enough—the Father
being able to accommodate fifty to sixty people in it
for the services."

At the outset Father Lacombe's mind was greatly
occupied by his house-tent, the newest idea evolved

[1] These twenty days included fourteen days on the trip out to find the
first encampment and six days later while again looking for other camps
of the Crees.

from his fertile brain and one with which he hoped
to astonish and delight his nomads.

For years the French priests in the west had
plodded along as best they could with nothing better
than a skin tepee. But if there was a brisk wind it
was often impossible to celebrate Mass in a tepee, because the smoke circled about the lodge half-way up
and filled the throat of a man standing.

Once Father Lacombe had to celebrate Mass on
his knees to avoid the smoke. Another day at the
elevation his crucifix hanging to the tent above his
head plunged into the chalice.

To avoid any such accidents he had designed his
house-tent of leather. He bought fifty tanned buffalo skins from Indians at St. Paul. With twenty
poles as big as his wrist in circumference and with
iron pegs got from the Company's blacksmith at Fort
Edmonton he contrived to pin the frame of his house
together and then fasten the peaked roof upon it.
The dimensions of the house-tent were 25 feet by 15.

The buffalo skins were shaped to make a deep covering secured about the base with banks of snow.
This last convenience served two purposes—it held
down the walls and kept out the thieving Indian dogs,
which were—he gravely stated once—"just bands of
devils." He had with him besides a small campstove as heater.

With Alexis and all this paraphernalia he started
out on December 4, 1867, from St. Paul, his two

horses drawing the equipment and an aged, destitute Blackfoot woman who had been thrown on their mercy at the mission. Under her tuition Father Lacombe hoped that winter on the prairie to increase his knowledge of the Blackfoot tongue.

He had a fresh reason for this study: he was planning for the next summer a *coup d'Etat* to be followed by a vigorous campaign of Christianity among all the warlike, stubborn southern tribes.

Provisions formed but a small part of the equipment on leaving St. Paul, for the supplies there had been about consumed by the sick Indians maintained through the autumn. They had some frozen fish and pemmican—enough in all to last them a couple of days on their journey to a camp of Crees near the Battle River.

There was no trail broken; the snow was deep and progress was slow. The second night, as they were deciding to camp, they saw a thin smoke rising from a clump of trees nearby. They went to it, and found a group of eighteen miserable Indians—men, women and children—"only skin and bones, almost starved. For many days not a mouthful of food—poor people! *Mon Dieu,* but they were *miserables*—so thin, and the children too weak to play or cry!"

They answered listlessly to Father Lacombe's questions but their very looks seemed to ask him what he would do for them. They had come down from the wooded country, where they had had no luck all autumn. Neither fur nor food had been found in any quantity, and they were looking for their kinsmen on the plains. They had eaten their horses and dogs. They were now at the end of human endurance.

XIV

THERE was only one thing for Father Lacombe to do. First he ordered Alexis to pitch camp beside them.

"Now, Alexis, and you, Suzanne, have you the courage to risk having nothing to eat for three days!" he asked his companions. "For my part, I am willing."

"Yes," each agreed simply; and "I have often starved before," the squaw added. So, too, had Alexis, but he was more sparing of words.

Then Alexis gave out the tea and pemmican, and five or six fish—all they had, altogether insufficient and rapidly devoured. As for Father Lacombe and his party they might be the proud guardians of the finest tent in the northwest but they went to bed that night without supper, and with little prospect of breakfast.

Next morning the journey was resumed, the priest and his party leading the way to break the road for the famished company straggling behind.

"Try and follow us," he told them. "But I have no more food, and I do not want to kill my horses yet. I need them too badly this winter."

The poor Crees taking heart from his sympathy dragged themselves along the beaten trail. All that

146

day the travellers found only one rabbit and a partridge. A mouthful for twenty persons! These morsels were cooked and given to the children.

That night they camped in a big snowstorm. The next day and still the next there was nothing but snow and cold, and the sad little section of humanity dragged its way slowly across the wide plains. Their stomachs shrank with the gnawing hunger-ache. Their tired hearts panted sickly forward to the camp-fires of their tribe.

The clamour of dogs and children, the smoky lit-tered tepees, the rank steaming kettles had some-times been repulsive to him, but Father Lacombe in his heart now felt he would never despise an Indian tepee again, even at its worst of dogs and vermin and dirt.

On the fifth day out they approached the rendez-vous indicated by the courier at St. Paul. . . . They came up to it before dusk—but to find the bit-terest disappointment awaiting them.

The Crees had pitched off to another point. The skeleton frames of their tepees were standing—that was all; and the wanderers felt even Hope desert them as they looked on these chilly witnesses of the vanished cheer.

A heavy snowfall had covered up the trail their tribe had taken. . . .

The disappointment was agony, and the torment of their hunger returned tenfold. The starving com-pany were free on the trackless prairie—yet their very freedom mocked them as the blindest *impasse* might have done. And above and beyond every other feeling was their hunger. They had not eaten at all that day.

Father Lacombe sent Alexis off with his gun to search for food: the others were past that effort. For his part he fastened snowshoes on and went to look out from a hill in hope of some guidance. There was nothing for him; and he, too, like the others was failing with weakness. . . . His sight was confused; his neck seemed to totter under the weight of his head. He was not racked any longer with hunger, but the faintness of death was on him. He rallied, and caught his mind wandering as if he were in delirium.

Yesterday they had eaten and drank—a bouillon made of the skins of old sacks, cords of sinews and old pieces of moccasins!

At nightfall they had scraped off the snow and were camped for the night—when the priest heard the creaking of Alexis' snowshoes, and by the sound of his steps felt sure he carried a burden. They all pricked up their ears at the sound, and when Alexis came into camp went eagerly out to meet him.

He had a burden—some pieces of meat from a buffalo bull he had killed, as he found it diseased and dying, abandoned by the herd.

The emaciated Indians threw pieces of the meat into boiling water and gladly ate their disgusting portion and drank the bouillon, but the sight and smell of it only filled Father Lacombe with nausea. He tried the repulsive stuff; his offended stomach refused to retain it.

That night the great lights of the north rose in such splendour that even Father Lacombe in his exhaustion could not forbear to marvel at them. To the Indians bred in the belief that these were the spirits of their ancestors, the ghostly white lights shooting across the sky were as spirits beckoning insistently from their skyey realms to the sickened, hopeless group of humanity huddled about the greenwood fire on the trail that led Nowhere.

For fourteen days in all this blind search and painful walking, with the griping fast continued. In all that time the disgusting meat that Alexis brought and an occasional rabbit or prairie-chicken was all that stood between the wayfarers and utter starvation.

"But, Oh, those horses getting weak—and those people dragging themselves behind!" . . .

In that heart-wrung exclamation of the old missionary decades later can be seen the whole painful picture that made so cruel a blot on the white prairies. Had the Master of Life no thought then for his children?—The birds of the air were sybarites compared to these.

"My dear friends and you who seat yourselves at tables covered with appetizing food whenever you need it, let me tell you," Father Lacombe wrote of this to the Forets, "how painful and torturing it is to know hunger in circumstances like these!   Up to that time in my sermons and instructions to the Indians— some of them lazy—I had said many times, I had proclaimed, that those who did not want to work— *should not eat.*

"But now, after such an experience, I have changed my ideas, and I have taken the resolution to share my last mouthful with anyone who is hungry.   After experiencing such hardship from hunger how clearly one understands these words of the Father of the Poor: 'I was hungry, and you gave me not to eat.'"   .   .   .

The starving band had reached the last point of endurance, though all were still living.   The horses were growing weak from the continual wandering and difficulty to paw down to the grass under the deep snow.

As a last resource Father Lacombe one night told the camp he was resolved to kill his horses one by one. He had made the resolution before, but had neither expressed it nor carried it out.   The following morn- ing—this was Sunday, as he recalls it—fresh hope came to him with returning light.   He told Alexis they would put off killing the horse until night. .   .   .   They could endure one day longer.

But the horse was never killed.

Two hours after midnight, the innocent prodigals came upon the hearth fires of their people.   There was joy on both sides—better still, plenty to eat in the camp.   This was something of which the newcomers would hastily assure themselves, but their people wise from similar experience gave them at first only bouillon with tiny pieces of buffalo-meat chopped in it.

Food, fire and the sense of Home was theirs: that was Heaven after the cold and pitiless uncertainty of the plains.

In three or four days they had begun to eat solid food and live like their brethren—which for that season and in that particular camp meant living very well, with dried meat in abundance, fresh pieces of rib-meat and buffalo hump. What more could the heart of the plainsman desire?

It was now Christmas Eve—*Ka-nipa-ayam-itiak* (The-time-we-pray-at-night). Although still weak Father Lacombe had to bestir himself. He had spent the first days in the lodge of Chief Sweet-Grass, but now he showed the materials for his house-tent to the Indians and asked them to set it up. They complied with delight; it was an honour to have anything to do in connection with this novelty.

The snow was cleared away by the squaws, while the men set up the frame and covering. The campstove was put in place, a pile of wood cut for it and the snowy ground of the tent covered with boughs and buffalo-skin. Such luxury and comfort had never been known on the plains before.

When Father Lacombe was installed the old men gathered about his doorway. Awed by the elegance of his domicile they were at first shy about entering.

But they soon found their way in with their pipes and philosophy and made themselves entirely at home . . . until Father Lacombe had to clear the room to hear the confessions of those who were already Christian.

For the first time on the prairie Father Lacombe was to exercise his priest's privilege of celebrating three Masses on this one day of the year. From his doorway, when the bell had called the camp to attention, he announced that all the chiefs and hunters were to attend the first Mass, the women the second, while the Mass after daylight was to be for the children.

Midnight found him at an altar made of poles surmounted by his chapel-box in which were the vestments, the altar-stone, the linen and vessels necessary on the altar. Every foot of kneeling-space was occupied by the men.

"As I robed myself for that Mass," he has written, "this is what passed in my heart. . . . 'The Holy Gospel tells us that the shepherds of the valley of Bethlehem came to the stable to adore the divine Child. And here to-night in this wild country in North America another kind of shepherds—the shepherds of the great flocks of buffalo—are kneeling down to adore the same Child Jesus, the Son of God, that lay on the straw in Bethlehem in the far east.'

"And when these old shepherds began to sing the canticles of the Church in their own tongue—'*Emigwa tibiskayik*'—'*Ca, bergers assemblons-nous*'—for some time I could not begin my Mass because the tears

came and I wept. Ah, that scene was a *poeme.*
. . . *'Sasay Manito, awasis.'* . . . Those
warriors and hunters singing the hymns that are of
the Church the whole world over, the same old melodies we sang at St. Sulpice for the *Noel!* Ah-h!"
He never spoke of this night without emotion.

"I have said Mass in Saint Peter's at Rome, in
fine basilicas in France and in many places—but I
say to you, this was the most solemn Mass—the most
grand of all."

When the Mass was ended, the young priest, so
happy that he was conscious of no fatigue, dismissed
the warriors with a glad—

"Bon Noel! My dear shepherds, go and smoke
your Christmas calumet and take your rest."

Then followed the Mass of the Dawn. Now it was
the women of the camp who came uniting their voices
in sacred song. The Sacrifice was concluded and the
women dismissed.

Father Lacombe, now thoroughly weak, felt his
head reel with faintness as it did during that awful
fortnight on the prairies, and in blind haste he packed
away the altar fittings and threw himself down on
the buffalo-skins to rest. The warm skins enveloped
him; the earth welcomed him and breathed repose
through him. Sleep closed his eyes.

No angels watched visibly over the sleeping camp,
but their message had penetrated to the hearts of the
Cree warriors. And the promised Peace-to-men-of-
Good-will had fallen in divine fullness upon Father

Lacombe lying exhausted by the fire on his bed of boughs and skins.

On Sunday night when the last hymn was sung in the chapel-tent Father Lacombe would fain say good-night to his warriors: he did not want to exchange stories over the pipes that night, for the air of his tent was hot and bad, and he still felt weak. But while the men lingered the doorway of the tent was suddenly thrown open and a Metis courier from St. Albert stamped in with greetings from that mission, and letters that had come by the Company's packet from the Red River.

As the Indians watched Father Lacombe read and re-read one paper they saw great joy and anxiety alternately master his mobile face, and the ready tears welled up. He seemed oblivious of all but one letter. This was from Bishop Grandin in Rome telling him of the condition of their venerable Pontiff attacked now on every side by enemies. Enclosed with this was a copy of the Papal decree convoking the twentieth Ecumenical Council. In the midst of his cares and humiliations Pius IX had grandly decided to hold another of the great Ecumenical Councils of the Church, the first of the imposing assemblages since the Council of Trent.

For these reasons smiles and tears were very close together on the priest's face. Chief Sweet-Grass, who was very fond of the Man-of-the-Beautiful-Mind, came quietly near him, and asked what news he had that moved him so strongly. Father Lacombe explained the letters reading from the decree some words of the grand chief of the Men-of-Prayer.

Immediately the warriors pressed forward to see it. Father Lacombe pointed out the pontiff's name and the heraldic device surmounting the sheet. One old man bent and kissed the page.

"What is the name of the chief of the Men-of-Prayer?" Sweet-Grass asked wonderingly.

"Pius IX is his name. Pius IX!"

Very gravely Sweet-Grass pursued his enquiries.

"May I speak his name—even though I am not a praying-Indian?"

"To be sure you may," Father Lacombe agreed, and Sweet-Grass had him repeat it for him until he felt he could say it correctly.

Then the chief stood up among his braves, holding the Pope's decree in his own hands; and he called out strongly, solemnly, as if he made an invocation:

"Pius IX! Pius IX! . . . Listen, all my people present—Pius IX! May that name bring us good fortune!"

Then sweeping an arm out over his seated braves:

"Rise!" he called to them, "and say 'Pius IX!' "

And they all rose and repeated after him—"Pius IX!"

This scene might have furnished another paragraph to Macaulay's admiring study of the Church of Rome. For while its Pontiff, the "Little Father of the Poor," was being driven to his last redoubt in the Vatican—only saved from the Garibaldian forces two months earlier by an army of men from every civilized nation—here in this western wilderness new races were enlisting under his banner, and a miserably clad but valiant soldier of Christ was moved to tears at the unlooked-for tribute to his chief.

In the following year Father Lacombe sent the details of the little incident to his early patron, Bishop Bourget, who was then in Rome. The aged Pontiff, profoundly moved by the happening, asked the Bishop to convey his blessing to Father Lacombe, his good chief and Indians.

XV

THE year 1868 opened upon Father Lacombe on the plains in the camp of the head chief Sweet-Grass. In a few weeks he returned to St. Paul de Cris, and later went up to Rocky Mountain House to minister to Indians there.

The time had now arrived to achieve his *coup d'etat;* consequently he called at St. Albert for the Sarcee captive. The Sisters who had become very strongly attached to Marguerite, as she had been christened, pleaded with Father Lacombe to leave her with them so that she might never know the hardships of camp life again.

"We love her," they said, "and she seems to be happy with us."

"Yes," said Father Lacombe, "that is all fine! But how long will it last? She will get tired of life here. Already when I spoke to her in Blackfoot she told me she was lonely for her people. . . . And, anyway, I must take her home. She is gold—*gold* to me!

"Her people of the Blackfoot nation are fierce and proud. They are my friends, though they do not love my teaching as the Crees do. . . . But when I bring Marguerite back to them. . . . Ah, *that is my day!*"

Father Lacombe had spoken with discernment. The Blackfeet did love him for his sympathy; they admired his courage and daring; more than once the chiefs had greeted the praying-man by running their hands over his forehead, chest and arms to absorb from him into their own bodies some virtue of the medicine which made him great. But they wanted nothing to do with the religion which had fired him to become the man he was.

From the Blackfeet trading at the Mountain House that spring Father Lacombe had learned something of the position of their nation's camp. With this, together with Marguerite's knowledge of her people's hunting-ground and their probable choice of a place of encampment, he had little difficulty in finding them.

His party included Alexis, the aged Blackfoot Suzanne and Marguerite. One day as they paused on a piece of rolling upland to rest their horses the girl's quick eyes caught sight of a big camp on the slope of a neighbouring coulee—blots of gray and brown against the first delicate green of the prairies.

Maybe this was the camp of her people, she said. . . . *Eh, bien,* said Father Lacombe, it was well to be prepared. Immediately the party pitched camp. Alexis was told to raise the Red Cross flag on a tent-pole. The Sarcee girl was ordered into the women's tent—under no pretext to leave until she was called—and then the Generalissimo folded his hands and waited.

But not for long: the Indians saw his signal flapping in the long prairie winds, and promptly recognized it. The flag in itself was famed among them, the man who carried it, revered . . . for had he not nursed them through the *rongeole* and the typhoid and stopped the battle with the Crees? Lassoing their horses lightly they sprang upon them and rode over in a barbaric, half-naked cavalcade to the priest's tent. Men and women rode galloping through the valley, up the hill, welcoming him with glad cries as they drew near.

"They did not want my religion," says Father Lacombe simply, "but they liked me. They were my friends."

In the crowd he noticed some whose faces were streaked with black paint and their hair cut, in token of mourning. This looked promising. He asked them whom they mourned?

"Six moons ago," they said, "your friends, the Crees, attacked a camp of our young men, killed some of them and carried off one of our young women."

"And did you go to find her?"

"Her brothers went, but did not get her. They carried her too far into the country of the Crees and she is dead maybe. We will never see her again!"

"Never again?" . . .

The psychological moment had arrived, and the dramatic instinct that had planned this seance recognized the fact.

"Marguerite," he called into the tent. "Come here!"

In a trice their lost girl—active, strong and radiantly glad to look on her people again—emerged from the dusky interior. With a searching glance through the crowd she ran directly to the arms of her mother. The astounded silence was broken with cries of joy, and women crowded about the mother who now lay silent in her daughter's arms: while the men pushed close to *Arsous-kitsi-rarpi*—The-Man-of-the-Good-Heart.

They touched his hands and face and gown. They told him their thanks in fervent language, and they shouted his name—*Arsous-kitsi-rarpi!* till the coulees rang. Then with the young men riding ahead as couriers Father Lacombe was brought in a savage procession to the Sarcee camp, where there were songs of triumph and orations by the chiefs.

Truly, this was his day. "An ineffable moment!" he says, and one that gave him more influence among these people and spread more desire for his prayer than many sermons or visits would have accomplished.

During this triumphal progress of Father Lacombe in the hunting-grounds of the Chinook-kissed south the priest of St. Paul found near the mission the bodies of two Indians who had perished of hunger. The only other item of interest Father Lacombe found in the Journal on his return was the record that at Easter "the famous old Na Batoche and all his family were baptised."

The items recorded in the Journal of St. Paul for the remainder of that summer are pitiful in their revelation of hardship from hunger. Père Andre who remained in charge during Father Lacombe's trips to the plains, could starve with composure, but he could not look on calmly at his inability to help the starving Indians begging for help, and he counts the days his stout-hearted, resourceful confrere is absent. He also chronicles in the Journal an interesting incident that marked the trip from which Father Lacombe returned on July 9. The latter had been spending several weeks with the Crees.

One day when the hunters came in with word that the Blackfeet were approaching, the camp was quickly put in a state of defence. Pits were dug to conceal their persons, the horses were hobbled within the camp. Small mounds of stones were piled outside the camp to shield the warriors.

At night the camp waited in readiness for attack.

"At last at half-past eleven, when we were all tired waiting," Father Lacombe tells, "I thought it may all be a mistake. Ha!—I take my horse and ride out of the camp up the hill. The young men said the Blackfeet were hiding in the trees across the valley, and the moon was shining full over the hill.

"Up there I call out—

"'Hey! Hey! Are you there and wanting to fight? Then my Crees are ready for you. Come on, and you will see how they can fight. They are brave, my Crees, if you come to kill their people.

. . . Come, they are ready.   Do not wait till the
dawn.'   .   .   .

"Oh, my voice sounded big over the quiet prairie.
But there was no cry; only the echoes answered.

"I ride back to the camp then, and I laugh.   'Let
us go to sleep,' I say.   'There is no danger.'"

The Crees decided to leave a small guard all night,
and the next day while the young men formed an
armed escort the band moved its camp north of the
lake.   While there were no further alarms it was discovered that this one had not been groundless.

Sixty Blackfeet had designed to attack the camp
that night, Father Lacombe learned soon afterward
from Big Eagle, one of their old men.   But they
would not fight when they heard the voice of *Arsous-
kitsi-rarpi,* who had been in their own camp at Three
Ponds.

That brief bold midnight harangue to the ambushed
Blackfeet warriors is worth noting.   It is a vivid
illustration of the instinctive art with which Father
Lacombe's Indian career was lit, as from day to day
he played on the Indian nature as a musician on his
harp.

To Father Lacombe the most important event of
the year was Bishop Grandin's arrival at St. Albert.
This marked the elevation of the half-breed colony to
the dignity of a episcopal see.   It also marked a long
advance from the arrival of Bishop Provencher just
fifty years before to establish the reign of Christ in
Rupert's Land.   Then there were two priests in the

whole immense territory west of Sault Ste. Marie.
Now there were three Bishops and close on to one
hundred missionary priests, nuns and lay brethren.

Toward the end of August the Bishop with his
caravan of carts was met at St. Paul by eight priests,
the Journal notes—by all in fact who were at work
in the diocese: Fathers Lacombe, Leduc, Remas,
Vegreville, Moulin, Gaste, Andre, Legoff.

On October 26th he entered St. Albert escorted by
a cavalcade of Metis horsemen who went out three
miles to meet him. He drove in under an arch of
greenery erected in his honour, while salvos of musketry and cries of welcome rang out with an enthusiasm rare in the calm wilderness. Father Lacombe,
who had hurried ahead to St. Albert to direct this
demonstration and then returned to Fort Pitt to meet
the Bishop, had exhausted his own and his confreres'
resources to make this entry memorable.

The new Bishop, who had so lately within the Arctic fringe chinked his own huts with mud, was doubtless fully impressed. The first day he officiated in the
little chapel, however, he found he must carry himself with discernment in order that his mitre might
escape being knocked off by the rafters!

His palace was of logs, sixteen feet by thirty. It
was uncomfortably crowded, and the diet was not
select. In a letter to his family one of the missionaries resident at St. Albert then has left a piquant
description of the external life. It is marked by a
gentle wit characteristic of the spirit in which the

French missionaries of the early days turned off their privations with laughter.

It however pictures St. Albert at its worst—when the mill was not working, and the vegetables were all consumed:

"Eight of us are living in the palace, and we are one on top of another. There are seven of us in one room which serves at once as a parlour, office, carpenter's shop, tailoring-place, etc. A buffalo skin stretched on the floor with one or two blankets— behold our beds! Mattresses and sheets are luxuries of which we know nothing. We eat bread only on feast-days and then in very small quantities.

"On the other hand we have *pemikan,* a species of pounded fat meat pressed into a leather sack ten or twelve months before. We cut off pieces with an axe—it is almost as good as a candle! We have also meat dried in the sun. It is as hard as leather: but with good teeth one finally tears it off. Our beverage is tea without sugar. With this not very recherche nutrition we nevertheless are looking well. I, especially—I am taking on flesh in such fashion that they call me Canon. . . ."

The new Bishop speedily attached his priests to himself, for he was a man of high principle, unselfish and notably amiable. With this he was possessed of a zeal for his work so ardent that during the past winter in France Louis Veuillot, the prince of French journalists, had said of him—"*Cet êveque des neiges fait bien comprendre que le froid brule. . . .*"

"This bishop of the snows makes one understand clearly how frost burns."

On the 11th of December Father Lacombe left once more for the prairies. He experienced no hardships in finding the Indian camps this year, for with all his dramatic instincts and emotional nature he had too strong a vein of practical sense and organising powers to make such a mistake twice possible.

During his stay in the camp of Sweet-Grass he was brought to a young warrior who, having his hand badly torn in the hunt, had amputated the useless member with his hunting knife, binding the stump with the cord of the sinew which tied his breech-clout about his loins.

Father Lacombe going to his tent was horror-stricken at the sight of the mangled arm. Up as far as the shoulder the veins and the flesh had darkened with blood poisoning, and at the wrist was a mass of inflamed, swollen and corrupt flesh in which the cord of deer-sinew was deeply buried. Putrified pieces of flesh had already dropped from the sore stump.

Father Lacombe felt helpless before this, but Sweet-Grass was relying upon him, so with a prayer for divine assistance he nerved himself to do what he could. For a few moments he studied the anatomy of his own wrist to avoid cutting into any of the principal arteries. Then insisting upon the young man turning his head away the priest made a deep incision with his razor into the swollen wrist—on, down—until he reached the buried cords of sinew.

This he cut and with the aid of two fine sticks removed it entirely. With the sudden resultant outflow of blood and matter the hitherto stoical Indian groaned pitifully; but the outcry speedily changed to a sigh of relief.

The onlookers murmured approval, and taking heart Father Lacombe bent again to his work. He cut away with his razor as completely as he could the mortified flesh about the wound and burned what remained with a stick of nitrate of silver—one of the few medical stuffs supplied to the missionaries and traders at that period.

He smeared the arm and stump with a thick layer of the balm-of-Gilead ointment which an old Blackfoot woman had taught him to prepare; then ordered the young man to lie in bed for days, forbidding him to eat meat. Dumbly wondering what would be the outcome of it all, he sent up fervent prayers that the man's life should be spared. For several days he visited him thrice daily, renewing the ointment and burning the rotten tissue.

To the delight of the whole camp, and to the surprise of no one more than Father Lacombe, the young hunter soon gave evidence of recovering, and in three weeks was convalescent! . . . Father Lacombe exclaimed with the great Parè, surgeon to four kings —"I dressed his wound; God cured him."

That winter again Midnight Mass was celebrated on the prairies in the house-tent. Father Lacombe did not return to St. Paul until late in February.

The St. Paul Journal records Father Lacombe's return on February 27th, 1869. One of the horses had died during the winter; the one that remained was as thin and jaded as its master. But he was satisfied with his latest ministry, exercised for the greater part of the time in a camp of almost 2,700 Crees lodged in 400 tepees.

Toward Easter he preached an enlivening mission for his former proteges, the half-breeds of St. Albert, and at its close gave them a rendezvous for a certain day to tear down his old bridge over the Sturgeon and replace it with a new structure—which they completed in two days.

Here again he combined with his spiritual ministry vigorous efforts for the material advancement of his flock; and as usual in the fields or pulpit he vitalized his followers by the spur of his own splendid energies.

XVI

THERE was now being debated at St. Albert a
question which had already been considered in February, when Father Lacombe returned to St. Paul de
Cris from the prairies and found Bishop Grandin
and Father Vegreville of Lac la Biche awaiting him.
It related to the improvement of their freight-trans-
portation. With the expansion of their missions the
amount of money paid out yearly to the Company or
freighters for this purpose was making terrifying
inroads upon their slim resources.

As early as 1854 Bishop Tache and his able lieuten-
ants at Lac la Biche had initiated a movement to
improve northern transportation by navigating the
Athabasca (hitherto avoided by the fur-traders as
too dangerous). This had now been successfully
accomplished by the missionaries, but there still
remained a possibility of bettering the transportation
system to the south.

As noted in the Oblate Annals, a new method had
been suggested to Father Lacombe and the Bishop
by "a certain number of adventurers . . . from
Benton, a quite new town of the United States built
near the sources of the Missouri." This method was
to ship supplies from France to New Orleans and
thence up the Missouri to Fort Benton.

168

It was obvious that Father Lacombe was the man to examine into the new enterprise, and on April 17th the task was formally assigned him by the Diocesan Council.

"Plein de courage et d'audace," he writes in a memorandum of that trip, he left St. Albert with three Metis. Each man rode a sturdy little Indian pony and in a cart they had packed their tent and some provisions. They soon left the tree-line, and for days travelled farther and farther south into the plains.

The Metis were very careful in choosing and concealing their encampments each night, for in spite of Father Lacombe's assurance of the Blackfeet's friendly attitude toward himself, they feared a midnight surprise upon their ponies at least. This was a dry season and many creeks were dried. So they always carried a small keg of water from camp to camp.

One day when this precaution was neglected nightfall found them parched with thirst. Father Lacombe, searching about in the dusk, found a marshy pool frequented by the buffalo. He brought a pail of the ill-smelling fluid to camp, but scorched and gripped with thirst as they were all refused to do more than moisten their lips with it.

One Metis suggested that they draw blood from the carcass of a buffalo killed that evening. In spite of some repugnance they refreshed themselves so, but Father Lacombe could not bring himself to it. All night he lay in broken sleep tormented with thirst,

which—at that distance at least—seemed to him more
difficult to endure than the hunger of his trip to Nose
Hill.

At dawn the party spreading out over the plains
to look for water came upon a small creek. They
had now reached American territory, as they knew
by that grim sentinel near the boundary, the Chief
Mountain—*Ninnistakow*—recalling to Father Lacombe his old friend, Rowand of Fort Edmonton.

The next day on the banks of the Missouri they
came to a straggling village of log-cabins. Small
steamboats lay along the water-front; fur-traders and
Indians dawdled here and there on the dusty street.
The whole aspect of the place was sunny, lazy and
cheerful.

As they hesitated enquiringly on the village street
a French-Canadian servant of the American fur-company approached Father Lacombe and offered him
the hospitality of his small home.

Benton then was the home of many dashing frontiersmen and traders whose names still linger in quaint
or exciting tales of the old trading-days. I. G.
Baker's log-store was the largest in the village, but
among the rough-shirted, big-hearted traders who
loitered about the sunny streets were Tom Powers
and the Healeys who later struck gold in Alaska,
Kaiser—and Harnois, who was to cross Father
Lacombe's life again—Joe Kipp and many another
who was to find his way across the border into British
territory.

The news soon went among them that Père Lacombe was in town, and as the Blackfeet had long ago carried his fame across the plains, his arrival created a stir of which the dusty and tired Blackrobe was quite unconscious.

As there was no money in currency along the Saskatchewan, Father Lacombe had brought a letter of credit from his Bishop to the Jesuit missionaries of Montana. Borrowing money for his fare to the mission he went there by stage, only to find that the Jesuits had no money either. He refused their invitation to wait until they could get some from St. Louis.

Instead, he returned to Benton, resolved to go forward to St. Louis at once, with or without money.

Two days later he was selling his pony to repay what he had borrowed for stage-fare and to renew his Metis' provisions. For himself, he was a guest of Captain Rae of the Silver Bow, who offered him a free passage to St. Louis. He was also the owner of a well-filled purse, made up for him by the Healeys and their friends in Benton.

The Silver Bow made slow progress down the river, because as "the traveller from the British possessions" recalls—"We were continually slowing down or running aground." Tree-trunks and sandbars frequently blocked the current.

"We did not travel by night for fear of accident in the shallows; the boat was tied up to the bank like a broncho. We passed the time talking, mostly in

English, of the experiences of each one." But their finest recreation was watching herds of buffalo come crashing through the trees on the river-bank and precipitate themselves into the current.

"Imagine our boat," Father Lacombe writes in vivid remembrance, "steaming into the midst of the bison crazed by the shrieks and whistling of the steam-engine, and the reports of rifles and revolvers. Imagine the tumult caused by such encounters! The water was sometimes red with blood, which flowed in streams from the bodies of the poor victims massacred only for the pleasure of killing them."

The night before the steamer reached St. Louis Father Lacombe's generous travelling-companions, miners from the new gold-fields, surprised him with a purse of over one hundred dollars. This with what the generous Benton traders had given him left him master of $300. He felt himself a prairie-Crœsus.

He was now in St. Louis, the birthplace of his friend Brazeau the Blackfoot interpreter at Fort Edmonton. He promptly made his way to the University, but paused outside its hospitable entrance, as though struck by his own temerity in thus calmly claiming lodging in what seemed to him magnificence embodied in masonry.

The massive portal and mullioned windows of the College were impressive to the prairie visitor to whom for a score of years the measure of architectural splendour had been the Big House at Fort Edmonton with its two score of glass windows. Glass! not parchment, let it be noted.　Was it possible, he asked himself, that he had thirsted on the plains for water and watched the miners slaughter buffalo only a few days before?

A warm reception soon made the northerner thoroughly at home.　He even found a close link between the University's dignified atmosphere and his own smoky house-tent. . . .　For that Père de Smet who had been a professor here forty years before, was the same who at Fort Edmonton in 1845 laid upon Father Thibault the mission of Christianizing the Blackfeet—and it was Father Lacombe himself who had eventually undertaken that mission.

Archbishop Kenrick received the Canadian *voyageur* hospitably on several occasions, and his whole stay at St. Louis was finely enjoyable.　But from his own observations and on the advice of the Archbishop he resolved before he left to report to Bishop Grandin against any change being made from the Red River route to the Missouri.

Amply supplied with funds now he decided to go on to Canada before returning.　His father had died the year before, and his heart urged him to go and see his mother again.

Entering the Palace in Montreal unheralded some days later he was greeted with heartwhole delight by the gentle Bourget.　Others hurried to welcome him, and coaxed for stories of the adventures and achievements of the *"petite sauvage Albert."*

He first looked into the circumstances and health

of his good old mother at St. Sulpice. Her son Gaspard was still wandering with the world for his pillow. There remained to Madame Lacombe near the old home a married daughter, another teaching school and her youngest child, Christine. The latter had developed into a bright helpful girl, and mindful of the missions' need of teachers her brother invited Christine to come west with him and teach.

Christine readily consented; and it was arranged that the mother should spend the rest of her days as a paying guest at the Grey Nuns' convent in Montreal. This was Madame Lacombe's own desire. A few months later, dissatisfied with even that amount of the atmosphere of a city which penetrates a convent, the brave old mother of the missionary, without informing him of her discontent, had friends arrange for her entrance again as a paying guest into the homelike convent of L'Assomption not far from St. Sulpice. Here she lived content.

On his return west with his sister Father Lacombe placed her in charge of a kindly Canadian woman at St. Paul de Cris, with whom she remained a few months before going to Lac la Biche to teach. As for himself, when he had reported on the Mississippi route to the Bishop, he resumed his ministry on the plains.

Shortly after the New Year he journeyed up by dog-sleigh to Rocky Mountain House to meet the Blackfeet Indians there. As chance had it, Jack Matheson, a young trader from the Red River, was going up to the Mountain House and he proved an interesting travelling-companion. For this lusty young giant from the Red River, grandson of John Pritchard the private secretary of Lord Selkirk, was brimming over with gay spirits, with lore of the hunter's world and tales of the early settlement of the Red River.

Jack Matheson was himself to come in time through many wanderings and a life of much colour to be an Indian missionary in the Church of England. But on that trip behind the dogs to Mountain House there was little thought of prayer or preaching in the rollicking young trader's head.

Disappointed in not finding the Indians at the post, Father Lacombe took a young Piegan as guide, and set out on an arduous trip in search of the tribes. They suffered from lack of fuel, heavy snow-storms and snow-blindness, finally being directed to the camps by a luckless group of Blackfeet who were murdered a few days later by a hostile band.

"Before these poor people had separated from me, I attempted to turn them back from the direction in which they were travelling: I coaxed them to come with me, but they were deaf to my invitation. It seems as though I had some presentiment of evil . . ." [1] wrote Father Lacombe.

"I could not remain more than three weeks at this camp. I occupied all my time in teaching them

[1] Letter of May 12th, 1870, from Father Lacombe to his Superior-General, published in Annals of Oblates.

prayers, the singing of hymns, the catechism and particularly in making further studies of the language.

"You will easily understand what trials I had in doing this: to grasp the sounds and fix them in writing, finding the meaning, discovering the grammatical rules; this is no little affair.   Nevertheless, I made a goodly number of discoveries in a short time, and I was happy in the progress which with God's help I had made.

"The Indians on their part showed themselves very willing—even eager to know something of religion.

"When the time came for me to return home I set out with fifteen families who wished to accompany me to the Rocky Mountain House.   After several days passed together at the Fort, I parted from them with regret, to return to St. Albert.   But before having the pleasure of embracing my dear confreres there my heart was torn with a painful spectacle.

"At some distance from the Saskatchewan River, as I travelled along the trail with my men, I came upon some Indians who ran to me weeping.   They had been despoiled of everything and they carried two of their number who were also wounded.   They were of the Blackfoot nation and were the only survivors of the group attacked by the Cree-Assinaboines near Fort Edmonton, eight miles from St. Albert.   They had not eaten anything for three days: they were floundering along almost barefoot in the slush and ice.

"Poor unfortunates!   I could not restrain my tears

at the sight of such misery. But that would not suffice; I had to give them some help. I distributed among them what remained of my provisions; I tended the wounds of the injured, gave them something to wear and then lent them my two horses.

"For myself, I had to go afoot, but I had only a few miles more to make. . . ."

The miserable Blackfeet who met Father Lacombe were the survivors of a small trading party attacked by ambushed Crees as they mounted the south bank of the river opposite Fort Edmonton. Seven of their number were brutally killed and two wounded. The survivors had fled for their lives leaving their goods behind them.

Their tribe immediately sought revenge. One night, before Father Lacombe left St. Albert for St. Paul, a courier from the Fort announced that a war-party of seven hundred Blackfeet was marching on Edmonton.

"The Father purposed to leave at dawn for the Fort to aid in averting this misfortune, but toward midnight a fresh courier arrived, and he departed immediately. . . ." [1]

[1] Letter of Father Leduc to Superior-General of the Oblates, December 22, 1870.

XVII

A BAND of Crees employed in cutting cordwood
had first brought word of the revenge-party to the
Chief Factor. They hurried to their tepees by the
Fort, and decked themselves for battle with vivid
streaks of vermilion.

Chief Factor Christie ordered every one within the
stockade and the gates closed. Malcolm Groat hur-
riedly crossed some traders from the south bank.
The cannons in the bastions were primed and every
man held himself ready to defend their stronghold.

A flash of humour relieved the anxiety when
Christie, fastening on the Chief Factor's ceremonial
sword-belt and sword, found that in days of peace he
had so put on flesh the belt was uncomfortably tight.

Malcolm Groat and Harrison Young came to his
aid in girding his solid form with the outgrown belt,
and the pinching and pressing process was rich in
mirth for the onlookers.

As we have seen, Christie sent a messenger galloping to St. Albert for Father Lacombe and some of
his Metis. Within the courtyard painted Indians and
anxious whites did what they could to pass the unpleasant hours of waiting. . . . The Blackfeet arrived
before dusk and lay in ambush among the trees on

the south bank. They announced their arrival and their intentions by repeated firing upon the Fort.

The bullets whizzed against the stockade; a few found their way over it into the courtyard, but their force was spent. With nightfall the real danger came, and the men in the Fort strained their hearing for signs of life from the ambushed Blackfeet.

Past midnight the trampling of horses' hoofs was heard along the St. Albert trail, and in a few moments Father Lacombe with thirty armed Metis hunters knocked on the rear gate for admission. Their horses were speedily corralled in the stable-yard within the stockade, while some of the Metis were sent up to the gallery and bastions to man these with the handful of traders and servants already there.

The firing had been discontinued, but those on watch feared that under cover of the darkness the Blackfeet would swim across the Saskatchewan, lurk in the low brushwood by the bank, and from there creep unobserved to the stockade to fire it. This was the Indian's most effective method of atttacking a Fort, and just such an undertaking as had destroyed Old Bow Fort decades earlier.

Father Lacombe, who never carried a rifle, felt his defence must be of another sort. Disregarding the order for all to remain inside the stockade, he went boldly out on the meadows around the Fort calling on the enemy in what Blackfoot he could muster. He asked them to fire no more upon the Fort, for he and the other white men were their friends.

He—*Arsous-kitsi-rarpi*—who had so lately come from camps of their people; who had given all he had to their wounded kinsfolk—assured them now that the Company was indignant with the Crees who had treacherously fallen upon their people. He demanded of the ambushed Indians that they depart in peace.

His absolute lack of fear for his own safety and his anxiety to pacify the Blackfeet came close to bringing disaster on himself. In the southwest bastion beside Malcolm Groat was stationed Donald McDonald, a new clerk who had narrowly escaped with his life from a Blackfoot's rifle at Fort Carleton not long before.

When Father Lacombe, crying out his friendly plea, came beneath this bastion—the closest to the enemy's encampment—Macdonald's ear caught the strenuous shouts in Blackfoot.

He recognized the language without its meaning; guided by the voice he took aim with his rifle   .   .   . and would have fired, had not Groat and a Metis standing near begged him to desist.

They assured him the voice belonged to Lacombe— Père Lacombe.   .   .   .   Even if he were new to Edmonton, didn't he know that voice?

The priest, meanwhile, unaware of his narrow escape, continued his way around the Fort calling out his message of peace.

Up in the bastions and sentinel's gallery all was silent—as still as the war-encampment across the river. They waited for some response to Father Lacombe's plea. There was none verbally, but when dawn came it was found that the Blackfeet had quietly foregone the attack and pitched off for the prairies.

Early in the spring of 1870 Father Lacombe in compliance with a request of Bishop Faraud went up to Fort Dunvegan to visit Father Tissier. The journey of over 1,000 miles, attended by unusual hardships and illness, was undertaken solely with this object of fraternal charity; as in the five years Father Tissier was stationed there he had not seen a brother-priest and had endured much in the performance of his ministry.

Father Lacombe travelled by pack-horse and canoe, with one guide most of the way, by the Athabasca and Lesser Slave Lake.

The trying difficulties of the journey were light-heartedly put behind him when he saw the welcoming form of his confrere hurry to meet him on the banks of the Peace. Father Tissier was still suffering from the effects of a journey to Wolverine Point during the past winter, when he had both feet frozen and for six weeks lay ill in an Indian tepee sharing the semi-starvation of his hosts.

On his return to Lesser Slave Lake Father Lacombe rallied the Metis of that post about him, and began the erection of a permanent mission-house at Stony Point.

From the lake he continued down the Little Slave, the Athabasca and La Biche Rivers to Lac la Biche, where he found his little sister Christine teaching school and striving to acquire a taste for dried meat and fish, the only food she had.

But he had no time for brotherly solicitude. Terrifying news awaited him: his Indians were attacked with a strange fatal sickness. He did not pause for rest, but hurried his borrowed pony along the St. Paul trail to the urging of this message: "Your Indians are dying like flies; and, running away from the sickness, they die along the trail."

The epidemic, which started early in July, had been carried by Metis from some infected Blackfeet. These in turn had taken the contagion from Indians and traders of the Missouri. An old Indian at St. Paul assured Father Lacombe the disease was smallpox, because sixty years before they had it in the country and it ravaged their camps in the same way.

Father Lacombe soon found himself in the thick of the epidemic. The only nourishment he could give the sick was bouillon made of dried meat, and they drank eagerly, for they were thirsty with a great fever-thirst.

Sometimes he was occupied until midnight with the sick. The hour before sunrise was the time taken to bury the dead. Then Father Lacombe would call the young men to help him, warning them that if the bodies were not buried every one would catch the disease.

Meanwhile up at Victoria the Rev. George McDougall, the Methodist minister who had come

into the country eight years earlier, was devotedly
helping the Indians around his mission to make a
valiant battle against the plague, until two of his own
children succumbed to the disease.

At St. Albert the battle was being fought with
such reckless devotion by four Oblates—Fathers
Leduc and Bourgine, Brothers Doucet and Blanchet
—that they were all in turn stricken with the disease.

In the midst of Bishop Grandin's work with the
stricken Indians near Fort Carlton he received a note
from Father Lacombe on the prairies. It was pen-
cilled on ragged brown paper:

"My Lord, I am in the midst of the dead and dying, and
am now hurrying to St. Albert where our own men are
overcome by the disease. I fear there is not even one priest
there able to assist the dying."

Father Lacombe's arrival at St. Albert was timely.
Father Bourgine was down with the disease; Father
Leduc was recovering, though marked for his lifetime with the honourable scars of this year's service.
Practically the whole settlement was affected and only
two or three of the school-children were able to be
about.

In the Annals of the Oblates we read in a letter
from Father Leduc, December, 1870:

". . . Father Lacombe was again near St. Paul
in the midst of the dead and the dying. When he
heard of our distressing condition, he passed the night
administering the sacraments to those Indians who

were in danger of death, then flew to our assistance. This act of fraternal charity moved me to tears; I could not refrain from weeping as I threw myself into the arms of this good Father, who arrived so opportunely to help us through our difficulties."

When his confreres had recovered Father Lacombe hastened to return to the prairie and like Father Andre, who also spent the summer among the Indians, he had many gruesome experiences during the epidemic. For the numerous graves he dug his only implements were knives and axes, the clay being scooped out with his hands or improvised wooden scoops. Sometimes ten or twelve bodies were placed in one grave, carried there from the tepees in blankets.

About thirty or more encampments on the prairies were affected and there were from twenty-five to forty families in each. Father Lacombe found his way to most of these camps, performing the same painful duties at each.

One morning when the young men were aiding him in the burials Father Lacombe sent them back for the bodies of two children, which he had laid aside and covered with boughs the previous night. The men went, but the bodies of the little ones were gone. The dogs had already been there; only the torn remains were found.

Father Lacombe heard one old man mourning tragically over this:

"Great Father," he kept repeating audibly, "is it possible that you let us die with this horrible disease? —and then we are eaten by *dogs?*"

Even Father Lacombe's doughty heart found here its limits of endurance and power to console.

"I could not say a word to comfort him," he says, "I could not speak. It was too tragic. What could be said?"

Instead he took his extra shirt and socks and bits of cotton out of the dunnage-sack that served as his portmanteau, and went out himself to the repulsive task of burying the torn remains.

The only precaution taken against the disease by Father Lacombe was to keep a quill with camphor in his mouth. He did not fear the disease for himself; he was too busy thinking of others. But one evening after his rounds from tepee to tepee he felt so deathly ill he told himself his hour had come. With his inherent belief in the efficiency of action he fought the nausea by drinking painkiller and taking exercise until he was ready to fall asleep from exhaustion. The next morning the ailment, whatever it was, had disappeared.

Before the close of September the epidemic was over. Father Lacombe estimated that over 2,500 Crees died. Others place the number of deaths among the Crees and Blackfeet as well over 3,000. It is impossible to obtain any very accurate figures.

At St. Albert most of the Indian children in the

Grey Nuns' orphanage died, as well as many Metis and Indians. In every camp on the plains someone was mourned.

To-day, 1870 is a year from which Old-Timers on the Saskatchewan date modern events, as previously along the Red River all dated from 1852, the year of the Great Flood.

XVIII

THE great progress made by Christianity this summer brought consolation to the Oblates after the scourge of smallpox had spent its virulence. Their absolute devotion to the Indian had not gone unrewarded. The pagan warriors were moved by the unpretentious heroism of the priests: it had shamed their own fear. The attitude of their dying friends enjoying religious consolation also had its effect.

An item in the Journal of St. Paul records 2,000 baptisms of adults and children on the plains that summer. Among the many conversions was that of Papaskis (Grasshopper), a noted medicine-man, who embraced Christianity when on his prayer to the Christian God his daughter, the wife of Chief Ermine-Skin,[1] was cured.

But the conversion that delighted Father Lacombe most was that of his friend, Sweet-Grass, the bravest and most esteemed among the Cree warriors—the Head-Chief of the whole nation of Crees. For many years the Little Chief had said, "Leave me alone; I will tell you when my time has come."

Now toward the close of the epidemic Father Lacombe, calling the stronger Indians to prayer one

[1] This Chief and his wife still live at Ermine Skin's reserve, south of Edmonton.

187

evening, was astounded to see Sweet-Grass and several of his pagan warriors enter and kneel with the rest.

After the prayer and hymn were concluded, Sweet-Grass, mindful of a chief's privilege of oratory, rose and asked if he might speak.   .   .   .

"My relatives, my friends," he said.   "You are surprised to see me here.   You have known me as a strong follower of the beliefs of our fathers.   I have led in the medicine-feasts.   To-day, in the presence of the Great Spirit and before our friend *Kamiyo-atchakwe,* I turn away from all that.   It is past, and I will hear the teachings of the Man-of-Prayer."

Then falling on his knees beside Father Lacombe, he asked his friend to make the Sign of the Cross on him.

The priest took the hand of Sweet-Grass, made the mystic Sign on the chief, and said solemnly:

"In the Name of the Father—and of the Son—and of the Holy Ghost, I receive you, brave chief of the Crees."

Father Lacombe then gave some hours daily to the instruction of Sweet-Grass and the band of followers he was bringing into the Fold.

One evening when night-prayer was finished and Father Lacombe sat outside his tent, smoking and chatting in Cree with the older men, their causerie was broken by Sweet-Grass enquiring abruptly of Father Lacombe:

"Are you going to baptise me soon?"

"The whole camp knows I have made you ready for that."

"But perhaps you would not do it, if you knew what a man I am and what evil I once did."

For answer Father Lacombe slipped his crucifix from his belt and looking on it said:

"He became Man and died on the cross for your salvation: He came to the world to save sinners. If you are sorry for your sins He will pardon you all— to the greatest—and the waters of Baptism shall wash away all the sins of your past life."

Sweet-Grass shook his head regretfully.

"Hah! . . ."

That Indian exclamation can breathe alike the deepest regret or the keenest triumph.

"I will tell you about one time of my past life; you will judge, and some of the old men here will know that I speak the truth."

No one spoke, and for a long time the evening silence—filled with the peace that had come again to the afflicted camp—was broken only by the low and pleasant voice of Sweet-Grass.

He told of his despised youth as a captive among the Crees. Friendless, neglected and taunted with his small stature the warriors would have nothing to do with him. He-Who-Has-No-Name, they called him—until one night he slipped from camp, went far and alone on foot into the south country, and returned with one Blackfoot scalp and forty-two

ponies.   Then amid shouts of triumph he held aloft
a tuft of sweet-grass dipped in the blood of the dead
Blackfoot-Councillor.   An old man cried out "Sweet-
Grass!   Sweet-Grass!"—and the whole camp took
up the name.

"Sweet-Grass!"

So he had won a name; he became a brave, a great
chief; but his soul was haunted yet by the thought
of the aged Councillor.

Father Lacombe heard his story.   It was not told
with bravado, but with regret.   His lonely childhood
had developed in Sweet-Grass a sensitiveness and fine-
ness of thought unusual in the Indian.

The wanton murder of an unoffending old man—
when in the act of worshipping the Great Spirit in
His symbol the Sun—had weighed on the mind of
Sweet-Grass for years.   He loathed the crime; the
thought of it had held him back from a Religion
of Love which taught "Thou shalt not kill!"   He
feared the missionaries would reject him when they
knew all.

Now with his story told he found no judge, but
a disciple of the all-comprehending Christ, the Man
of Sorrows, who had said:

"Let him who is without sin cast the first stone!"

A few days later Sweet-Grass was baptised, receiving the Christian name of Abraham, and his marriage
was blessed by Father Lacombe.

Two years later the latter took Sweet-Grass with
him to Saint Boniface and in the Cathedral there this

esteemed chief was confirmed by the chief of the
Blackrobes in the West.

In November, 1870, Father Lacombe with Father
Scollen went by dog-train from St. Albert to Rocky
Mountain House and spent the winter there collecting and revising notes he had made for his Cree dictionary and grammar. In his many goings and comings, by the firelight in Indian tepees or log missions,
he had contrived with persistent labour to make
voluminous notes on the Cree language. They were
not always of the most accurate, but they were the
best he could obtain.

He now put these in shape, as Bishop Grandin
wanted to have them printed. At the Bishop's
request also he undertook to write a score of sermons
in Cree, embodying the whole Christian doctrine.

Early in December his work was agreeably interrupted by the visit of a "young Irishman,[1] an officer
in the British Army—a pleasant, fine-looking man,"
Father Lacombe recalls, "who passed several days
with me. I enjoyed his company, and on the eighth
of December he served my Mass at Rocky Mountain
House."

Butler's impression of Father Lacombe is clearly
conveyed in his recent work—"The Light of the
West"—where he says:

[1] This was Captain Butler — the late General Sir William Butler, honoured veteran of many campaigns in Africa and India. His book,
"The Great Lone Land," a classic of Western literature, was published
as a result of this trip, which he was making as a Commissioner of the
Canadian Government to report on the conditions of the Territories.

"In the winter of 1870 I met at Rocky Mountain House—a post of the Hudson's Bay Company—Père Lacombe. He had lived with the Blackfeet and the Cree Indians for many years, and I enjoyed more than I can say listening to his stories of adventure with these wild men of the plains. The thing that left most lasting impression on my mind was his intense love and devotion to these poor wandering and warring people—his entire sympathy for them.

"He had literally lived with them, sharing their food and their fortunes and the everlasting dangers of their lives. He watched and tended their sick, buried their dead and healed the wounded in their battles. No other man but Father Lacombe could pass from one hostile camp to another—suspected nowhere, welcomed everywhere; carrying, as it were, the 'truce of God' with him wherever he went."

While Father Lacombe at Rocky Mountain House had withdrawn himself from his picturesque *mission ambulante* and was studiously at work upon his book, cataclysmic events were shaking the nations of the Old World. Marvellous as it may seem these were conspiring to take the unknown Oblate missionary away from the plains and the tepees. They were going to place him in a field whose limits should outrun all Canada.

Perhaps Bishop Grandin in his sentinel outlook upon the needs of his diocese was the one instrument directly shaping Father Lacombe's course; but the causes were more remote. These western missions

MAP
showing
THE FIELD OF
FATHER LACOMBE'S
ACTIVITIES
1852 to 1872
and
1882 to 19

had up to now been maintained by the gifts of friends in France and by the alms of the Council of the Propagation of the Faith—the funds of this charitable society being mainly contributed by the French race.

But France was now upset by the losses of the Franco-Prussian war, and Pope Pius IX was the subject of most persistent and disastrous attacks. The administrative forces of the Church, confronted with such problems at the very centre, had little time or means for these remote missions of the west. The future looked almost as dark as in 1849, when the Superior-General of the Oblates decided to recall his men from the west, until the touching plea of young Alexandre Tache caused him to change his mind.

To add to their distress, the western missionaries experienced an unpleasantness that is one of the inevitable results of the world's pitiful division of creeds. Some of the non-Catholic traders and a couple of other missionaries took advantage—perhaps naturally —of the others' weakness to tell the Indians that the Chief of the Blackrobes was now a prisoner; that their religion had been humbled and they would themselves be recalled.

This spread among the Indians, and some unfriendly spirits among them taunted the poor priests repeatedly. But they were not without sympathy among their friends: and Father Lacombe recalls with tender amusement the martial proclamation of Sweet-Grass that if the Pope's captors sent traders among them his warriors would not give them their furs: they would fight the rascals!

The missionaries' condition this year is referred to with feeling in a letter [1] written by Father Lacombe at St. Albert on May 20, 1871, to a member of the Oblate Order in Montreal.

He is appealing to the Canadian House to secure aid for the missions, since nothing can be expected from France. He repeats the taunts they have lately had flung at them on the Saskatchewan, and adds:

"For my part, and I can say the same for my brethren of Saskatchewan and the north, we will die of hardships and privations before we will abandon our Christians and our poor catechumens. Already for a long time I have led the life of the Indians, and the greater part of each year I have been at their mercy; this will not then be anything new for me. Provided I have what is necessary to offer the Holy Sacrifice I do not ask anything else."

He announces in this letter his intention to spend the entire summer on the prairies with the Crees and Blackfeet.

The latter, he states, are in an alarming condition, being demoralised by American whiskey-traders who are bringing in liquor from Fort Benton.

"Since last autumn," he writes, "the process of demoralisation has, alas! made very considerable progress: the disorders of all kinds which have taken place among the savages and these miserable traders

[1] Annals of Oblates.

of rum are frightful. We have done our best to inform the American Government of these unhappy infringements of its laws; while on the other side the Government of the Red River has made a very severe law prohibiting intoxicating liquors throughout these territories. But while we await the coming of some impressive force [1] to compel the fulfilment of this wise law, we suffer unceasingly."

He goes on to cite an instance of which word was brought during the winter to Mountain House.

"While more than two hundred lodges of the Piegans and Bloods were drinking with the Americans on the Belly River last October a war-party of Crees composed of two hundred and fifty men fell upon them through the night; but the Piegans, although taken unprepared, did not let themselves be beaten. The Crees were almost all killed by those whom they had ventured to attack . . ." a result which was perhaps due to the repeating rifles supplied to the southern tribes by the Americans.

Father Lacombe left for the prairies very soon after the writing of this letter, for he was anxious to reach and bring into the Christian fold all those bands on the plains that were still pagan. With him he took his famous half-breed, Alexis Cardinal, who had continued to be the most faithful of servitors

[1] The representations of Father Lacombe and others resulted a few years later in the organization of the now-famous force of Mounted Police.

and religious to the degree of eccentricity. Alexis'
oddities would not permit of Father Lacombe receiving him into the Order as a lay-brother. He
regarded himself as a missionary, however, and wore
a semi-clerical gown of black stroud, made by a half-
breed woman on his own instructions.

Without accident and without hardship from
hunger these two in 1871 ranged far and wide over
the plains lying south of Edmonton along the Red
Deer River, the Battle River and well into the country of the Blackfeet.

In some of the Cree camps visited were already
many Christians, and in each the missionary spent
about two weeks while he instructed the people and
fulfilled his ministry generally. He baptized several
children and some adults who had been catechumens
and were already prepared.

In a few cases he performed the marriage ceremony, blessing the unions of "men of reputation"
upon whom he felt he could rely to keep their word
to reject polygamous practices. Several warriors
who were willing to accept Christianity had rebelled
at a form of marriage which required them to bind
themselves to one woman for life.

"If we marry, and find we cannot agree, we may
want to leave each other. Then what will we do?"
they argued.

That was to the Indian the one great drawback
in this strange and pleasant Christian religion: its

Men-of-Prayer not only objected to a brave having two or three wives—in whom he sometimes took even more pride as a man of means than in his band of horses; but they insisted that taking one woman he should cleave to that one through good and bad seasons and good and bad tempers.

Truly there were more things in this Christian philosophy than ever chief or warrior among them had ever dreamt of before!

One such protest Father Lacombe recalls in detail. A man of middle-age, who had embraced the Christian religion, continued to live with Margaret, a Christian Cree and the mother of his children; but he refused to bind himself to her by any such solemn promise as the marriage ceremony required. This was all the more strange because he had a high regard for Margaret and had never taken any other wife.

The woman had for some time been anxious to be married according to Christian rites; the man held back. Finally Father Lacombe told William if he did not make up his mind during that visit to the camp, he would not permit him to enter the House of Prayer. William thereupon consented to be married next day.

Next morning, when Father Lacombe threw open the skin doors of his tent to invite the people to Mass, he found William and Margaret with two witnesses sitting there stoically waiting. The four rose and stood before him on the prairie. Father Lacombe again spoke briefly upon the duties of marriage. When finally he declared they should cherish each other till death parted them, the man was visibly excited.

"At last," says Father Lacombe, "I said—'William, do you take this woman, Margaret, to be your wife forever?'—and oh, that sound so terrible! . . . you cannot know how . . . in the ears of the Indian man. He say quickly to me,

" 'Stop, Father, that's all fine for you to say those words, for you will not have the trouble with her. That's all fine . . . that you push me so for marry her: but if she give me so much trouble all these years when she know I can put her away any time—what will she do when she knows I cannot put her away?'

"I told him that she would be a good Christian wife, as she had just promised, and will give him no trouble. . . . But he talk on . . . and as I wait I get cross—myself—and I say sternly to her—

" 'Well, Margaret, you go leave him. You must separate then. You leave him to make his own moccasins, to cook his meals, to pound his pemmican. Yes, Margaret, you go!'

"William softened—as I know he would—at that thought of separation, for Margaret was a smart, good woman, and he say quickly again:

" 'No, I do not want that. I have said I will marry her, and I will. But I want to speak my mind first about what trouble she may make for me.' "

So the ceremony went on. And Father Lacombe was always happy to know later that William and Margaret lived together as contented as before, until death took one away.

XIX

FATHER LACOMBE spent part of the summer of 1871 with the Blackfeet Indians in the heart of their own country. The camps were pleasantly pitched, and buffalo were abundant in the valley. The time was favourable for teaching Christianity.

Unaware that Bishop Grandin was then planning a new course for him, he was working out in his own mind a distinct campaign for himself: just as ten years earlier he planned the establishment of St. Albert and St. Paul de Cris.

These missions were now in touch with civilization; he could leave them to the younger priests; for himself—with his partial knowledge of the Blackfoot tongue and warm friendship for the race—he would select the mission of converting the Blackfeet.

Up to this time he had been their only missionary, and his ministry had been necessarily interrupted. Now he felt he must devote himself entirely to them. The very difficulties of the work appealed to his high spirit. He already saw in his dreams a prosperous Blackfoot mission on the Bow River. He would consecrate it to Our Lady of Peace as a token of the pledge his Blackfeet must give him to cease warring upon their old enemies, the Crees.

In a campaign of instruction that summer, Father

Lacombe found that his Blackfeet were not docile and appreciative as his Cree neophytes had been. One afternoon along the Bow, when he had tired of the Indians' camp and company, he walked away by the river to read the day's office in his breviary, and to pray there in quietness.

After a time of this pleasant retirement he looked up to see two men standing near.

"What do you want?" he asked, with a touch of impatience.

"We watch you pray. Are you praying for us?"

"Yes; for all your people."

Then they sat with him, questioning him about the Creator, the world, its age, how the world was peopled—and a number of questions that had not worried his Cree friends at all. These warriors were more interested apparently in history than in doctrine, and he felt that unlike most savage tribes they were to be won through their reason and not through their hearts alone.

At last he felt he had got a foothold, and he turned to his task with fresh enthusiasm. He spent the afternoon answering their questions and explaining difficult points to them. As he defined the Trinity he drew a circle in the sand with a triangle set in it, making of this a symbol of Eternity, without beginning or end, and of the divine Person revealed to Humanity in three phases.

Father Lacombe continued drawing pictures in the

sand—and the interest and understanding of his war-riors developed more rapidly than he ever hoped it would.

"That night I went back to my tent," he says, "and a new plan was with me all the time. I dreamt of that. The next morning I took a parchment of buffalo-skin and with a dead coal I made all those signs again on the skin, with many more. I nailed it on a pole in the middle of the camp and called the people about me. Every day after that while I stayed among them I made my instructions there, and the Indians learned so fast I was happy.

"At St. Albert, where I spent a part of that winter with the Bishop, I made with ink and paper a longer history [1] with these pictures. It started at the Cre-ation, and went down through Bible history to the coming of Christ; then through the history of the Church and all Life on our pilgrimage to Heaven. The *echelle*—the Ladder—the other priests called it for its shape, and they laughed at my plan. But they liked it too.

"When I went to Montreal the next year the Sis-ters of the Congregation made a fine copy for me in colours, and I had many thousand copies of it printed in France."

[1] This Ladder (a Bible and Church history in pictures) of Father Lacombe was shown a few years later to Pope Pius IX, and its in-genious plan so appealed to him that he ordered several thousand copies made, that they might be available for Mission-work among the savage tribes in different parts of the world.

This summer, marked by the invention of his picture-catechism, was destined to be the last of Father Lacombe's *mission ambulante* on the plains.

Up to this time the Saskatchewan Valley had smiled to Heaven in the virginal freshness that moved Franchere to rhapsody a century and a half earlier.

The seventies ushered in the beginning of the end of the wilderness. Outside forces were moving to its wakening. Well-based rumour had it that the railway to the Pacific would pass through the Saskatchewan valley. Canada was in honour bound to keep its Confederation-promise and give British Columbia this railway connection with the east; and to all who knew the west it was apparent that the logical route lay through the fertile Saskatchewan belt and across the easy grades of the Pine River Pass.

The Hudson's Bay Company—every man of the ancient corporation, from stately directors at Fenchurch Street to the traders in the outposts—looked on with dismay. A railway to be built into the heart of their best fur-country! Appalling! . . . the fur-trade would vanish in its wake. The calamity must be averted—as the diplomatic and powerful company knew well how to avert any peril to its interests.

Bishop Grandin likewise heard the rumour with anxiety, but with no desire to postpone what he considered both inevitable and just. His anxiety was due to the conviction that this railway would bring a great tide of immigration, the consequence of which would be serious for the Indians if they were left unprepared to meet it.

The Bishop had made a comprehensive study of his diocese. He was now thoroughly acquainted with the conditions and dispositions of his Indians. As a result he had determined to provide both Indians and Metis with schools: and these must be adequately equipped schools in which the white man's civilization might be inculcated in the children.

In this way he became the originator of the existing system of Canadian Indian Schools.

On April 2, 1872, the Bishop received Papal Bulls erecting a separate diocese of St. Albert, and defining the ecclesiastical province of St. Boniface which was to become a metropolitan see. Now that he had attained to the undivided responsibilities of a large diocese he felt impelled to take up with Father Lacombe this pressing question of Indian schools.

For some reason he chose to impart his plans to his associate by letter rather than in person. Perhaps he felt that he could do it more easily so, since it was a hard task he was about to impose and he regretted the necessity for it. He knew that Father Lacombe had his heart set upon Christianizing the Blackfeet, but that project must remain in abeyance for the greater need.

Father Lacombe was the only man for the new work. Of the fifteen missionary priests then in St. Albert diocese he alone was of Canadian birth, and it was to Canada this new appeal had to be made.

France was doing, or had done, her part: the Church in Canada should now face her responsibilities.

The Bishop's letter here translated from the original French, sums up the needs of the diocese and is in itself a notable document:

"ON THE BANKS OF THE BEAVER RIVER, April 21, 1872.

"My reverend and dear Father Lacombe,

"I am spending Sunday here on the left bank of the beautiful Beaver. Last night after being in the water up to our knees for two hours fording the smaller stream, we arrived here too late to undertake another crossing. . . .

" . . . As a member of our Order you are my adviser and my first counsellor . . .

"So I nominate you by these presents my Vicar-General. It is not an honorary title that I desire to give you. It is a charge I impose on you, the difficulties of which will soon confront you; but with the grace of God you will surmount them.

"At the present moment you know as well as I, what we can do with the resources which we have at our disposal. We can, it is true, live in a poor way, but we cannot inaugurate anything. You are begging me to establish the mission of Our Lady of Peace among the Blackfeet; also another among the Crees. And how many other places there are where our missionaries are on the rack and appealing for help?

"It is necessary then to procure resources in some way; our zeal will be paralyzed for lack of means to carry on the work. Notwithstanding the number of missions which we ought to establish, we are reduced to employing several

Fathers simply as school-teachers; is it not a desperate state of affairs?

"It is necessary, *mon cher*, for you to abandon your Indians for this year: I shall myself so·far as I am able, go in your stead to dispense the bread of the Divine Word.

"And you, where are you to go?   Go I pray you, into your own country holding out your hands to your friends and mine.

"It pains me to impose this onerous mission on you.   It is, I know, an imposition on Canada, which has already shown so much interest in us; but it seems to me that we cannot stand on our dignity—when it is as now a question of life or death—if we would avoid seeing the young Church of St. Albert diocese die at its birth.

"When, in the last Council of Quebec, there was question of asking Rome to erect the ecclesiastical province of St. Boniface, I opposed it, fearing that once separated from the mother Province we should be somewhat abandoned by her. The Reverend Fathers of the Council reassured me on this point: I am convinced that they will all now regard your operations favourably.

"I shall ask one other service of you.   It concerns the extreme need for schools.   It is the important work, the only real means of civilising our Indians.   .   .   ."

He here details a plan of raising money through a charitable association.

"This project blessed by the Bishops and by our Holy Father, would also be blessed of God and would be one of the most powerful means while conserving the savage tribes, of civilising them—this taking hold of the rising generations in our schools.   With the permission of the Ordinary try also to find some good missionary priests and some young men to come to our aid by entering our Order. Finally, pray much for us; if God be with us we must succeed.

"I am not giving you a *celebret*. This letter will prove to those who have the patience to read it that you are not interdicted nor suspended, and that you have the confidence of your Superior and Bishop.

"Go then, my very dear Father; God is with you. Do not regard God's work in the diocese of St. Albert as my charge exclusively; *it is also yours*. More, it is the work of the Lord, and we are his instruments.

"*Bon voyage!* dear Father. I embrace you and bless you affectionately.   "Your devoted brother,

                    "VITAL—J,
                "Bishop of St. Albert."

This letter, written with difficulty in the Bishop's tent on the banks of the Beaver, was both a shock and stimulus to Father Lacombe, totally absorbed as he was in planning the spiritual conquest of the Blackfeet. He took it as a disciplined soldier, however, for here verily were his marching orders.

He was by no means enchanted with the prospect. To his spirited and at the same time sensitive temperament the rôle of a mendicant naturally did not appeal. His own knowledge of the needs of the diocese and his sense of obedience left him no choice however. Bishop Tache had collected $6,000 in Quebec in 1861, when his diocese was in such extreme need after the fire; why could he not do as well for St. Albert? he asked himself. . . . And if he succeeded, of what moment were his personal humiliations?

He went down to St. Paul de Cris early in May, closed that mission and set out for the east.

He made the long journey across the prairies on horseback, arriving at St. Boniface for the conferring of the pallium on Archbishop Tache. St. Jean Baptiste's Day was included in the celebration, which took the form of a tourney of speech-making. Father Lacombe delivered his oration in Cree.

He found the past two years had brought many changes along the Red River. On the bank opposite the twin-towered cathedral of his friend, the frontier town of Winnipeg had grown up about old Fort Garry.

Mariaggi, the epic-caterer of the frontier, had already opened the first of his chain of western cafés. An empty hall in the sprawling town had actually been turned into a theatre—while newcomers were being pressed to buy town lots for $50 each! Winnipeg, in very fact, was a lusty infant creeping toward its disastrous boom period.

At St. Boniface he turned his back on the west and entered upon a new life of service in which he was to traverse continents as before he traversed the plains.

It was a life in which he would learn that the cold splendour of European courts could shelter more heart-hunger than the smoky lodges of his Indians; and that the *Gros-Bonnets,* the Big Chiefs of the white men, were no more formidable on acquaintance than his old friends, Natous and Sweet-Grass.

PART II

"Pursue the West but long enough, 'tis East!"

I

WHEN Father Lacombe returned to Montreal, fresh from the life of the plains, he surveyed the changing east with some awe and a great deal of appreciation.

Behind him he had left the "tall young Adam of the west," struggling along its Red River fringe to a consciousness of its own possibilities—but for the rest a wilderness overrun by insouciant Indians, Metis and fur-traders.

Before him in the east he saw a new Canada rising out of the grave of Old World feudalism: a superb figure that, reaching out to closer union with the spectacular young giant of the west, would soon stand forth as a nation.

The score of years that had elapsed since he went away had been fruitful of changes in the gray streets of Montreal, but in himself the alteration was even more striking. He had travelled a long way from the timid young Levite who wept as he said good-bye to the gentle Bourget in 1852.

To easterners his strenuous personality and his stories were alike unique and pleasing. Wherever he went he was welcomed royally. It was a strangely cold heart into which this "spoiled child of Providence" could not creep.

His first duty was to call upon Archbishop (later Cardinal) Taschereau of Quebec, to lay before him the needs of St. Albert diocese, and to urge the establishment of an Association to assist its schools. This plan did not seem practicable to the Archbishop at the time, but he recommended Father Lacombe and his cause very warmly to all the clergy under his jurisdiction.

"Ah, he was kind to me—that Cardinal—the first time I pass on Quebec to beg," Father Lacombe recalls. "He had an appearance very severe, you know, and a face like ice. But behind that I found his heart was very warm."

Father Lacombe hated the rôle of beggar. Each time he ascended a pulpit or made an address for this purpose the free spirit of the "little Indian" revolted. He had lived so long in a primitive land, where a man yielded almost without the asking what another's need claimed, that he found this work particularly humiliating.

In addition he dreaded those great audiences of critical palefaces, as he fancied them to be. His method of nerving himself then, and even years later, when this feeling arose in him was unusual but characteristic:

"Why am I afraid?" he would demand of himself sternly. "I come here to speak the word of God, to carry on His work. . . . Ha, I am *stu-pide, stu-pide*, but . . . ! these people are more *stu-pides* even than I!—Now I will talk."

In a letter to a friend, written from the Archbishop's Palace on Christmas Eve, 1872, Father Lacombe anticipates his first public appearance in the ancient Capital:

"You can imagine that at this moment I am not very much at ease, haunted as I am by the thought of my exhibition tomorrow morning under the vaulted roof of the old Cathedral. My body groans in anticipation; what will I do when I stand before an audience to which I am so averse?

"But what petty pride! What miserable human respect! Is it not sad to see so much self-love in an old Indian—such a blockhead as he is too!"

When the Congregation nuns had reproduced his picture-catechism in colours he took it to the Desbarats house, whose head had 500 copies gratuitously printed for him. The Ladders, as he always called them, were then straightway shipped back to the missions and were soon to be found in every corner of the West, where an Oblate had penetrated.

He received considerable sums of money during his season of begging and remitted all happily to his Bishop; but no benefactor, as previsioned by the latter, came up now on Father Lacombe's horizon to assist him in publishing his Indian dictionary.[1]

[1] This was the first book printed in Cree, but not the first in other Indian dialects of the West. The priests of the Hudson Bay district had books in syllabic Indian printed by Palsgrave several years earlier, while the Rev. Mr. Evans, the Wesleyan minister who invented this syllabic method, had some books printed even earlier. Bishop Tache, who originated the Chipewyan characters, had a book of prayers and hymns in this tongue published by Palsgrave in 1857.

Finally an inspiration came to ask the Government's assistance.

"Surely this much aid is due the missionaries who have been so strong a civilizing influence in the west," it was suggested.   And the Government, fortunately falling in with the idea, made a grant of $1,000 toward the publication of the dictionary.

It was found necessary to defer the publication of the book, as Archbishop Tache wrote now asking Father Lacombe to employ all his energies in securing new French settlers for the west.

After a brief campaign of begging and colonization he expected his recall to the west.   Instead, at the close of the winter he sailed from Portland for Europe, having been appointed the representative of his Archbishop at the General Chapter of their Order.   His Grace was too ill at the time to leave St. Boniface.

When he arrived in France Father Lacombe, like all brother-missionaries who had preceded him, went from city to city addressing large congregations upon the needs of the western missions.   Likewise he visited numerous seminaries, endeavouring to inspire some of the students to volunteer for the western field.

A copy of his Ladder, which he presented to the Superior-General, so pleased that dignitary that he recommended the publication of 10,000 copies.   But during his stay in Paris M. Letaille, a benevolent old man who was the head of the publishing-house of that

name, printed 16,000 copies for him at a nominal
cost.

Interesting glimpses of the impression made by
Europe upon the free-lance of the plains-missions are
to be had in his letters to Father Poulin, who was then
living in retirement at a Montreal hospice, failing
in health and threatened with blindness. It was characteristic of the western priest's sympathetic nature
that his longest letters were to this shut-in friend.

From London, where he is learning metropolitan
modes of transport, he writes on April 16th:

"I have already commenced to plough London—under the
earth and along the streets and over the streets and on the
Thames. . . ."

He speaks of visits to museums, to the Lords, the
Commons and Westminster. . . .

"What do you think of all that? I tell you, I do not
know what to think of it. It is doubtless very fine for you,
civilized men, who love these useless statues and walls gnawed
into by Time, with all the shapeless stone towers which lift
themselves into the air amidst numerous gables and turrets—
and the more knobs and holes in them the finer they are considered!

"Yes, it is very beautiful certainly. But all that seems
nothing to me in exchange for our forests or our prairies or
even our poor chapels. You may put me down as profane or
savage, but would you have me think otherwise—*moi*, a poor
missionary to those whom people in a sort of disdain call
savages."

Cartier, the invalid Canadian statesman, Count Bassano and others entertained him here, but his visit to Archbishop Manning was to him the most impressive part of his stay in London.

He writes of Manning with enthusiasm:

"How this man pleased me! What a worthy Bishop! I made him a present of one of my 'Ladders,' and he seemed enchanted with this new plan of teaching the catechism."

Could the sympathetic Archbishop be other than enchanted with the ingenious Ladder, which the missionary showed him gravely as his one tangible achievement? He likely forgot to be amused at the picturesque jumble of men and porpoises in the waters that conveyed the image of the Deluge, or with the lurid rain of fire that is seen to drown Sodom. He admired instead the wonderful ingenuity of his mind so appropriately fitting the lesson to the pupil.

During their conversation Father Lacombe must have made some reference to the unseeing sight-seers in the once-Catholic temples of London—or in some other way introduced the subject of non-Catholics; for many years after as he spoke to me of this visit he recalled that the future Cardinal talked to him a long time about their separated brethren—urging him to love them as warmly even as he did his own people of the prairies, and to pray for them.

" 'For I was one of them once,' the Archbishop said to me, 'and I know how they believe in their souls they are right—so there is no blame for them that they do not see the Truth.'

"Of course, I have pray for them before, but—" added Father Lacombe with delightful naivete, "that was the firs' time I truly understand the Protestant, and I begin to love them—not only a few like Mr. Christie and Mr. Hardisty, my good friends, but all of them: to pity them and pray for them, because I love them."

As naïve a comment as any he makes is contained in his first letter from Paris, though it must be remembered that as yet the writer had met New World English only when travelling:

"Before leaving England let me tell you, for your satisfaction and mine, that I have been enchanted with the good manners and politeness of the English of England. How very different they are from our wooden English of Canada and the United States. To your great surprise, doubtless, I shall tell you that not once from Portland to Dover has anyone given me the tiniest trouble nor shown me the least rudeness. This is a big avowal, is it not?—for me, who find it so difficult to be pleased with the manners of 'civilized' people."

Paris he styles satirically "the Metropolis of fashions and good government." In the French houses of the Oblates, where so much had already been heard of the Indian ways and daring of their *"fameux Père Lacombe"* he was an object of curiosity at first. His Superior-General spent a whole recreation near him one evening, he chronicles:

" . . . and at the end I believe he was convinced that this Père Lacombe, whom they said they had awaited with so much impatience, was like other mortals and fed on the flesh of animals—not human bodies."

But the civility of his French cousins bores him—

"I have begun to get lonely, having no one to argue with me. It is shocking; they always agree with me . . ."

He concludes this letter with *"un salut à la mode Parisienne."* At dinner with Louis Veuillot, the noted journalist, where he met several people of distinction, the meal did not pass without an amusing contretemps. He writes to Father Poulin:

"At the close of the dinner they brought bowls filled with some liquid. I thought this was to drink and was on the point of swallowing it, when I had the sensible thought to ask my neighbour, the good Mdlle. Veuillot, what it signified. She laughed and said, 'It is to wash the fingers, *mon Père.*'

"Pugh! how they laughed, and I cried '*Vive nos sauvages!*' ——who do not need to wash themselves so often."

The itinerant missionary spoke in churches and seminaries at Strasburg, Nancy, Vichy, Autun, Brest and Metz, so lately ceded to the Prussians. After the address in the Seminary here "the Superior came to me, and said if the Prussians had heard me they would have put me in a dungeon!" . . . A fresh adventure to which the *voyageur*-heart of the missionary would not have been averse!

Father Lacombe did not, however, meet with the

success of either Bishop Faraud or Bishop Grandin. He could not speak of his mission-life from the viewpoint of a Frenchman. Consequently while the addresses of this unusual missionary echoed like pages from a medieval romance, the young French seminarian was not drawn to emulate him on the prairies.

Father Lacombe was somewhat discouraged. He writes that he is continually travelling to new points, working "like a negro, when he is not on the trains"; that he meets with little success, and if the tide does not soon turn he will become desperate. As a nameless unrecognized Indian brave might do, he exclaims:

" . . . I will become a Prussian, or I will declare myself a Jesuit and declaim against Bismarck, so that I may be imprisoned, *and then I shall make myself a name.*"

By June 9th at Nancy he feels that he is civilised "almost to the degree of these proud Frenchmen"; but when he is asked to dine with the Bishop of Nancy he lapses—and describes the occasion in concise Metis terms of the camp and trail: "We made *grande chaudiere!*" (We had a well-filled kettle of food: a feast).

All through Brittany, which had sent so many missionaries to the west, he met with the most hearty welcome. He found that the Canadian Zouaves passing through Brittany on their way to Rome had made a lasting impression. He met many like the Bishop of Varennes, who said:

"Send for your baggage: you must stay with us.

For we Bretons love the Canadians.   They are our brothers."

To a government official who enquired concerning the Indian form of government Father Lacombe replied:

"We have the true Republic.   God is our President, and we hold no debates.   There is to be had only   among   us—Liberty,   Equality,   Fraternity. *Vive la Republique—sauvage!*"

In Paris he witnessed the splendid reception accorded the Shah of Persia.   But the heart of the plainsman is homesick; he is gorged with sight-seeing, with the man-made splendours of cities, and he is tired of it all.   He writes:

" .   .   .   It is true that notwithstanding all the beautiful things which I have seen in this France and England I have looked on sights as fine in the beautiful valley of the Saskatchewan or on the borders of some of our fine lakes.

"Say what you will, you can not take this belief from me. I am writing you to-day from a nobleman's palace, but it is not as precious as my *poetique* tent in the wilderness, where I wrote on my knees my sermons in Cree and Blackfeet."

This is the instinctive Indian in Father Lacombe speaking now, as it frequently did throughout his life. .   .   .   Is it a reversion to type—some strong strain of one of his Indian ancestors?

Still another side of his character is charmingly revealed in another communication to his friend.   On the receipt of the good news that instead of being doomed to total blindness Father Poulin may now hope to recover his eyesight, this letter wells up from the emotional heart of the Canadian abroad:

"   . . .   What gave me most pleasure in your letter was to know that in the next there would likely be a few lines written by your own hand!

"Thanks, my God, a thousand thanks; and you, my good Mother. . . .   My friend is going to recover his sight! I could weep with the joy and consolation of it. . . .   O, my Lord, Thou art satisfied with his sacrifice and especially with his heroic resignation.   Thou hast said: 'It is enough. I know you now. . . .   Finish what you have undertaken.' . . ."

And at the end of the letter he prints in large round letters:

"NOW READ YOURSELF.   I SALUTE YOU—I KISS YOUR FINE BLACK EYES. IN THE SACRED HEART OF CHRIST, I AM,
            "YOUR DEVOTED FRIEND,
                  "ALBERT LACOMBE,
                        O. M. I."

Vichy did not enchant him.

"When people have bathed they soon end by having a fit of blue devils, if they are not of the number who go to the theatre and other pleasure-parties which they put in the way of strangers to kill time. . . .   For, *voyez-vous*, the great school of Vichy does not suit me at all.

"It has for a principle, and it teaches this in huge letters— one of which alone would fill one's vision—that when at Vichy to take the waters, in order that they may exert all their influence upon you, you must not occupy yourself with anything serious, not even with much praying to God.

"We must simply float along the Boulevard, go on the minute to the spring assigned to you; look up and down the fairy parterres and salute right and left the butterfly-ladies in their afternoon toilettes, which give them truly the appearance of those insects [1] we call in Quebec 'les Demoiselles,' and then—*voila!*—when you have looked up and down, confused and disheartened at all these imbecilities—then to tone up your system mentally and physically again, you go and throw yourself in the Bath   .   .   .!"

By August Father Lacombe was openly pining for the Northwest:

"I am thinking very much of our missions, and my imagination is continually with my dear friends, the Indians.   This loneliness takes my appetite from me and sometimes makes me melancholy."

He is expecting a visit from the Superior-General, and he decided to ask to be ordered back to Canada. . . . "I am horribly lonesome," he declares.

In his next letter he relates an incident to amuse his shut-in friend.   His brethren in Paris tease him about it, he says, but he assures Father Poulin gravely that this has been the one disagreeable incident of all his travels.

The story is that on one of his numerous railway

---

[1] Quebec countryfolk call butterflies *les demoiselles*—the "young ladies."

journeys he one day entered a compartment without noticing that it was reserved for women.

"Soon," he writes, "several women came in, but none took the liberty of pointing out my mistake. At the first station these women left, and I was alone. Then at the next depot a fat little man, accompanied by a lady, opened the door into my compartment.

"Perceiving me he made big eyes at me, and angrily told his wife not to enter until I passed out. Then I saw the mistake I had made and rose to leave the carriage. But my scoundrel called out aloud to the guard, before a large crowd:

" 'Guard, come here, there is a Curé in the ladies' compartment!'

"I now saw that this admirable philosopher was bent on making a little scandal. The guard arrived just as I stepped out on the platform, and he very politely asked me to enter another carriage. Already quite agitated I said to him:

" '*M'sieu le Garde,* I am a stranger, and I did not know this compartment was reserved.'

"But my insolent fellow, not yet willing to leave me alone, said roughly: 'You ought to have known it!'

"You understand that I had contained myself now for a long time. I did so no longer. Now before the whole crowd I gave him something to think over:

" 'Sir,' I said, 'I want to tell you that you are an *insolent* fellow. I can read in your face and speech that there are many things which *you ought to know.*

You ought to know what courtesy is; but you do not. You are an unmannerly churl. Moreover in calling me a Curé, you are also mistaken: for I am only a poor missionary from America.

" 'I have not the honour to be a Curé. However, if I knew your Bishop I would go and ask him to kindly name me your Curé for some weeks—and then, to make you *know,* if that were possible, I should *scour* you down, body and mind!'

"*Et puis, voila!* the whistle announced the departure . . . ": and Father Lacombe hastened to find another compartment.

But his indignation was appeased by the outburst. The man who had defied Rowand, and worsted the sorcerer White-head was not likely to cower before a noisy little Frenchman of unclean mind. While the plain western speech dealt out to the fellow was probably beneficial.

II

On his return to Montreal that autumn Father Lacombe met Archbishop Tache there. The latter had been called east to confer with the Government concerning the amnesty for the agitators of 1869–1870. More particularly they dealt with the likelihood of Riel, the leader of the Metis government, contesting the vacant seat of Provencher for the Federal house.

Riel and many of his friends desired this; and he could easily be elected. But his presence in the House of Commons would embarrass the Government and endanger the peace of the Dominion—at least, of Ontario, which had become the storm-centre after the Metis had come to terms.

Sir John Macdonald and Sir Hector Langevin met the Archbishop in the former's office. They were naturally anxious that the Archbishop should make Riel drop out of the electoral contest. They knew he could prevail on him, for like all the Metis of Manitoba Riel regarded Alexandre Tache as the warmest friend of his race among the whites.

The Archbishop informed the two Ministers decisively that he would not help them, because he had already been too often deceived by them in regard to

the amnesty.   He would agree to do what they asked
only on one condition—that they now definitely grant
the amnesty instead of putting him off with fine promises!

Sir John, with one eye on Ontario's outburst of
mingled loyalty and fanaticism—and with the other
on the coming elections, hesitated.   At last Tache
told him he would do nothing in the matter—*"until
Sir John had given him a written guarantee of what
he said."*

Was ever a more suggestive alternative presented
to that charming old sinner of diplomacy, who could
indicate a promise with one eye and wink it off with
the other? This was a wall Sir John could not get
around: and he did not want to leap over it. . . .
So he retired—somewhere out in to the gray corridors
or stately chambers of the Gothic building.

As he went, we can imagine him smiling. For,
however annoyed or nonplussed for the moment, he
admired this Tache as one great and generous man
can always appreciate the strength and ability of his
peer.

His colleague was left behind to make more promises and win over the ruffled ecclesiastic.   Langevin
consequently was magnificent in his assertions, cap-
ping them with the statement that if Sir John did
not take the steps promised that day toward securing
the amnesty he, Langevin, would "resign from the
Cabinet and take Quebec with him."

"I do not want your resignation: I want the amnesty!" was the Archbishop's only response. And the interview ended in an unsatisfactory manner.

The Archbishop and Father Lacombe now returned disheartened to St. Boniface, and the Macdonald Government went forward to its overthrow.

The new Government reluctantly inherited the white elephant of Riel's political aspirations. They also approached the Archbishop: he repeated his claims to an amnesty for the Metis agitators as promised him in 1870. They were not—for the same political reason as the Conservatives—prepared to grant this. Sir Aime Dorion now appealed to Father Lacombe. The latter, who was in Montreal at the time, declined to interfere. He wrote the political friend who approached him:

"I have been reflecting more and more upon what you said to me yesterday, on behalf of Mr. Dorion, asking me to intervene with Riel to secure his pledge not to present himself at the next general elections—because his doing so would do a great injury to the new government, making it lose twenty-five constituencies in Upper Canada; and that on the other hand his presenting himself as candidate and his re-election for the County of Provencher would compromise still further his cause and that of his compatriots.

"A stranger to all political revolutions and occupying myself only with my poor Indians of the Northwest I could scarcely anticipate that men would cast their eyes upon me for this mission. . . . I have concluded that the wisest part for me . . . would be to abstain from interfering in any way in these elections. . . .

"The affair would seem to me to be more easily arranged

by some one of yourselves with the member for Provencher,
and I could facilitate the interview if you desire it. In making this advance you have more chance of succeeding than
I, although I fear that Riel will only answer you as he did
me recently:

" 'What candidate is there in the entire Confederation who,
if elected by acclamation in his constituency would consent
to sacrifice himself to forward the interests of his colleagues?
And furthermore, there is no such candidate representing a
principle of nationality as I do.' . . ."

Riel had fled to Montreal from St. Boniface in
1873, when the warrant for his arrest was issued.
When Father Lacombe met him there in 1874 he was
in a state of mental derangement, due it was believed
to the continual fear of assassination and arrest prey-
ing on his mind since his first hurried exit from St.
Boniface in 1872. It fell to the lot of Father Lacombe as the Archbishop's representative in the east
to visit the unfortunate Metis occasionally at Longue
Pointe Asylum outside Montreal, where he was
finally kept under supervision.

From this house Father Lacombe transferred him
this year to an institution at Plattsburg, N. Y., where
he was kept under some restraint. His mind continued to be affected at intervals—always upon religious and political questions. One night in
particular he astounded the community by running
into the dining-room scantily clad and proclaiming
himself to be the Holy Ghost.

Notwithstanding his eagerness to go and civilise

the Blackfeet Father Lacombe permitted himself to become absorbed in work for Archbishop Tache. This prelate was then bending his energies to promoting colonization of the west, and Father Lacombe seemed the one man equipped to be his lieutenant. His knowledge of the west and persuasive personality both fitted him for his new duties.

On July 22, 1874, Father Lacombe returned from a colonization campaign to Winnipeg as parish-priest of St. Mary's in the growing frontier-town. This was to be his headquarters while he continued his work of colonization. A large log-building served as a church and residence for himself and curate, Father Baudin. The church situated on the second floor was only reached by an outside stairway.

The building had been erected for him, and for once Father Lacombe stepped into a mission-house which he did not have to construct or chink. This was an aid to bodily comforts; but in other ways the missionary did not enjoy his early ministry at Winnipeg. The people he met in his own parish or out of it seemed to him to be rarely as good or kind as his Christian Indians; while to sections of the population he found his priestly garb was offensive.

Of these he used to ask indignantly:

"Why shouldn't I wear my soutane if I want to? We have done much to civilize this country wearing these soutanes: they are the Oblates' uniforms as soldiers of Christ. The policemen, the trainmen and the Queen's soldiers wear their uniforms—and no one

objects.   Why shouldn't I wear mine without remark?"

More than once insulting, jeering remarks were
thrown slyly at him as he passed through the streets;
and usually then a very unpriestly desire came to
thrash the man or boy who flung the jeer at the crucifix or robe.   There never was anything of the turn-
the-other-cheek Christianity about Father Lacombe.

In the spring of 1875 he brought out a large number
of excellent settlers.   In 1876, in response to his
efforts in Quebec and Massachusetts fully 600
French-Canadians arrived in Manitoba.   New parishes were formed at numerous points on the prairies,
and Father Lacombe—rejoicing in the pleasure this
gave his invalid Archbishop—applied himself to colonization with zest, as though he really enjoyed it.
In reality he found it very ungrateful work.

In 1877, accompanied by Father Fillion and two
others, he continued his work.   This year 400 families
were settled in Manitoba.   On one trip west Father
Lacombe accompanied ten families from Lowell.
The weather was depressing, and the band of emi-
grants discouraged.   On their arrival he left them in
the immigrants' quarters promising to go with them
next day to select their farms.

The next day was radiantly fine. . . . "But
such mud! The oily mud of Winnipeg in the days
before there were pavements," Father Lacombe
shuddered to recall it.

The newcomers sat outside the Hall smoking dole-
fully. Inside the building their womenfolk were
complaining steadily. They clamoured to go home.

"How do things go this morning?" Father Lacombe
asked them.

"Oh, no better. It is a poor country you bring us
to. It is always raining—raining; and then mud!
Look at that mud! We will go back east."

The words and manner alike were impertinent;
and when they would not listen to his placating remarks all Father Lacombe's patience fled, and he
cried to them:

"Then go back, since you have not more sense than
to judge a country before you have looked into it.
If there is deep mud here it is only because the soil
is fat—the richest in America. But go back to your
Massachusetts if you want to, where the soil is all
pebbles, and work again in the factories!"

His outburst acted upon their flagging ambitions
like a cold douche. They decided to stay in Manitoba, and in a few years they had no reason to regret
their decision.

"This year of 1877," Father Lacombe notes in his
letters "was one of events on the Red River. . . ."
And not the least was the arrival of the first locomo-
tive-engine brought on a decorated barge down the
river by the steamer *Selkirk*. During the last four
miles of its journey the whistles of the *Selkirk* tooted
joyously: the bells of St. Boniface added their peals,

waking the echoes of vanished days along the historic river. And Winnipeg turned out *en masse* to welcome the harbinger of the new Era.

Apart from the ordinary round of his ministry and his eastern work this period of Father Lacombe's life was marked with the formation of several notable friendships. Friends have always been to his warm nature the jewels strung along the rosary of his years, and these of the seventies made no exception.

In St. Paul he met Jim Hill, then a man in the prime of life and already marked out as one of the coming men of the west. Two qualities drew Father Lacombe's regard to him—the excellence of the man in his domestic relations, and his commanding genius for business—coldly daring, keen and unfailingly accurate in his judgments.

One day driving down the winter trail to St. Paul Father Lacombe met Donald Smith. He also was in his prime, a man of greater abilities and more stupendous plans than the Red River yet realized. The priest, who had always a keen scent for the note of distinction in a man's character, soon felt himself drawn to a friendship for Smith which was to be permanent.

Mr. Smith was delicately thoughtful for the missionary during their long cold drive. As habitual he was strikingly pleasant in voice and manner: wherefore Father Lacombe adds:

"But ah, he was determined behind that pleasantness. For the Company he was the ideal man:

smooth but so firm!   He fulfilled always their motto
—'*Pro pelle cutem.*'   Also he was the most lucky man
I ever knew—and one of the most agreeable to ap-
proach."

Another interesting man of the early days of
Canadian rule in the west was Luxton, the brilliant
founder of the Manitoba *Free Press.*   His first meeting with Father Lacombe was made picturesque by
the circumstances and the strong individuality of the
two.

This is the story of their meeting, evoked by a
question concerning an old letter.

"When I was at St. Mary's of Winnipeg, you understand that was hard work for me, making the
foundation of a new parish with a melange of all kinds
of people—*Ontariens,* Metis, Scotch, Irish, French
and some Indians.

"Well, when I was there in Winnipeg a newspaper
was organized—what you call the *Free Press,* and
Luxton, that was the man at the head.   He did not
care much about us, you understand.   He did not
know anything of us priests nor our faith, and he was
prejudiced.   From many little things I see that.   So
I decide to go and talk with him.   .   .   ."

Father Lacombe's old eyes twinkled at the memory
of that interview and of Luxton's laughter at the
audacious Blackrobe.

Like everyone else to whom this naïve, warm-
hearted priest cared to show his real self the keen-
witted newspaperman was captivated with his amusing

jumble of fun and diplomatic wile. Luxton eventually came to regard Father Lacombe and his entertaining friendship as one of the mental oases of his new life! The regard was mutual.

"I admired that man," Father Lacombe recalls; "he was so honest and sincere and upright."

Later on Luxton felt it in his conscience to attack the Canadian Pacific for what he believed to be monopolistic methods; likewise he defended the Catholics' claims to maintain their own schools upon their own taxes, if they so desired. Both courses were unpopular with the powers and the first ruined him. So when Luxton's uncompromising independence and sincerity had brought him to hard days, and when many former friends had deserted him it was to Father Lacombe he came one day; and that warm heart, touched to the quick, saw him over the darkest days until new hope came. . . .

Here is the letter that had lain forgotten while Father Lacombe talked—one written years after Luxton left Winnipeg.

"St. Paul, Minn., Sept. 23, '99.

"*Rev. Father Lacombe, Edmonton, N. W. T.*

"My Rev. and dear Father: I have seen in the Winnipeg papers that just about now the fifty-year jubilee of your entering upon your holy work is being celebrated. Though I am not sure that it is not somewhat of an impertinence on the part of one who is not of the same fold to do so—I cannot forbear tendering my congratulations on the occasion. Your humanising work—not to mention the strictly Christian part—has been such that it cannot fail to command the admiration of all good men who know anything of what it has been.

"My dear and venerable Father, permit me to assure you of my most fervent hope, that you may yet be spared many more years of valuable life to be more or less an active participant in good work, and to enjoy seeing the fruits before you are called hence to whatever reward is in store for the most holy of men—for that I know is yours.

"Respectfully and affectionately,

"Yours truly,

"W. F. Luxton."

The restraint over the warmth of this letter tells its own story of Luxton's attitude toward priests, before he came to know this one. When he wrote the letter he was manager of a paper in St. Paul; since then he has passed away, while his octogenarian friend remains.

During Father Lacombe's incumbency of St. Mary's Church a young Metis named Angus Morrison was committed to gaol on a charge of murder.

As chaplain of the Penitentiary Father Lacombe one day met his half-breed there—all half-breeds were *his,* it will be noted. Angus was a good-looking youth of twenty who always protested his innocence of murdering a Scotch settler for robbery. Many believed him innocent, and general sympathy was felt for him.

During his imprisonment Father Lacombe was his spiritual adviser. When he was finally sentenced to be hanged Father Lacombe circulated a petition praying the authorities to commute the sentence. Eventually an imposing list of names went down to Ottawa, but it was decided that the sentence should be carried out.

To Father Lacombe's distress, when he conveyed this news to the prisoner, the lad fainted. Again when Angus took leave of his widowed mother the scene was so pitiful that Father Lacombe felt he had known nothing of human grief before.

This is his story of Angus in part:

"Hah! I prepared him then to be strong and courageous, but I told the Bishop I would not consent to go to the hanging. . . . Ah, I could not do that. I made a plan—in a Metis parish nearby they had wanted me for many weeks to preach a retreat. This was my chance. . . . 'Now,' I said to the Bishop, 'I am going.'

" 'But that will take you away some days,' he said: 'You forget your Angus.'

"I beg him then to let me go away: some stronger priest would go with Angus.

" 'No,' the Bishop insist with me, 'you prepared him; he loves you now like a father. If you go away he will be discouraged. This is *your* work for him. . . . It is your *duty* as a priest.'

"Then I go home and say to myself: 'No, I cannot; it will kill me.' . . . Some days I was thinking that, but at last one day at Mass I feel to myself I can go now, since it is my duty. . . . But again when I think of it—it was like killing myself. Always I felt that on my mind.

"That night before the execution I stayed all night in his cell with Angus. He was a frightened lad, my Angus—very nervous and affectionate. I told the gaoler he must not put the irons on that night: I would be responsible. He did as I said.

"After we said the prayers Angus slept all night, but I could not close my eyes. I just watch that poor lad and pray for him. . . . At four o'clock I roused him.

"When he wake to that day and know it—he cried; my poor Angus! And I let him cry well at first. Then I help him dress. Outside in the hall before his cell I offered the Sacrifice of the Mass, and gave him communion. . . . He would not take any breakfast.

"That was a fine day—cold but fine, and the scaffold was built outside the window on the second story. When we came to that window I felt I was going to faint myself, because going through the corridor I saw the hangman coming all in black.

"Outside, it seemed all the people of Winnipeg were there: that was one of the first hangings in the town.

"I was afraid for Angus, and I say:

" 'My boy, show yourself a brave man to those white peoples—'

"They told the prisoner to speak, but he could not. I spoke for him, just to say that Angus was dying all right with his God, and he asked pardon from any one he had ever hurt.

"Now—ah, God came upon me, and my weakness changed. No more nervous—I was all master of myself! . . .

"Over us there was a big black flag, and down below I knew there was a coffin . . . and across the river the bells of St. Boniface were tolling.

"It was nine o'clock—the hour.

"Angus knelt, and I pronounced over him a last absolution. . . . Ah-h! . . ."

The old priest's head fell forward in silence, and as I waited I heard echoes of Eternity. . . .

"The body of my Angus was brought to St. Boniface that day—and the Bishop Tache made one of his finest sermons over that poor boy. That text he took from the *Dies Irae;* you know that grand sentiment in it.[1] . . . *'Tantus labor non sit cassus?'*—'Shall such love meet no return?'

[1] The reference here is to one verse of the *Dies Irae,* the superb requiem hymn of the Catholic Church composed many centuries ago. Its rhythm has the swing of a tolling bell; chanted, it is one of the most affecting and beautiful things in the world of music. The verse from which the text was taken is in full:—

> Quarens me sedisti lassus,
> Redemisti crucem passus:
> Tantus labor non sit cassus?

> Seeking me Thou sat'st forlorn,
> Saved me on the tree of scorn:
> Shall such love meet no return?

III

EVEN in the pampered ways of civilization Father
Lacombe lost none of the vitality which had so distinguished him on the plains. One day in the
spring the small riverboat *Swallow,* on which he was
returning from Selkirk mission, suddenly careened
off Point Douglas in a bitter wind and snowstorm.
All hastened to the small boats. Father Lacombe
missed his footing and fell into the river.

As he was about to sink a second time a man
caught him by the hair and pulled him into the boat.
Numbed and icy after a long walk on reaching land
he found shelter in a Metis cottage, while a messenger went to St. Boniface for the Archbishop's carriage.

"I went to bed about five o'clock that day maybe;
next day I rise about seven, all right. That was
nothing—a dip in the river!"

But while Father Lacombe was spending himself
in moulding into shape the elements of his town-par-
ish and in colonisation work—events were moving
marvellously on the plains among his own people.

The Government of Ottawa, recognizing that a
new period of western development was at hand,
mobilized and despatched to the Northwest—in
1874—a semi-military force of Mounted Police.

The intention was to pave the way for new forms of government, meanwhile suppressing cattle-stealing and the illicit sale of liquor on the Montana border.

Having profited by the lesson of the Red River agitation the Government also sent commissioners into the country to deal with the Indian tribes before the change came about. By these treaties the Indians agreed to live within fixed limits of territory called reserves, and in lieu of certain annual payments and rations they yielded all claim to the wide hunting-grounds of their fathers.

It was at Treaty No. 6, near Fort Pitt, that Father Lacombe's Cree friends made their surrender. Sweet-Grass was still Head-Chief, and that day he spoke worthily for his people, urging them to come peacefully into treaty-relations and learn to farm like white men. The Treaty stipulated not only money payments but the provision of schools on reserves and practical instruction in farming.

In 1877 Governor Laird brought the Blackfeet into treaty. Father Lacombe was invited by the Federal Government to be present as counsellor and friend of these Indians, in the same capacity Bishop Grandin had attended the Cree treaty-ceremonies. He left Ottawa in August intending to travel by St. Paul and Fort Benton to Macleod, the new Police post in the Blackfoot country.

Unfortunately he fell ill at St. Paul and after a severe sickness of weeks was obliged to return to St. Boniface. The treaty-commissioner meanwhile secured as his substitute his former assistant, Father Scollen.

The preliminaries of the Indian problem being disposed of and the Indians established on their reserves the Government was reprehensibly slow in carrying out its whole programme. They were to teach the elders to farm and the children to read: they lagged in doing both.

The buffalo, steadily decreasing in numbers for some years, suddenly disappeared.

Nothing could have more effectively broken the links of the Past for the Indian. The buffalo had been their living manna. Emerging each spring from the earth, as they once believed, the Indians looked on the buffalo as a manifestation of the Great Spirit's care for his people.

With the coming of the whites this was gone!

They did not stop to reason why; or to what extent their reckless slaughter was accountable. They preferred to blame the extermination of the buffalo upon the Sioux and American trader with his repeating-rifles.

It was in the winter of 1878–1879 the Indians' best friend disappeared entirely, and the Hunger-Moon of the Blackfeet did not last for twenty-eight days that year, but for months.

The Crees, more fortunate in their northern hunting-grounds, had resource in other game and in goods exchanged for furs at the Company's posts. But the Blackfeet did not live in a fur-country. As in John

Rowand's day the buffalo had been their all.   They were now in a most desperate plight.

Twenty years before Father Lacombe had begun to Christianize the Blackfeet, and it was ten years since he had planned to give himself entirely to civilising them.   In all this time he had lost none of his original interest in these Indians, and it was with poignant grief that he heard of their present condition through letters from Father Scollen.

He had known them in their pride—kings of the open plain in their barbaric power—brave and proud, honourable and hospitable; dwellers in frail skin-lodges yet Lords of all the outdoor world.   Now he heard of them as miserable dependents upon the charity of the Mounted Police and the missionaries.   Owing to the difficulties of transportation supplies could not be brought in readily.   Moreover in spite of the best efforts of those in the country it was difficult to bring Ottawa to understand the acute distress that prevailed.

Father Scollen in his voluminous letters related that the Indians were devouring their dogs and had even eaten the carcasses of poisoned wolves and soup made of old buffalo bones gathered on the prairies. A few of the aged died of starvation and he had seen men leaving their lodges because they could not provide food for children wailing with hunger.

They had begged all they could from the few whites in the settlements.   Now he feared they would be driven to steal the range-cattle.

In a letter by the same writer forwarded to Ottawa by Major Irvine, N. W. M. P., the harrowing condition of the Indians is strongly set forth. He demands farming implements and seed for the Piegans, as promised at their Treaty two years earlier. He concludes with the hope that if not palatable his letter may at least be useful—"for I can assure you I have written it with all frankness." Which statement no one who has read the letter will doubt!

Jean L'Heureux, an interesting character who had applied, but was rejected by Father Lacombe, as a catechist at Lac Ste. Anne in the fifties, wrote an appeal from the camp of Chief Natous. He implored the Princess Louise at Ottawa, as the daughter of the Great Mother, to take pity on the starving women and children.

Bishop Grandin in one letter to Father Lacombe —to whom he is always prompted to turn when in distress—sums up the tale of misery among the northern tribes:

"   .   .   .   To-day again we have learned very sad news of these poor inhabitants of the plains. The Metis would have been able to keep off starvation with the provisions they laid by last autumn, but the starving Crees threw themselves on their mercy. The latter were reduced to eating their dogs and horses: dying with hunger, to eat the carcasses of poisoned wolves and dogs.   .   .   .

"   .   .   .   At St. Albert, too, we have had reason to feel want to some degree. A band of Assinaboines passed a part of the winter camped around us. Their hunt had not been successful and we did what we could to give them aid. Without the Company, without our missions and others, many would have died of hunger. . . . Our dear Father Leduc, who hoped he had provisions ahead for two years, fears we will be short of food before the spring is over."

There could not have been more painful news for Father Lacombe than this, repeated in letter after letter from his confreres. It was the more distressing that he had no means with which to send relief; and he could almost reproach himself that he was living in some degree of comfort while they suffered.

Acting on the information contained in his letters he demanded from Ottawa that they hasten relief to the west. In the case of human suffering his temperament never would brook the delays of red tape.

As a consequence of the many representations from the northwest relief was hurried to the Indians in the spring of 1879.

On June 2 Father Lacombe sailed for Europe. He had been delegated to represent Archbishop Tache at the General Chapter of their Order assembling in France. Visiting Rome, he presented the Pope with a copy of his Cree-French dictionary.

The happiness he experienced in meeting for the first time the Commander-in-Chief of their scattered missionary forces reveals itself joyously in letters to the Archbishop. The latter affectionately assures him that he is glad his own illness has given this opportunity to his friend.

The glories of Rome's art and architecture found
a more appreciative spectator in him than the splendours he looked on during his first visit to Europe.
He confesses he is again *civilisé*.

But one day in a Roman crowd he finds that a
purse with one hundred and thirty francs has been
abstracted from the wide pocket of his soutane, and
he satirically notes that he is not in the west—where
men are not sufficiently civilised to steal!

Still another day the Saskatchewan is vividly recalled to him: up on the great cupola of St. Peter's,
enjoying a superb view of the city built on the Seven
Hills, he meets two priests from Louisiana and from
them hears of Father Frain.   This was the delicate
young ecclesiastic whom twenty years before he
brought on a dog-sleigh to Fort Edmonton to con-
sult Dr. Hector.

Now the same Père Frain is somewhat of a per-
sonage in his southern home—

"*Monsignor* Frain!"—the old Indian missionary
notes expressively in his diary.   His friends are all
becoming Bishops or Monsignori; he remains only the
old Father Lacombe.   But what of that, since he is
also to his Indians *Arsous-kitsi-rarpi*—the Man-of-
the-Good-Heart?

In Paris on his return he again visits the old publishing-house of Letaille and arranges for the publication of a new illustrated catechism for the Crees.
It is a fine edition, of which Father Lestanc receiving

a first copy in his remote mission exclaims—"Truly you are of the Age of Progress!"

Father Lacombe, while in Montreal on his return early in 1880, arranged a loan of $20,000 for the College being built by the Archbishop of St. Boniface. In the same year constructon began upon a stone church for his parish of St. Mary's and upon a girls' academy adequate for the needs of the growing popultion.

From these facts it is obvious that Winnipeg was rapidly growing too commonplace and civilized for Father Lacombe to be quite happy in it. Writing to a friend on January 8th, he says:

"Here, my dear Father, I continue to do penance by remaining in the midst of modern civilization. More than ever I long for the Indian missions. . . ."

But even as the monotony of his parish-work troubled his peace of mind a new field was opening for him.

Destiny was afoot on the plains, knocking at the great gates of the west. The steel head of the new trans-continental was pushing its way out to the prairies, bringing in its wake all the seeds of development the west was to know in the next two decades.

Fully one-third of the workingmen engaged on the construction-work were recruited from the Manitoba settlements of French-Canadians. There were other Catholics among the workmen and staff, and the Archbishop occasionally sent a priest out to visit them.　This man had reported the navvies in a sad condition through the bad influence of whiskey-peddlers, "bad-men" and other demoralizing agencies that follow close upon railway construction.

At the request of several of the contractors the Archbishop arranged they should have a permanent chaplain.　His judgment promptly selected Father Lacombe as the one man for the service.　A man who had always made his way with the plains-nomads was not likely to be discouraged or repelled by the unlovely conditions of railway-camps.

On November 2, 1880, with Sir Charles Tupper as a fellow-traveller, Father Lacombe went out from Winnipeg to his new mission.　He travelled by wagon-road and construction-train to Rat Portage—then the terminus of the road.　Here, cordially welcomed by the contractors, he established himself in an unfinished building, with an old box-car for a temporary chapel.

His first impression of navvies pertained to the extent of their blasphemy—vile utterances thrown about as lightly as a man calls for pick or axe.　To him, at once reverent and aggressive, this was a tocsin.　His rebukes and appeals were as impassioned as their utterances were hardened and criminal.　He made indeed of his own faith and love and reverence whips to drive the fear of the Lord into their neglected souls.

It was after one such castigation that he made this entry in his diary:

"It seems to me what I have said is of a nature to bring reflection to these terrible blasphemers, who have a vile language all their own—with a dictionary and grammar which belongs to no one but themselves. This habit of theirs—is diabolical!"

He had entered upon a wandering pastorate in which he would find the moral condition of the whites inferior to that of the pagan Crees. In later years, with the memory of this period softened by Time, he was unwilling to say that these construction-gangs were exceedingly disorderly. He would recall little of them except their unvarying kindness and respect for himself. But a truer picture of conditions is had from his diary, which is made up of brief, vigorous notes.

He actually found the camps reeking with blasphemy; hideous on occasions with the drinking of smuggled liquor and with immorality. This was true, although accidents were numerous, and the reckless navvies going out could never tell who would next be brought in dying.

IV

FATHER LACOMBE could not remain indifferent in the face of such disorder. He promptly threw himself into the fight; his strong heart with its powers of sympathy and scorn; his faith and authority—against the dare-devil lusts of the navvies. He fought with such good effect that in time most of the contractors, and the President of the Canadian Pacific, personally expressed their appreciation of his remarkable services.

But the contest was not waged with a light heart. . . . *"Que c'est triste de voir l'etat des choses ici!"* he concludes one pathetic entry in his diary.

A fortnight after his arrival a big dance was given in the village—"a disorderly and scandalous ball," he terms it. Through the greater part of the night he lay awake compelled to listen to the shouts and ribaldry of drunken men and women.

He finally went himself to the house where these dances were given each week, and where all the week moral disorder prevailed. He implored the woman who owned the establishment to change her life—to cease her work of debasing men through liquor and vice, fattening her purse upon their degradation.

Woman can fall so low that this harridan answered the earnest priest with insults and jeers. He turned from the door in disgust and heartbreak—for the first time in his missionary career thoroughly baffled.

The powers of evil impressed him as overwhelming. Father Lacombe could now understand why the contractors had so urged the Archbishop to send them a priest to clean up the Augean stables of vice in which their men wallowed.

The sense of near-Despair that possessed him after this first conflict with the navvies' evil-genius endured for a time. But other days were coming in which the Vampire of the frontier was to see her grip on men's souls somewhat weaken as the indefatigable little missionary drew them to himself, and whipped their rude souls into a fresh realization of life as Life.

Father Lacombe had recourse to prayer. "My God, have pity on this little village where so many crimes are committed every day!" was the entry he made one night in his diary after the day's work was done. Again some days later he recorded:

"I am convinced more and more that the sins committed in this little corner of the world are enormous. Since I cannot stop all the evil, at least I have the power to pray for these sinners and arrest the divine anger."

This statement was made in no arrogance of soul, but in the absolute belief that God would not refuse a prayer for grace.

From camp to camp he went blessing, rebuking, exhorting, cajoling. Gradually his first shock at

conditions modified, as he saw more clearly into the
hearts of the men who toiled in this

> " Land of the wilful Gospel,
>   Thou worst and thou best;
> Tall Adam of lands, new-made
>   Of the dust of the West."

The Archbishop had appointed him a chaplain: his
own good nature made him a Bureau of accommoda-
tion: as his slim diary gives evidence. It is dotted
with commissions entrusted by the labourers—all
duly crossed out in token of fulfilment.

One wants a dictionary; another a prayer-book;
others send subscriptions to newspapers. One
Hudon wants the Father to look up a house in Winnipeg for his family; another, Berube, asks him to
deposit $250 in the bank. Amounts from $40 to
$100 are sent by Father Lacombe home to the fam-
ilies in Manitoba and Quebec. And all these commissions were scrupulously fulfilled.

> "Received from ... . of .... in Quebec, $...., to
> deposit in the Bank of ... ."

so the entries frequently run.   Or again—

> "A.... .... sends $.... to his father, ..., of
> St. ——, in the diocese of ....; write to his mother."

Another entry marks his promise to look into the
cabane of John Ward left untenanted at Whitefish,
and to report conditions to the said John. Still fur-

ther memoranda remind him to procure entertaining reading-matter for such a camp and medicines for such another. Nothing is too small to note or do, if it contributes to the welfare of *his men*—his big heart having speedily adopted them as his own.

He brought their letters in to them when possible, and carried their answers away to post. He read and wrote for those who could do neither—and in this way frequently obtained a strong hold over the younger men inclined to yield to the worst influences of life.

Once after reading a letter for a lad from his sweetheart, the young man dictated a pleasant response not without such vows of constancy and affection as the heart of the maiden in Quebec was doubtless hungering to receive. This done, Father Lacombe cast a knowing eye on the young man and informed him that he was now going to add a few facts about the lad's real life.

He only agreed to the young fellow's prayer to refrain—on condition that his gay young compatriot make it possible for him to send a good report next time. The bargain was made and the lad lived up to it.

"More than once," said Father Lacombe years later with a tender smile for the garçons and their perplexities. "I would say to those garçons—'If your conduct here is not that of good Christians, you will see. I will write and tell *Her*. . . . And then it's all finish with you!'

"Ha-a-ah! how they beg me not to do that—what fine promise they make always if I do not! I was teasing them, of course, but they do not know that for sure. They did not know how much I mean. So they try to be better—and that was all what I want!"

The routine of his ministry was similar in each camp. At dusk when the men came in from work to the lights and rude cheer of the log eating-house they would find this sturdy little man in the black cassock waiting for them. He was welcomed and treated reverently by all the men. To the French-Canadians his coming was that of a beloved and benevolent relative.

A hearty supper soon disappeared before the attack of the men upon the rough fare in tin bowls and plates on rough-board tables. Then over their pipes as they lounged against their bunks there was the blessed interchange of news and comment which makes the visit of an outsider to a woodland camp memorable.

After the pipe those who would attend the evening-service remained in the cook-house, while hymns were sung and Father Lacombe in his picturesque manner talked to them in both languages. Then confessions were heard—a blanket across a corner forming a confessional-screen—and it was rarely before midnight that the tired missionary could roll himself up in his blanket and find rest in one of the bunks.

Before the foreman's stentorian reveille had tortured the ears of the slumbering navvies the priest was afoot again preparing an improvised altar for the divine Sacrifice, and at five the men trooped in clumsily but devoutly to the service and communion. By seven the Mass was over, the men had breakfasted and were ready for duty.

As they swung off to their work Father Lacombe was wont to stand in the doorway and bid God-speed to these companies of Labour's world-army, as they moved off into the morning mists.

Sometimes the railway-chaplain travelled between camps in a hand-car, a chilly means of transport in winter. On February 10, 1881, he went on such a trip, and his note-book tells its own story:

"11—Sick; like pleurisy. I am paid for undertaking this trip."

"12—I continue to suffer."

The three following days are summed up in the entry—"I suffer all day."

"16—My God, I offer you my sufferings."

He is roused from thought of self, however, on the following day by a horrible accident in which three men were killed and four injured by an explosion. He went out to these at night as soon as the word came.

That year his Lenten visits to the railway-camps covered all the territory between Port Arthur and Winnipeg. In May he began the erection of a church at Rat Portage. Then he travelled hundreds of miles by canoe with an Indian guide visiting the Indian camps in the back-country.

This summer—1881—the Marquis of Lorne was welcomed to the Portage with all the pomp the woodland depot could muster.

The Governor-General, travelling by canoe from Thunder Bay, was met down stream by a flotilla of Saulteau canoes which as they advanced moved in and out in a bewildering series of manœuvres. Swaying to the paddles the canoemen sang the old melodies of the *voyageur* days.

The maze of canoes steadily approached the envoy of the Great White Mother: in the van rode Father Lacombe glad to participate again in an Indian ceremonial.

From the prow of his canoe fluttered a Red Cross flag—the banner he had waved in triumph to the Sarcee camp when he restored the captive Marguerite; the Red Cross he had held up as a sign of truce to the warring Crees on the morning of the memorable battle.

Here where Progress was taking its first sinuous hold upon the land of the vanished *voyageurs*—remote from his beloved plains and painted nomads— the Red Cross had reappeared. It dipped in salute to His Excellency, who stopped to talk a while with the bronzed eagle-eyed missionary in the shabby black cassock. He was unaware that he held converse with one whose name would yet fill a larger place than his own in Canadian history,

Throughout the summer the entries in Father Lacombe's diary indicate the steady routine of his trying ministry. One sentence—"I want to rest"—
occasionally interjected tells a story of days too weari-
some to note their events. One day in November he
confides one cause of his weariness to the intimate
little note-book:

"My God, send me back again to my old Indian missions.
I am longing for that."

But his day of deliverance is still remote. The
Archbishop can not release him.

At Christmas he celebrated Midnight Mass in an
abandoned sleep-house. The trader lent him cotton
for decorations, and the navvies built a roof of ever-
greens over the altar to symbolize the Cradle of Bethlehem. Everyone within range of the lake lent
themselves to aid with the rare joy of Christmas-
tide.

They were a rough lot of men separated there
from all that they valued most on earth, but there
was a heart-drawing power in the ancient rites celebrated by this unique Blackrobe in his evergreen
temple in the woods.

When Father Lacombe went to Winnipeg in
March, 1882, he learned that at last he might return
to his Blackfeet.

For several months Bishop Grandin had been
urging this, for he still claimed Father Lacombe as
his Vicar-General and a missionary of his diocese.

The Archbishop reluctant to part with Father Lacombe wrote Bishop Grandin on September 12, 1881:

"This dear Father desires to go to you, among your savages. . . . If the state of his health had not prevented me I should have used him here with the Indians as you desire to use him. I have need as you have. . . .

"In fine, my responsibilities as a Bishop do not permit me to send away an individual who does so much good, and although the work done in your diocese rejoices my heart, you understand that it is not the fulfilment of my first duty as a pastor. This you will admit—but we have a Superior common to both of us: he alone has authority to do what you ask."

It was decided that Father Lacombe should return west, and the Archbishop applied to the Canadian Provincial for another missionary priest. His reply to the Provincial's letter is interesting:

"You say you have no one to send me at present; but after an ordination you may have perhaps a newly-ordained priest to give me to replace—*my premier counsellor, my adviser, my Vicar-General, a missionary who speaks four languages, one who has thirty years of experience!* Confess, *mon cher*, that this is not generous. . . . If I were sufficiently near you to embrace you *en pincette*, I assure you I would pinch you hard."

On April 24th Father Lacombe resigned his post as chaplain to the Canadian Pacific construction-camps. He acknowledges to his diary-confidant:

"If I have had many difficulties and sorrows here I have also had many consolations."

On the eve of his departure a fine team of horses and buckboard-wagon were driven out for his inspection. Before he could guess his good fortune the generous contractors presented him with these and a tent. Their thoughtfulness thus provided him with transportation and lodging on his long drive across the prairies.

On May 15, 1882, he left St. Boniface. He parted from his beloved Archbishop and confrères with regret, but lay down gladly the responsibilities of his post as Curé of St. Mary's. He felt he was turning his face away from the troublesome white newcomers, and that he should now go to his Blackfeet to make them ready for the coming of the palefaces.

V

On his return to the Indian field Father Lacombe saw a reprieve from uncongenial surroundings, such as he had surely merited after thirty years of devoted work. His buoyant nature lifted to the tune of expectation, and at fifty-six he felt himself entering on his work with the freshness of his first years in the west.

For eight days out from St. Boniface he travelled along the railway grade to Qu'Appelle mission. Here with the powers transferred by the invalid Archbishop he confirmed sixty children. His route now lay north across the prairies by Battleford, the seat of Government, and Fort Pitt.

He had believed himself returning to his beloved wilderness, but he regretfully noted that even here were evidences of the white man's invasion. Out of old Pile-o'-Bones in the Qu'Appelle valley the infant settlement of Regina was stirring to life, and along the grassy cart-trails he passed groups of newcomers, fleeing from the plagues of grasshoppers and early frosts of Manitoba's pioneer period.

As his buckboard rattled up the trail to the old headquarters of the Beaver District—the post where he had disembarked from York boats with Rowand in 1852—he blinked increduously at a new Edmonton. The Big House—Rowand's Folly—had been torn down, and a new residence built outside the palisades on the hillcrest.

Stockades, bastions and sentinel's gallery had all ingloriously given way to a low plank fence. Up on the hill log-shacks were set down in clearings. There was even the semblance of a village street at an elbow in the trail as it wound eastward up the valley from the Fort. It could boast a log schoolhouse and shops of free-traders.

A telegraph wire ran into the village bringing messages from the great Outside. More wonderful still to the man who had looked for the old wilderness— a tidy little printing-press was publishing weekly editions of a newspaper on sheets as large as notepaper!

At St. Albert he found another small village growing up in the vicinity of The Bridge. . . . Where was his wilderness gone?

He met his sister Christine here, for the first time since she had become the wife of Leon Harnois. The announcement of this marriage in 1875 had distressed Father Lacombe, as one of his confreres—a merry Breton fond of a joke—had written him then that Harnois was one of the most reckless of the frontier-traders and adventurers, as a maimed hand and seven bullets somewhere in his body testified.

Father Lacombe wrote Christine that if she contracted this marriage he would hold no further communication with her. . . . Mail moved slowly between the Red River and Edmonton House then: the letter reached Christine only after her marriage.

"And when it came," Leon Harnois told me thirty years later, "and Father Lestanc with his good heart said to us he would write Father Lacombe and tell him the truth, I only laughed and told him to say—'That is all right. We hold no further communication, if you wish. . . . I have your sister: that is all I want.'"

For Leon Harnois—adventurer, ex-trader and Indian fighter though he might be—was no desperado, but a debonair well-mannered young Frenchman of good principles, whose adventurous soul caused him to drift away from old Louisville years before.

He was a nephew of Papineau's friend, that Ludger Duvernay whose *Minerve* had sounded the tocsin of independence through the parishes of Quebec in 1837. And as one of the Harnois of Louisville he was not inclined to sue for favour, especially from one of such comparative insignificance as a brother-in-law. However Father Lacombe's hasty indignation had spent itself in the writing of the letter, and he was soon reconciled to the marriage.

In the straggling groups of Indians met at Fort Edmonton in 1882, Father Lacombe found traces of what he feared. The buffalo were gone. The Cree braves were no longer free or independent. They were officially restricted to reserves that were but patches on their old hunting-grounds.

Their old motives of race-pride were gone. Their

faces and forms had taken on a cast of subjection and servility. They were a dark fringe on the ranks of Humanity.

Father Lacombe could see the Indian of the morrow disregarded, uncared-for, unwelcome, thrust back further and further from his old territory. His heart brooded over it all, and he felt himself called to give the remainder of his life to their protection—as he had once given his years to their evangelization.

He continued his journey south. Marvellous! . . . If the new Edmonton had impressed him with the advent of a new regime, he was still more astounded by what he saw as his buckboard and bronchos carried him down the trail past the Red Deer River—through the borderland of the Cree and Blackfoot territories into the Bow River country.

It was little more than twenty years since he had first come here with Alexis to nurse the Blackfeet through the epidemic: then the Crees and traders had warned him not to go among the murderous Blackfeet. Even ten years ago he had traced his *Tableau Catechisme* on bark in the Blackfoot camp by the Bow and taught his childlike naked warrior friends from it.

Now there were white men's horses grazing on the rolling prairies and long bridle-trails led to the shacks of young English and Canadian ranchers. In the beautiful valley where the Bow and Elbow meet he looked down to the slim palisades of Fort Calgary.

Here too he met a single red-coated horseman.

The erstwhile missionary-Crusader who had ranged the plains armed only with his crucifix and Red Cross flag, could appreciate the grandeur of the figure of this solitary Rider of the Plains.

Two great agencies met there near Calgary—in the trim young horseman and the aging priest whose bronchos jogged as peacefully down the Trail as if they were the traditional fat ponies of the clergyman of civilized lands and their driver were as commonplace.

He drove in between the straggling shacks and tents already spreading across the prairie in anticipatory welcome of the approaching railway. Here in addition to the mission of his confrères were the white barracks of the Mounted Police and trading-posts of the Company and I. G. Baker. Numerous prospectors and fortune seekers had drifted in to make a new home: the village radiated bright prospects.

But there were sad associations about Calgary for the returned missionary . . . memories of his "*fameux* Alexis," who achieved the distinction of erecting the first building here. He left Edmonton in 1872, after Father Lacombe's departure for the east and built a house on the Elbow 25 miles from the junction of the Bow and Elbow.

Since he could not accompany the master he loved with such doglike fidelity he found some consolation in settling here among the Blackfeet. He was realizing as best he could the mission so long planned by Father Lacombe. His new home was at one of the shifting centres of population on the plains, a rendèzvous for the Bloods occasionally visited by American whiskey-traders.

The following year Alexis gave over his house to Fathers Scollen and Fourmond who came to establish a permanent mission for the southern tribes. In 1874 a larger house was built here and another at Fort Macleod, where the new soldier-police were established.

In 1875 Alexis, under the priests' direction built another house of logs at the junction of the Bow and Elbow, with a roof of spruce bark and door of buffalo hide. It was here the Mounted Police received hospitality on their first arrival in Calgary.

In the autumn a larger house was built by Alexis on the plateau across the river. That winter the buffalo roamed over the neighbouring plains in incalculable numbers. Whenever the cupboard looked lean Alexis strapped on his snowshoes, set off with sleigh and rifle—and came back with delicious fresh buffalo-meat.

But in the spring the longing for his old master grew too strong for him to rest contented there. He heard that Father Lacombe was in Winnipeg and would not return west. One day he told Father Doucet he must go and join him.

Instead, poor Alexis went wandering over the prairie from camp to camp. His mind, previously somewhat unbalanced, became unhinged in a form of religious mania with a belief in a divine mission for himself. He declined to live in the Palace at St. Albert. . . . At last word came one day to Father Lacombe in Winnipeg that his Alexis had been found dead on the trail near the far-away mission of Cold Lake.

Two years later with the disappearance of the buffalo, famine stalked over the plains: and in 1882 Father Lacombe found that while most friendly relations had been established between the priests and Indians there had been little progress made in evangelizing them. His brethren had scarcely acquired fluent command of Blackfoot before the wretched Indians were painfully absorbed in a prolonged search for food.

From Fort Macleod, where he was warmly welcomed by the Mounted Police officers he pushed on to the Blood Reserve. Here even the nonchalant Piegans and Bloods unbent to enthusiastic expressions of delight, when they learned that the Man-of-the-Good-Heart was going to give the rest of his days to them. His reception was like the return of some great medicine-man to his tribe.

Other Blackrobes might be their friends and they could respect and love them, but this fearless, high-spirited, tender old man was their own; and they loved him greatly. The Journal of Macleod mission, which record his re-entry to what was now the Territory of Alberta, note that it was easy to recog-

nize the ardours and enthusiasm of the former shep-
herd of the plains.   A ten-years' sojourn in another
milieu had not altered him.

The mission-house, fifteen feet square only, now
served as "a reception-hall for the Indians who
flocked from all quarters to see their former missionary and talk with him of the good old times.   The
air was continually saturated with tobacco-smoke,
and the calumet made the rounds continually."

Father Lacombe pitched his tent.   The resident
missionary slept on hay on the earthen floor inside
and cooked their meals in a clay fireplace.

At Fort Macleod, where he located the headquarters of the Mission, Father Lacombe found only a
bleak Police-post whose constabulary found their
spice in life lay in exciting chases of whiskey-smug-
glers and cattle-rustlers.

The old forts of the whiskey-traders at Whoop-
Up, Stand-Off, Slide-Out and Whiskey-Fort had
ceased their more flagrant operations in 1874, when
the Indians brought them word that red-coated
Britishers were riding over the prairies to chase them.
Yet some daring frontiersmen lingered to trade a
little bad whiskey for buffalo-robes while these lasted
—and later to satisfy the desire of the very thirsty
whites coming out to the plains.

The efforts of Father Lacombe and his fellow-
workers were at first directed mainly toward the protection of the Indians.   Whenever and however they
could they got whiskey to drink.   Even poverty did

not secure them against the firewater, which they
loved so fatally and which was rapidly completing
the downfall begun by their loss of independence.

There were always ways of obtaining liquor with
or without money for men and women. In fact, the
one great reproach repeatedly made by Chief Crowfoot against the whites was that liquor was continually used by them in the demoralization of the Indian woman.

Following speedily upon the arrival of Father Lacombe in 1882 a definite change came over the Blackfoot mission-field. The Indians seemed to enter upon
a new phase of existence in which they undoubtedly
owed much to the firm direction of their *Arsous-kitsi-
rarpi* and his lieutenant, Father Legal.

In the latter, a new recruit to the western field,
Father Lacombe found a personality as strong as his
own. This meeting with Father Legal indeed was
an event in his life as his meeting with Bishop Tache
thirty years before had been. It marked the beginning of a friendship that was to endure for his lifetime and in many ways contribute to his comfort in
his latter days.

The strong administrative powers of the young
Breton afforded the necessary complement to Father
Lacombe's unusual ability for planning new movements and securing the co-operation of everyone
needful. As a result each enterprise they undertook
was markedly successful.

The two spent the winter together in the little log-

house on the Blood Reserve. When they had dug
their potatoes in September they set about chinking
the house with mud and laying a floor in it. This
done they began work upon a Blackfoot dictionary,
employing William Munroe—*Piskan*—as interpreter.

In the afternoon Father Lacombe taught a class
of fifteen children and a group of adults each evening. The mornings were devoted to the dictionary,
which they completed before spring. During the winter they went to Macleod and there superintended the
construction of a small mission-house. Whilst there
the two priests occupied a log-house lent them by
Col. Macleod, but which they also had to chink with
moss and mud to keep out the elements.

The coal areas in the vicinity of the Belly River
were now about to be developed by an English company in which Sir Alexander Galt was interested.
The latter visited the west about this time, and as
the Journal of the Blood Mission notes, Sir Alexander agreed to saw for his friend Father Lacombe
10,000 feet of lumber from logs hauled to the Company's mill.

Father Lacombe could now enter upon a campaign
of construction. He began with a building at Blackfoot Crossing, but while here his summer plans were
broken into by a virulent epidemic of erysipelas among
the Blackfeet. He and his colleagues spent most of
the summer tending the sick Indians. His plans
had so far progressed by September, however, that

visiting his Bishop then he could declare himself well satisfied with the year's work.

He received about this time a letter from his mother which is the only one of hers remaining among his correspondence. The venerable woman was spending her last days in cheerful serenity, and although close on to eighty was still knitting socks for her son.

L'Assomption, Nov. 4.

"My very dear Albert: I received your pleasant letter on October 20th, and it was very welcome. You may imagine the great joy I felt in receiving it; for, *voila*, you are again back among your poor Indians. I am glad of this for your sake, because you have wished for so long to return to them.

"I often journey in spirit to your poor cabin; although age creeps on me I hope to see you once more: but if this may not occur here below—there Above I know that we shall meet again. . . .

" . . . Do not be afraid to let me know of your work and cares. I am glad to be able to share your sorrows with you as well as your pleasures. . . .

"I can no longer see at all with that eye, but I am hoping that the right one will remain to me, for I can see as clearly with it as with the two. I read, sew and knit as before—I should like to send you a little bundle of socks. . . ."

VI

THE three great civilising forces of Western Canada—the strongest factors in its development from
the days of Verandrye up to 1880—were the Hudson's Bay Company; the scores of French Oblates
who had devoted their lives to civilising the Indians,
and the Northwest Mounted Police.

They were men of heroic stripe, all three types of
trader, priest and constable: each deserving of the
Homeric epic that should some day enshrine their
deeds in a living monument.

With the first large wave of immigration the Company practically ceased to be a potent factor in
western life. But promptly on the eclipse of the
Big Company there emerged another power, which
was also to exert a notable influence in the consolida-
tion of the Dominion.

This was the Canadian Pacific Railway, which
separated the prairies forever from the hazy period of
travoix and canoes. Already the steel head of the
road was advancing on Calgary, justifying the faith
of the men who had built it.

The opulent latent spirit of the young Northwest
was like the legendary Princess sleeping: this road
the daring Prince that broke through every obstacle
of rock and chasm on the rugged North Shore—then

flung itself into the prairies lying in virgin enchantment. It wakened the Spirit of the land—and the
transformation that followed forms the first chapter
in the history of the New West.

To Father Lacombe's impressionable mind the
Canadian Pacific looming on the Calgary horizon
made an unforgettable picture. Years later he
lapsed into reminiscence in forceful French:

"Hah! I would look long in silence at that road
coming on—like a band of wild geese in the sky—
cutting its way through the prairies; opening up the
great country we thought would be ours for years.
Like a vision I could see it driving my poor Indians
before it, and spreading out behind it the farms, the
towns and cities you see to-day.

"No one who has not lived in the west since the
Old-Times can realize what is due to that road—that
C. P. R. It was Magic—like the mirage on the
prairies, changing the face of the whole country.

"We know of course it was not built without the
hope of some day bringing in much money to its
builders and directors—that is the way of mankind.
But I say to you of the men I met those first days of
the road—there was more than money-making in their
heads.

"There was courage; yes, and daring. . . .
Hah! that did make us all admire; and there was a
great faith and pride in this country. They believed
it held great possibilities, those men who fought so
hard to carry that plan through, and they had the

prescience that is the gift only of the great men of every age.

"Then the men who controlled it when it was built —the order, the discipline they demanded from their employes. . . . Smith, George Stephen, Van Horne and Angus, hah! . . .

"How we admired that man Van Horne! He was a Napoleon in the planning of his work, in his control of it and in the attachment of the men who worked for him. . . . 'Politeness is business,' that was his maxim. He gave that road from end to end of the continent one spirit—like the old Company used to have from London to Oregon."

Weathered frontiersmen grumbled that the railway would destroy all the freedom of the good old days: the red man looked on with awe and suspicion. One day Father Lacombe was called from Calgary to quiet the Blackfoot nation. These Indians were indignant that grading was being done upon their Reserve without their permission. They threatened they would not submit to this invasion of what little land remained to them.

Father Lacombe hurried there, and requested the railway-men to cease operations until he could settle with the Indians. With the confidence of ignorance they pooh-poohed his warning, and continued work.

Meanwhile Father Lacombe hastened to the chief's camp with 200 pounds of tea and as much of sugar, flour and tobacco. Through his friend Crowfoot he called a council of warriors. He first "opened his mouth" with the gifts; then urged them to permit the grading on their land. He promised them Governor Dewdney would come and arrange all with them.

The Head-Chief insisted his braves should heed the words of a friend who had never lied to them, and after many rumbling threats the council ended satisfactorily.

The construction-gangs proceeded peacefully with the grading, incredulous of any danger; unaware that but for Father Lacombe's intervention the construction of the first Canadian transcontinental would have been attended with deliberate bloodshed.

The Governor came to the reserve before long accompanied by Col. Macleod. They formally ceded to the Blackfeet another portion of land in compensation for what had been taken by the road.

.   .   .   .

Father Lacombe had returned west with the expectation of spending his days on the plains with the Indians. A year later he found himself pastor at Calgary labouring with whites as at St. Mary's in Winnipeg.

His disillusionment was complete when in August a newspaper was set up with western enterprise in a tent, and in the same month the first train reached Calgary. The arrival of this last was heralded by a telegram to Father Lacombe from George Stephen (later Lord Mountstephen) the president of the Canadian Pacific, saying:

"Come to lunch with me to-morrow in my car at Calgary."

Father Lacombe had known Mr. Stephen since 1881 and at Rat Portage once advised him to build the road through the Pine River Pass. He traced the route he recommended upon a map hanging in Stephen's car, but while the directors present conceded his advice was good other counsels prevailed.

Now in Calgary the president triumphantly reminded Father Lacombe of his prophecy that the Company could not find a favourable pass over the mountains at the Bow. He rejoiced, too, that while his own car was within sight of the Rockies construction-gangs were successfully pushing their way through the Kicking-Horse Pass.[1]

At the luncheon the busy Curé of St. Mary's found himself in a rare company: a *"pleiade d'hommes"* he calls them in appreciation of their individual brilliance. In this group of men who were binding Canada together with rails of steel were President Stephen, Donald Smith, William Van Horne, R. B. Angus and Count Hermann von Hohenlohe, after whose estates in Germany the nearby station of Gleichen had recently been named.

The repast was a pleasant one for many reasons. The directors were delighted with the progress made in construction. The missionary was charmed to enjoy again the company of men of such parts.

[1] This Pass received its name from an accident occurring there to Dr. Hector of Palliser's party, and who was Father Lacombe's guest at Ste. Anne in 1858.

This first train to Calgary marked an occasion, and was celebrated with toasts and merry speeches. The cream of the day came at last: Mr. Stephen resigned as president of the Canadian Pacific and upon motion of Mr. Angus Father Lacombe—whose services, as chaplain and again on the Blackfoot Reserve, were gratefully recalled—was then unanimously voted to fill the position. For one hour the picturesque missionary of the plains was by courtesy and vote of the executive the President of Canada's greatest corporation.

Father Lacombe has always rejoiced in a graceful *tour d'esprit.* He promptly accepted the honour and the President's chair—and once there he mischievously nominated Mr. Stephen to the rectorship of St. Mary's. The election was proceeded with amid laughter and applause, and the ex-President accepted his new dignity with a glance over the village and the simple speech:

"Poor souls of Calgary, I pity you!"

A pleasant echo of this luncheon-party is had in a photograph and note which Father Lacombe received soon after from Cardinal von Hohenlohe:

              "SCHILLINGFUERST, October 18, 1883.

"Very Reverend Father:

"My cousin Hermann tells me that you desire my photograph. I hasten to send it to you, recommending myself to your prayers.   I have the honour to be,

         "Your very devoted servant,

           "G. CARDINAL VON HOHENLOHE."

The luncheon that day in August was a cheery social affair, but the day did not pass without its serious
moments of discussion. In these was mention of a
plan to bring out other French settlers to the west.
The one primary need of these solitudes and of the
traversing railway was inhabitants. Mr. Stephen desired Father Lacombe's co-operation in the work.

The plan there agreed upon is outlined in a letter
written by Stephen from Montreal on January 25,
1884, to Father Lacombe at Ottawa:

"Now, as to my proposed French colony, I do not know
that it is necessary for me to say anything more than that I
will be ready to expend the sum of $500 on the homestead of
each of the 50 families it is proposed to settle, taking a lien
on the homestead for the repayment of the money at such
times and such interest. . . ."

as agreed upon. He suggested that houses be built
for the settlers after Father Lacombe had arranged
with the Interior Department for the reception of the
newcomers.

Here we have in 1884, between George Stephen
and Father Lacombe, the idea of the ready-made
farm which attained successful realization in the Bow
valley in 1909.

Several letters of this period from half-breeds indicate that one of Father Lacombe's new duties was
unofficial arbitrator in horse-thefts.

This crime was the chief plague of western life.
The Crees sent protests to Father Lacombe that his

people in the south were stealing their horses, and the Blackfeet went either to the Mounted Police or to their old missionary. In the supine days on which these Indian warriors had fallen a brave might no longer seek revenge on the war-path.

After a theft concerning which Father Lacombe made diligent enquiries through a trusty Metis he finally sent the man to the Crees of Red Deer Crossing. The Metis reported:

"They know nothing of the horses stolen from your people, the Blackfeet!"

In a second letter he assures the priest in his almost untranslatable patois that:

"Since the Spring the Crees here have stopped this business of horse-stealing that they used to carry on with the Blackfeet; but among themselves they continue to steal. There was one of them caught. They sent him to Winnipeg to prison for five years. The Government is very hard on business of that sort—it is reported at the Red Deer Crossing that twenty-five Piegans are in prison for stealing horses. . . ."

—indicating that the Police not only maintained the law, but spread a very wholesome fear of punishment through the Reserves.

On one occasion a Cree who lived north of the Red Deer lost his entire band of horses. He promptly had recourse to Father Lacombe, and the almost illegible scrawl written for him is very quaint.

"RED DEER CROSSING.

"*Rev. Père Lacombe:*

"I am very angry because some young Blackfoot men came to steal my horses when I was camped quietly here among my friends. They say, these men, that they came at night intending to steal back the horses lifted by the Crees from them at the Cypress Mountains. But they were lying for nothing, says Gabriel Leveille who came in yesterday from the Hunt; and he passed by the Cypress Mountains.

"You who are down at the Old Man's River, I pray you to take some trouble to find and return my horses to me."

All of these communications are significant of the new spirit abroad on the plains, where was now a definite form of government by the whites, with the details still sketchy.

At Calgary, where the town-site was still unsurveyed, men hurried to secure locations with an idea of making fortunes out of town-lots. The air was full of rumours about the location of the town; no one knew definitely, but each man squatted on the spot he considered likely to be chosen.

In the closing months of 1883 Father Lacombe and Father Doucet as priests in charge of the mission claimed not only squatter's rights for the mission-buildings, but as male citizens of the Dominion they felt themselves each entitled to a homestead. Father Lacombe accordingly selected two quarter-sections about the old and new missions on either bank of the river.

A few of the newcomers who were building where

they chose set up shacks upon his homestead, refusing to admit his right to hold it over them. Father Lacombe warned them to move off; they persisted.

"You priests, do you want all the country? I warn you, you can't have this bit," said one to him—with probably the idea that the priest's frock prevented him from locating a homestead as every other man on the ground hoped to do.

With resistance growing Father Lacombe felt he must secure his holding, and as the claim could not be registered outside of Ottawa he decided to go there. There was no time to wait for permission from his Superior—without which no Oblate or other community-member makes an important step. Father Lacombe, the advisor of Bishops for fifteen years, took on himself now the authority of a Superior and left for Ottawa.

VII

Sir David MacPherson was Minister of the Interior then. One morning as he sat in his office shut off from the commonplace world by noiseless baize doors and the imposing quiet of long Gothic corridors, a priest in a dusty black cassock was ushered in to him.

The priest's hat and stout umbrella were equally shabby, but the strong frame, the statuesque face and long straight silvering hair would have been remarkable anywhere.

The doughty Scotch-Canadian was impressed, and curious. The eagle eye and commanding profile of the visitor were at variance with his modest bearing and studiously respectful speech. But MacPherson understood when he heard his visitor's name. . . . Père Lacombe.

This then was Père Lacombe; the very name carried weight. MacPherson had not met him before, but the fame of the pioneer was already spread over the official world of Ottawa.

The plainsman laid his case before the Minister. It sounded reasonable: Sir David felt inclined to comply with his request. But the dignity of Governments must be upheld—delays and red-tape being the traditional safeguards. Father Lacombe was in-

formed that his request would receive most favourable consideration, and if he returned in a few days he
would receive definite confirmation of this.

That did not meet Father Lacombe's wishes at all.
Each day that passed meant more likelihood of newcomers building on his land, and the piling up of
abuse or inconvenience for poor timid Father Doucet
—"God's lamb."

His next statement, blandly made, took away Sir
David's breath.

"*Non, monsieur,* I cannot go until I receive that
settlement of our land.   I came hundreds of miles to
you just for this.   I will wait here with your permission.   .   .   .   I am used to camping on the prairie,
on the floor—anywhere.   .   .   .   I will just camp
here until I get my papers!"

He looked about him.   After the mud-chinked
shack at Macleod or the shedlike house in Calgary
this office was regal.   He seated himself with the air
of one who settles himself comfortably for a length
of time.   .   .   .

Sir David felt the force of a personality quite irresistible, and let the red-tape bandages of dignity
relax.   He immediately wrote out a guarantee of the
homestead locations on the sections indicated by
Father Lacombe.   The patents for the land were to
follow when the conditions were fulfilled.

The westerner in bowing himself out from the
courtly MacPherson was as shabby a figure as when
he came; but he carried himself like a chief return-

ing from a victory. . . . One wonders what ex-
ploits might have been his, cast in another mould of
the frontiersman—the adventurer instead of the
priest!

He hurried to telegraph his good news to Father
Doucet; then went to Montreal. Here he did a
quaint stroke of business: upon his own initiation he
had hundreds of statuettes of Archbishop Tache cast
from a mould by young Louis Herbert, and sold to
that statesman-prelate's numerous admirers. The
proceeds he turned over to the missions of his friend
at St. Boniface, who was greatly amused and touched
by this new enterprise of *"ni matchi Albert."*

Whilst in Montreal he issued a letter to the priests
of Quebec begging them for books from their library:

> "I will say from experience that one can endure well
> enough a poor dwelling, coarse food and coarser manners;
> but to have few or no books—you will agree with me that
> this is something to which a priest can resign himself with
> difficulty. You will say to me perhaps—'Why not buy
> some?' Ah, yes, *voila*, a just question. . . . But we
> have no means to buy them. That is why I take the liberty
> of knocking at your door."

Books literally streamed upon him, the Curés joyfully finding a place for their antiquated numbers,
and Father Lacombe returned happy. He wired
ahead for his brethren to meet him at Calgary to share
his good fortune, and Father Legal records in his
Mission Journals that their Superior returned—

"successful to his heart's content" in all his affairs—homesteads, schools and books.

The homesteads were divided into portions—for a future church, hospital, academy and cemetery; while the proceeds of town lots later sold from them furnished the diocese with money to erect buildings.

Calgary meanwhile was taking shape as a town with marvellous rapidity. Its population numbered five hundred, and new citizens arrived weekly. Men foregathered and elected a town Council, which promptly crossed swords with the railway company to which the little town owed its existence: there was no lack of spirit in the new frontier.

With the white population monthly taking a stronger hold upon the land the establishment of Indian Industrial Schools became the dominant idea of Father Lacombe.

Bishop Grandin had originated a campaign for schools in the mission he laid upon Father Lacombe in 1872. It appealed to him as the final phase of his own work for the west, and though enfeebled now he determined to carry it through at any cost to himself.

The bishop insisted that the few schools in existence should be developed and extended, teaching the Indian boy to till the soil and his sister to keep a house: in this way to reach the adult through the children. To do this schools must be conducted on a large scale. But how? For ten years he had exhausted every effort to secure money for this in Canada and France. He was still without means.

It was then that Father Lacombe, growing in
worldly wisdom and knowledge of public life, im-
parted to the bishop the idea of petitioning the Government for funds.   These might appropriately be
had from the Indian funds held in trust by the Government.

Father Lacombe, though corporally in Winnipeg
during the seventies had been much in spirit back on
the plains, and at every feasible opportunity was
helping Bishop Grandin to forward their school
project.   The plan was communicated to Archbishop
Tache and the latter met the bishop early in 1883 at
Ottawa to press the educational needs of the Indians
upon the Government.

That spring the ministers' offices and the corridors
of the Parliament Buildings were for some days
haunted by first one and then another of the western
prelates.   Representations were also made to the
Prime Minister by Father Lacombe and by Sir Alexander Galt at the request of his missionary friend.

The result of these combined efforts was that the
Government authorized the establishment of three Industrial Schools—at Dunbow, south of Calgary, at
Battleford and at Qu'Appelle.   The Government
agreed to erect the buildings, pay the principal a fair
salary and make a per capita grant toward the main-
tenance of the pupils.

Sir John Macdonald writing from Riviere du Loup
on August 1, 1883, to a friend of Father Lacombe—
who forwarded the letter to him—says:

". . . I am down here getting a little rest and fresh air, but amuse myself occasionally by looking over my correspondence in arrear. . . .

"With respect to the most important of these, the establishment of Industrial Schools among the Indians, I may say that all difficulties have been overcome and three Industrial Schools are to be established—one Protestant at Battleford where the government buildings will be available, and two Roman Catholic schools—one under the patronage of the Archbishop and the other of Bishop Grandin. The Order in Council has been passed. Mr. Dewdney has been instructed to take steps for their establishment and Sir Hector Langevin has called the attention of their Lordships to the importance of the Principals or Heads of the schools being good administrators. Learning and piety, however necessary, are not all-sufficient. Good business ability is, if possible, a greater requisite than either of the other two. . . ."

In 1884 Qu'Appelle and Dunbow schools were opened. Father Lacombe, although still supervising the southern mission-field, was given direct control of Dunbow school. He had already chosen the site and directed the construction of the building. On its completion he rode out among the Bloods and Piegans asking the parents to send their boys to the school. Father Legal and Jean L'Heureux did a like service at Blackfoot Crossing.

The Indians however absolutely refused to part with the younger boys for whom the schools were intended. Eventually after much persuasion the missionaries succeeded in assembling seventeen boys from 15 to 17 years old.

Father Lacombe received the boys at Dunbow. As a preliminary they were shown to a room containing washtubs. They were directed to bathe. Their long hair was combed by Father Lacombe and his assistant, for the parents had refused to have it cut. New clothes were supplied to each boy, and his own tattered garments rolled away in a bundle to be returned when he went home again.

About as much at home as wildcats in a beaver's well-ordered domicile the young Indians were given a supper which they appreciated more than the grooming. Then they were sent out to the prairie for a playhour. This was Bedlam.

The lid of a repression imposed by awe of their surroundings was thrown off, and in all his experience of Indian children Father says he never witnessed anything like this. The boys ran wild in a riot of horseplay. . . . But a bell rang; and at its unwonted sound the poor young mavericks of civilization were rounded up and sent to a dormitory to sleep.

Here were compensations for the broken playhour. . . . The stairway was a novelty, and the boys found rare amusement in running surreptitiously up and down the steps. In the dormitory they were invited to undress, and each put in possession of a little bed decently equipped with bedding. After the first shock of surprise there was another Carnival for the seventeen dusky human mavericks!

They laughed and sang, and with all the Indians'

power of ridicule made light of the odd furniture. They examined the beds, explored them above and below and punched their pillows. Some crawled under the beds and found there a new vantage-point from which to hurl missiles and ridicule at those who ventured to lie on the beds.

There was no sleep in the dormitory for hours. Father Lacombe, old now to the ways of Indians —sympathetic always to youth, merely controlled them from his own apartment without any effort to repress them. Through the night however he was awakened by a hilarious rout in the hall below the stairs, where some of the boys had elected to finish their frolic.

On the following day the teacher went about organizing a class. With the consuming curiosity of their race the boys were interested in its first session. They were then and always reverent and quiet at prayers—but when their first recess came there was pandemonium again, and reluctance to return to the class.

It was so during all the early weeks of the school.

"You could open the doors and look inside and see —*Hell* that first winter," said Father Lacombe twenty-five years later.

The main difficulty was that these boys were too old to be broken to school ways, but they were the only boys available. All winter they continued to be as wild as young elk. Sometimes they would turn

the playground into a battlefield; more often they
would slip way to a big hill a mile distant and play
there well away from the shadow of the school.

Occasionally the teacher on ringing the bell for his
charges would not find one in sight. In an instant,
so it seemed, they had hidden themselves about the
yard, ready to lope off to the prairie if the teacher
would not come out to round them up. During the
winter some of the boys ran home. When spring
came they all clamoured to be free.

Father Lacombe went north and obtained boys
from Cree reserves. By degrees the Blackfoot elders
acquired clearer ideas of boarding-schools. They allowed a few of the younger children to go with Father
Lacombe—some girls as well as boys; and the work
was considered established.

In this way the first Indian Industrial school of
Alberta took shape.

The Grey Nuns who had volunteered as teachers
quickly secured control of the younger pupils and
held their affections. Little by little a regular school
routine was formed, the children lending themselves
more readily to manual training than to books after
the first novelty wore off.

This was the beginning of a system that has since
spread throughout the west, an honest endeavour by
men with the best interests of the Indians at heart to
solve their problem. The schools were designed
to bridge for the Indian the Transition stage from
barbarism, so that at least the children's children of

the warriors of Natous and Sweet-Grass should be fit
to cope with the Caucasian civilization that threatened
to overwhelm their race.

In the autumn of 1884, after this Industrial school
was opened, Father Lacombe as Superior of the whole
southern district had the delight of welcoming Archbishop Tache to Calgary.

Aware of the Archbishop's invalid state and anticipating his anxiety to witness the marvellous development in the remoter west the president of the
Canadian Pacific had courteously placed a private
car at his disposal. On September 21st he arrived,
and found there to welcome him—Father Lacombe
and Father Remas, who had made a retreat with him
in the northern woods thirty years before; Fathers
Legal, Doucet, Claude and Foisy, with several lay-
brothers.

The venerable prelate heard the story of each. He
marvelled. He could scarcely credit that this organized district with new buildings at each mission-
point and prospectively valuable property in the town
was the same field to which Father Lacombe had returned two years earlier.

There had been then only two missionaries and two
log-huts, mud-chinked and floorless. To-day . . . !
The Archbishop looked about him, and recognized
the old powers and organizing genius of his friend—
"ni matchi Albert."

VIII

THE frontier town of Calgary was rapidly rising
from its first semblance of a tented village. Primitive restaurants, pool-rooms and shops lined the Main
Street with false fronts and aggressive signs behind
which the newcomers laid plans for future fortunes.

Meanwhile elsewhere on the plains, in the homes
of the Metis Old-Timers, there was much sullen discontent.

The insurrection of 1885 was impending.

It was no summer thunder-cloud coming out of
clear skies. Grievances had been rankling for at least
five years. Repeatedly in letters and interviews the
Saskatchewan Metis, and Bishop Grandin in their
name, had urged the Canadian Government to meet
their claims to land-scrip similar to that granted to
Manitoba Metis; likewise to initiate measures [1] for

[1] The formal list of claims of the Metis included:

(1) The division of the North-West Territories into Provinces;

(2) A grant to the Metis of Saskatchewan of the territorial privileges
conceded to the Metis of Manitoba;

(3) That persons already located be secured in title to their holdings;

(4) The sale of 500,000 acres of Government land, the proceeds of
which were to be devoted to the establishment of schools, hospitals
and other institutions for the Metis—together with a grant of seed and
agricultural implements to the poorer of their number;

(5) The reservation of 100 townships of land to be distributed in
time to the children of the Metis;

the improvement of the Indians' condition as well as their own.

Differences with minor officials of the government and instances of misunderstanding concerning their right to hold land on which they were located were causes of irritation among the Metis. A consciousness that they were retreating before the dominant newcomers had set the hidden fox of envy gnawing the vitals of a race still free and proud: the Federal Government neglected their communications. . . . Here was sufficient material to fire a Metis rising.

Manitoba Metis, who had sold their holdings to unscrupulous white men for trivial amounts, had emigrated in poverty to the Saskatchewan. They were now living examples of what their brethren might expect in the future. . . . The Saskatchewan Metis resolved to make a stand for themselves and their children.

Gabriel Dumont, a noted hunter and relative of Louis Riel, a recklessly brave, dashing and hospitable fellow, was now pushed to the leadership of the French-Metis; while James Isbister of the Scotch-Metis made common cause with him against the new Regime. The united halfbreeds held an assembly in May and there delegated Dumont, Isbister and others to go into Montana and bring Riel back to lead them.

Louis Riel was then employed peaceably earning a

(6) A grant of at least $1,000 for the establishment of an Academy at each settlement of Metis;

(7) The improvement of the conditions of the Indian nations.

livelihood for his family as a schoolmaster in the parish of St. Pierre. He did not leap with enthusiasm to the offer of leadership at first, but he finally made up his mind to accept. Honore Jaxon (Henry Jackson), the young Ontario aide of the Metis and graduate of Toronto University, joined Riel on his arrival in Canada and assisted him in framing what they termed a constitutional agitation.[1]

A number of white men were now interested in the movement, urging on the more ignorant Metis. Some of these were probably moved by envy of the newcomers' progress. It is still believed along the Saskatchewan that others interested themselves in promoting agitation in order that the country might be flooded with negotiable script. Out of this the Saskatchewan man of affairs might hope to make a fortune as easily as his prototype of the Red River had done.

When word came to Bishop Grandin that Riel was again in Canada, and greeted by the Metis as a Napoleon returning from Elba, the bishop hurried down to Prince Albert. For fifteen days he visited

[1] Jaxon stated to me in Edmonton in October, 1909, that Isbister and Dumont brought Riel letters from leading white men among the old-timers and business men of the Saskatchewan valley, urging him to come back to curb the ambitions of the newcomers and secure the rights of his own people.

These letters Jaxon saw burned at Prince Albert at the close of the Rebellion before he fled to the United States and freedom. A prominent statesman of Western Canada also informed me that he knew of those letters held by Jaxon and burned by a relative of the latter at Prince Albert in order that the writers might not be compromised should an investigation be held.

among the Metis, pointing out the dangers of a course that might lead to combat and the forfeiture of all rights instead of securing them.

Seriously alarmed by what he had seen and heard the bishop wrote a formidable warning to the Prime Minister:

"I have seen the principal Metis of the place, those whom we might call the ringleaders; and I am grieved to realise that they are not the most culpable. They are pushed forward and excited not only by the English half-breeds but by inhabitants of Prince Albert—persons of some prominence and opposed to the Government, who hope without doubt to profit by the regrettable steps of the Metis. These must certainly be strongly supported to act in this way without the knowledge of their priests, who have now been represented to them as sold to the Canadian Government.

"It will surely be easy for your government to suppress this sort of a revolt—which might later have painful consequences; because the Metis can do as they please with the Indians. . . .

"How many times have I not addressed myself in letters and conversation to Your Honour—without being able to obtain anything but fine words . . .! I have written at their dictation the complaints and demands of this discontented people; I send them to you again under cover with this.

"I blame the Metis and I have not spared them reproaches. But I will permit myself to say to Your Honour with all possible respect, that the Canadian Government is itself not free of blame; and if I had the same authority among its members that I have with the Metis I should tell them so—more respectfully doubtless, but with the same frankness. . . .

"I implore Your Honour not to be indifferent to this and to act so that this evil may be checked."

He gravely warned Sir Hector Langevin:

". . . Once pushed to the limit, neither pastor nor bishop can make them listen to reason, and they may proceed to acts of extreme violence. I beg you then to instantly employ all your influence to secure for them whatever is just in their demands."

The bishop's letters were written in September, 1884—in ample time for the Ottawa Government to have averted the Rebellion of 1885. Ottawa did not unbend. Why they did not—why they paid as little heed to this solemn warning as they did to Tache and MacTavish in 1869 has gone down into the grave with the men who were in authority then.

On March 18, Riel, whose weak brain was again unbalanced by excitement, called his followers to arms. He had already in his madness set himself up as a sort of Pontiff, had a new scheme of religion planned and proposed to reorganize the Catholic Church and reform Canadian Government in the west.

Swiftly following upon Dumont's encounter with Crozier at Duck Lake came news of Big Bear's depredations and the massacre at Frog Lake, where the Agent Quinn, Father Fafard and Father Marchand were murdered.

Canada was now awake to the urgency of the Metis question!

Father Lacombe hearing the news telegraphed into Calgary mourned again that he had not been left on the plains in 1872 to continue the work of Christianizing the Indians. Had he done so the missionaries would have had Big Bear and Poundmaker under their influence to a degree that even Dumont or Riel could not prevail against.

Chief Crowfoot he felt confident could be relied upon to help him keep the southern tribes at peace. He wired this assurance to Sir John Macdonald, who stated [1] in the Commons on March 26:

"I had a telegram from the Rev. Father Lacombe to-day, and he vouches for the loyalty of all the Blackfoot Indians at Carlton and the west."

The Prime Minister's idea of western locations seems to have been very inaccurate. The news he conveyed was received with applause however.

Father Lacombe's confidence in his Blackfeet was presently tried. On the evening of March 27th grave rumours spread through Calgary of fatalities near Prince Albert. Though remote from the disturbance, the townspeople grew afraid.

It was known that emissaries from the Saskatchewan Metis and Crees had been skulking in the camps of the Blackfeet for some time. It was realized too that if the Blackfeet and their allies, the best fighters on the plains and the least docile of all western Indians, should unite with Riel they could

[1] Debates, H. of C. (March 24), 1885, Vol. 2, p. 745.

temporarily destroy white settlement in the country. Calgary had reason to be cautious.

A Home Guard of 104 men was organized, and the leaders telegraphed Ottawa and Regina for arms. That evening the almost incredible news was flashed from Langdon station that the Blackfeet were about to attack Calgary. The Guard was sworn in for service; armed patrols were set to watch the town by night.

The routine of life was rudely broken; people gathered in groups on the street to discuss the shocking news. Timid hearts could see visions of the painted and feather-decked Blackfeet riding down on them. Excitement was intense in the little town.

In their extremity the people of Calgary turned that night to Father Lacombe. He agreed to go out to pacify the Indians, though protesting there was no truth in the rumour.

"That's only humbug!" he said. "Crowfoot would never let his braves attack Calgary."

Men shook their heads. Not all of Calgary shared his belief then in the Head-Chief.

The following morning at dawn Father Lacombe departed in an engine lent him by the Canadian Pacific. Arrived at the Crossing he sent for Crowfoot, who enquired in amaze the cause of a visit so early on Sunday morning.

"Oh, it is lonesome in Calgary without my Blackfeet. I want to visit you, and meet Father Doucet."

"He gave me the news of the camp," Father Lacombe recalls. "Then he asked if that news was as he heard—that the Crees and Metis of the Saskatchewan were killing all the whites. This is what the Cree runners from Poundmaker's camp had told him!

" 'A few have been killed,' I said, 'but this is a small fight that will soon pass.' "

Father Lacombe then had the camp assembled. He gave them news of the rebellion, telling them what fools the Crees were to fight the white people who had so many big guns and armies they could send into the country. For even if the Crees conquered now. . . .

"Those strong white people would come back like a great sea that could not be stopped and the Indian nations that killed their brethren would be swept off the earth."

Crowfoot was a man of reason. He exhorted his warriors, took counsel with them—and finally promised Father Lacombe that his Blackfeet would on no consideration take up arms in this rebellion.

"Then," says Father Lacombe, "I decided to send a telegram to Sir John saying the Blackfeet would be loyal to the last. . . . By-and-bye I heard from one of my friends at Ottawa that the telegram was brought to Sir John when they sat in Council. At once he read it to his colleagues, and they clapped their hands with pleasure. They had not much good news from the west in those days!"

"Soon after that a telegram came from Sir John telling me to do anything I liked concerning the Indians—to make them keep the peace: the Government would approve everything."

Sir John evidently had profited by a second bitter lesson. The "big chiefs of Ottawa" had at last glimpsed their own limitations as rulers of the people by the voice of the people. They could now appreciate both the danger of the western situation and the good intentions of the missionaries—as well as their influence over the Indians.

Father Lacombe's report on his return from the Crossing on Monday, March 30, was reassuring to Calgary; as noted in George Murdoch's terse diary—

"Lacombe came to-night from the Crossing and reported all well."

The same day Sir John Schultz, who had travelled a long way from the Red River physician of 1870, wrote him from Ottawa. The letter is significant of the attitude of Canadian public men toward Father Lacombe at this period. It likewise reflects the fatuous complacency of the government, which will not recognize the results of its own dilatoriness:

"The Senate, Ottawa, March 30, 1885.

"*Dear Father Lacombe:*

"Since I had the pleasure of hearing from you or writing to you, what sad events have occurred in the northwest; and though our information is very meagre as yet, I am afraid that a great mistake has been made in coming to armed collision with Riel's men before an effort could be made to obtain a peaceable solution of the difficulties.

"Of course we cannot judge very well at this distance, but that is my opinion; and I told one of the Government yesterday that had no collision occurred and had they tried to avail themselves of your services, so respected as you are by Indian, half-breed and white alike—you might have solved the difficulty with not unreasonable concessions on the part of the Government.

"At the last meeting of the House of Commons I was glad to see that Sir John quoted you as high authority for the hope and belief that the Indians would remain quiet. I took the liberty of recommending that your services should be, if possible, secured at once and if they are I feel very sure that my modest friend, Father Lacombe, will show himself of great service to the peace of our young Dominion. . . ."

Following upon his interview with Crowfoot both Father Lacombe and the Government thought it well there should be an impressive peace-contract made with the Blackfeet. Consequently about the middle of April Governor Dewdney came from Regina to Blackfoot Crossing, accompanied by Father Lacombe, his personal suite and Captain Denny acting for the Indian Department.

The good-will of the Indians was that day conveyed to the Canadian Government in a lengthy telegram inspired by Father Lacombe and signed by Crowfoot. The practical result of the day's ceremonies is had from an address [1] of Sir John Macdonald in the House of Commons:

[1] Debates, House of Commons, 1885, Vol. 2, p. 1038.

"I may as well now inform the House that there is no further news from the North-West that would interest the House except the fact that Mr. Dewdney, the Lieutenant-Governor, accompanied by the Rev. Father Lacombe, missionary to the Blackfeet, has held a meeting with the great band of the Blackfeet, headed by their Chief Crowfoot.

"Father Lacombe says they had a most enthusiastic reception, that the Indians pledged their loyalty to the utmost extent, and I have received a telegram signed by Crowfoot, which I will read. It is not in Blackfoot:

'FROM BLACKFOOT CROSSING, VIA GLEICHEN, N. W. T.

'11th April, 1885.

'On behalf of myself and people I wish to send through you to the Great Mother the words I have given to the Governor at a Council here, at which all my minor chiefs and young men were present. We are agreed and determined to remain loyal to the Queen. Our young men will go to work on the Reserves and will raise all the crops they can, and we hope the Government will help us to sell what we cannot use. . . .

'Should any Indians come to our Reserve and ask us to join them in war we will send them away. . . .

'The words I sent by Father Lacombe I again send: 'We will be loyal to the Queen whatever happens.' I have a copy of this, and when the trouble is over will have it with pride to show to the Queen's officers: and we leave our future in your hands. . . .

'CROWFOOT.'"

To this Sir John telegraphed the reply:

"The good words of Crowfoot are appreciated by the big
Chiefs at Ottawa. The loyalty of the Blackfeet will never be
forgotten. Crowfoot's words shall be sent to the Queen. All
Mr. Dewdney's promises shall be faithfully carried out."

From the time of Father Lacombe's hurried first
visit to the Crossing until the Rebellion ended he
spent his time mostly out on the plains seeking to
keep the Indians pacified.

A rumour came to him that Ermine-Skin's Indians
were rising in the north. It was even reported that
the Metis at St. Albert district were threatening—
but this Father Lacombe did not take seriously. He
knew too well Bishop Grandin's influence over them.

He departed for the north, when he had no longer
any fear for the south. He believed Crowfoot would
keep his pact of peace and, keeping it, would strongly
influence the allied tribes. Moreover Fathers Legal
and Doucet, as also Captain Denny the Indian
agent, were industriously at work on the reserves
keeping the tribes quiet.

This was absolutely necessary; as the records of the
Blood Reserve mission note:

"These Indians had a very efficient despatch service and
they were fully informed upon all that passed. They remained loyal and at peace, but it was easy to recognize signs
of uneasiness in them; and if the Metis and their savage allies
in the north had been able to maintain the campaign longer,
it is difficult to say what might have resulted."

A letter in April from Father Scollen at Bear Hill reserve greatly disturbed Father Lacombe. He related that a courier riding from Edmonton passed through the reserve at a steeple-chase rate, warning all the whites as he went. The half-dozen white people there fled to Edmonton. Father Scollen and his lay-brother remained alone with the Indians who were now hugely excited.

They believed that Riel was about to pass through the country with an army, sweeping all before him. The days of the whites were numbered, they said, and the buffalo would return. A band of painted warriors looted the store in the village. The older, staider men supported Father Scollen in his protest against any brave joining Riel, and with one of the chiefs he succeeded in breaking up a war-dance of the young men.

This letter caused Father Lacombe to realize afresh the imminent dangers and the slight weights on which everywhere the balance might turn. He at once departed for the north with an old Metis to pacify any restless Crees he could meet, and to visit the bishop.

He arrived at St. Albert at noon. The bishop was pacing slowly through the grounds before his log-palace lost in thought. . . . When his glance fell upon the unexpected visitor the surprise so affected him that he tottered to a nearby seat.

His unhinged nerves cried out that Father Lacombe's arrival meant some fresh trouble had befallen their Indian charges or their own men. The massacre of the two young priests at Frog Lake—the knowledge that others were even then imprisoned—and the grief he felt over the whole uprising had completely worn him out.

He was so pitifully broken with this fresh emotion and so nervous that at first Father Lacombe would not let him talk, but soothed him with assurances of the peaceful condition of the south. Always strong and optimistic, without an enfeebled nerve in his entire makeup, Father Lacombe was a tower of strength to the bishop then.

This period assuredly was a Golgotha to the sensitive prelate, mourning his own helplessness to stem the insurrection. He could not leave St. Albert, for the Government had requested him to remain there to ensure the peaceful attitude of the large colonies of Metis in that district. Many persons from Edmonton and the surrounding country had taken refuge near him. So this physically-broken man, who dominated the position in one portion of the west, had to chafe at home in inactivity.

On his return journey Father Lacombe met many Crees at Bear Hill Reserve, among them his friend Chief Ermine-Skin. The latter was not content to speak his loyal intentions to the missionary. He desired to communicate them to General Strange, the commander of the Canadian soldiery encamped nearby.

Father Lacombe brought him to the camp.   It was dusk when they approached the lines, and they were challenged by the sentry.

Father Lacombe did not know the pass-word.   To the challenge—*"Qui-va-la?"* he answered only:

"Père Lacombe."

The name proved a Sesame here, as in the camps of the Crees and Blackfeet!

The soldier immediately stepped aside to let him pass.

Lacombe was one of the watchwords of this camp, whose occupants—the 65th Regiment from Montreal —were familiar with Father Lacombe's services to the west.

Meanwhile the fate of the rebels was being worked out on the plains of the Saskatchewan.   When Riel and Poundmaker surrendered in May the insurrection was virtually over.

A letter written by Father Legal to his Superior after a summer spent with the Indians reflects conditions in outlying camps:

"MACLEOD, August, 1885.

"Dear Father Lacombe:

"I received yesterday at Macleod a few lines which you wrote to me on the envelope of a letter from France.   *C'est bien;* I will remain here awaiting your orders.   .   .   .

"I have passed the last two weeks with the Blood nation. I camped in a tent in their midst.   The villages are abandoned.   .   .   .   The Indians are quiet, but they are far from being persuaded of the defeat of the Crees and Metis.

All sorts of rumours, more or less resembling the truth, are being circulated among the two camps.

"For instance lately an Indian who came from Blackfoot Crossing related that the Police and Blackfeet were on the point of attacking each other at Calgary—and that the shedding of blood had only been prevented by your intervention . . . that seven cannons had arrived—three for Calgary and four for Macleod . . . and that Crowfoot was very exasperated [1] against the Whites . . . that he threatened to assemble a multitude of Indians whom he would bring from across the Mountains. What is there of truth in all this?

"I have told them that your letter, which I had just received, told me nothing of the kind. The Indian pretends to have his information from Crowfoot himself—'Who,' he said, 'knows whereof he speaks and is not a child.' It is in this way they excite one another."

[1] The talk of Crowfoot's exasperation may have arisen from some hasty expression of this Chief—though he was in act loyal throughout the Rebellion. It is related in Father Doucet's manuscript Notes of the Blackfoot Missions that Crowfoot was greatly annoyed when Poundmaker (his adopted son) was imprisoned after his surrender—and it was reported that this likable Chief would be put to death.

It is possible that Crowfoot was then provoked to hasty remarks of a threatening nature.

IX

THE services of Father Lacombe in the interest of public welfare during the Rebellion were generously acknowledged in public and private by various Canadian statesmen, by congratulatory letters and otherwise.[1]

The Government now secured Father Lacombe as census-enumerator for the first census of the Blackfeet and their allies. The resultant statistics indicate clearly a transition stage: as on the Blood Reserve the population of 2,251 possessed 1,500 horses, lived in tepees most of the year but had already built 220 permanent dwellings on their reserves.

In his activities here, however, Father Lacombe did not lose sight of the misguided Crees and Metis who were now chafing in imprisonment for participation in the Rebellion. The opening months of 1886 found him at Ottawa urgently pleading for the release of Chief Poundmaker and others.

He was most favourably heard by the Prime Minister and his new colleague, Sir John Thompson, the young Catholic judge upon whom Sir John—pre-

[1] It was with Father Lacombe and his confreres in mind that Sir John Macdonald said in a public address in England in 1886: ". . . The finest moral police in the world is to be found in the priesthood of French Canada."

eminently of a subtle wit—had bestowed a portfolio and with it the responsibility of explaining Riel's execution to Catholic Quebec.

Father Lacombe was joined in his representations at Ottawa by Archbishop Tache. They were entirely successful, and on March 4th Father Lacombe could return to Winnipeg. Without waiting for food or rest he hastened out to the Penitentiary to bring the good news to Poundmaker and his men.

"Ah, the scene in that Penitentiary when I went with Governor Bedson to tell our Indians they were free to go home to the plains again," Father Lacombe recalls. "They were so happy—like little children. Bedson, my good friend, made them a banquet and gave them presents. To Poundmaker he gave a watch—and we drove away in carriages to the Archbishop's Palace.

"We stayed there overnight. Then we went by train to Qu'Appelle, the Government paying all the expenses of the journey. The passengers were very curious about us and asked many questions. But my Indians thought of nothing except that they were going home. At Qu'Appelle I gave them over to our Fathers there, and they took them north into their own country.

"I was sorry I could not take a pardon to all of the prisoners that day; but I could promise it to the others soon. Before the year they were free. Big Bear was one of the last to leave—one year after Poundmaker went home."

During his visit to Ottawa this winter Sir John Macdonald invited him to return with Crowfoot and others of the allied chiefs who had remained loyal to the Government. He desired to show his appreciation of their conduct. Likewise it was felt that the chiefs' visit might serve as an object-lesson of the white man's power.

Crowfoot and his brethren—Three Bulls and Red Crow—were now made ready as befitted chiefs of their rank, and their people assembled *en masse* to watch them ride away on gaily-caparisoned ponies to the Crossing. Here they committed themselves to the demonlike horse which was to carry them a long journey many days from their own people.

They did not take this step without hesitation. They were reassured only by the fact that the Man-of-the-Good-Heart was to be their guide; for though Crowfoot would not accept his Christian teachings he loved and trusted the man himself.

The party was provided with transportation over the Canadian Pacific, to Ottawa, Montreal and Quebec, and their passage was something of a royal progress. People everywhere crowded to see them. Hotels vied to secure them as guests and different theatres were anxious to have them occupy boxes.

At Ottawa they were received by Sir John in the Parliament Buildings—then entertained at his residence. The Governor-General was waited upon at Rideau Hall, the Archbishop at his Palace; and everywhere the little bronzed missionary and his silent warriors were welcomed with impressive friendliness.

At a public reception given by the city of Ottawa, Crowfoot's fine manner and physique astonished the assembled multitude. His address, which was delivered with superb gestures was translated into English by Jean L'Heureux, whose services Father Lacombe had thoughtfully rewarded by including in the party.

At the close of his speech Crowfoot placed his hand affectionately upon Father Lacombe's shoulder, and looking down at him, said:

"This man, *Arsous-kitsi-rarpi,* is our brother—not only our Father, as the white people call him—but our brother. He is one of our people. When we weep he is sad with us; when we laugh he laughs with us. We love him. He is our brother!"

It was a simple summing-up of a whole-hearted devotion.

At the hotels these veteran warriors would not occupy the fine suites of rooms reserved for them: they felt safer in one apartment. They were uneasy when Father Lacombe was out of their sight and insisted he should sleep in the same room as they did.

One day when Sir John Macdonald telegraphed Father Lacombe to come from Montreal to Ottawa on business, the Blackfeet were genuinely distressed.

"Do not go. We will be alone," they protested. "And what will we do alone in this big country?"

He persuaded them to let him go to Ottawa in the

morning and he would return before night. Meanwhile they had him order their meals served in their
own room, and they did not leave it nor would they
close their eyes in sleep until he returned.

To a Roller Rink the party went one day, the
chiefs exclaiming with laughter at the whirling
whites as a Canadian might find amusement in a
whirling dervish. They went another day to the
Royal Theatre, but soon tired of the bright lights and
scenes that were merely new phases of the drama of
civilization unfolding itself daily to them.

At Quebec the visitors were guests of the Officers'
Mess at the Citadel; they were guests at a sham battle at Levis, and Crowfoot with the military commander reviewed a regimental parade on the Champ
de Mars. The Government judiciously desired that
Crowfoot should return home with a vivid realization
of the fighting power of the white race.

Perhaps the most demonstrative reception of their
tour was accorded them at a bazaar held in Montreal. Clad in skin garments, feathers and brass
ornaments the warriors and their cicerone were the
chief attraction of the festivity. Here as elsewhere
the stately Crowfoot was the Lion. A group of
Iroquois chieftains from Caughnawaga only served as
foils to show up the primitive grandeur of Father
Lacombe's proteges.

On the final night of the bazaar Crowfoot was led
to the stage and there presented with a stack of rifles
and ammunition. He astounded his hearers by

rejecting them with a magnificent gesture, as he said:

"I do not want these guns you would give me. I did not come here to make war—nor to defend myself; because I am with friends here. I have not even a small knife to defend myself. . . . Keep the guns; we have many guns in our country!"

Translated into French by Father Lacombe the chief's pronouncement was greeted with wild Bravos! and cheers. His apparent hurt at the gift, the sincerity of his avowal of friendship struck to the hearts of the impressionable audience. . . . To their aroused sympathies his words thrilled with the rude chivalry of the plains: they were seized with the strength of his personality. . . . *Vivat Crowfoot!*

Flowers and shawls and handsome gifts were then suddenly showered on the stage at his feet by the wildly enthusiastic people. These, they assured him, were the tokens of friendship he was to bring back to the allied tribes from the French-Canadians of Montreal, and Crowfoot accepted the new gifts with cordiality.

On their return home the lodges of the Blackfeet echoed for months the tales of the wonders of the east and the cities of the white men: for the Indian's face may be impassive, but his eye reaps its harvest and his memory is long.

The closing months of this year and several in 1887 were spent by Father Lacombe in supervising the mission-work of his southern district, with several visits to Edmonton to secure Cree children for the Dunbow School. There was one pleasant interval of relaxation, when he led an excursion by rail to the Pacific.

This was a tour especially planned by him for the benefit of Archbishop Fabre and Archbishop Tache, but he also invited Father Maisonneuve now old and frail and deaf, resting at St. Boniface after years of hardship along the Saskatchewan.

Here and there at the points tended by isolated missionaries an Oblate brother, shabbily clad, brown with exposure but light of heart, boarded their car— to be swept into a whirl of fraternal greetings, to marvel at the grandeur of their equipage, then to drop back into the routine of everyday work as the train sped on.

At the Columbia in the Rockies where that river winds north about a mass of mountains, Father Lacombe recalled his prophecy to the promoters of the Canadian Pacific that they would be unable to make a desirable passage through the Kicking Horse Pass. He saw now that while the Columbia River falls back before the Selkirks the engineers of the Canadian Pacific, more daring than Nature, had thrown their iron road triumphantly over the obstacle.

At Vancouver, then the crude young terminal of the C. P. R.—the visitors were given a civic reception. Toward evening they were conducted to the harbour, where a beautiful spectacle awaited them.

An Indian village across the bay was fantastically illuminated with Chinese lanterns and on the harbour a flotilla of Indian canoes spread out. Chinese lanterns attached to the slender rigging gemmed the floating parade which formed and re-formed in bewildering manœuvres about the boat of the Bishop's party.

As the dainty craft darted here and there across the water there rose from hundreds of breasts the wild melody of Indian hymns. Three great cannons added their voices to the tumult of joyous welcome as the procession moved across the Bay, until at last the visitors stepped ashore at the Indian village and in the square before the church were formally welcomed by the chief of the tribe.

On the following day Archbishop Fabre blessed the first Catholic Church to be opened in Vancouver where decades earlier French *voyageurs* of the Company and Indians had worshipped at woodland shrines erected by Father Demers and Father Blanchet.

On the afternoon of the same day the party went by steamboat to Victoria. They found the city in mourning, the Palace and Cathedral draped in black —news having just come in from the north that Archbishop Seghers, the head of the diocese, had been murdered in November of the previous year by his servant whilst travelling on mission work in the Yukon District.

On their homeward way, as the train passed Calgary again, the party regretfully took leave of their "dear Indian," Father Lacombe, who picked up the threads of his work refreshed by the holiday.

Toward the close of this year Father Lacombe was again compelled to take to the road. Like a soldier he travelled with light knapsacks and never required long marching-orders.

On this occasion he was asked by his bishop to accompany him on a tour of the Eastern States, where in the French-Canadian parishes and elsewhere they might beg alms for their missions. Even to Father Lacombe's "holy audacity," as his ecclesiastical friends in Quebec termed it, this mission was not a pleasant one: to Bishop Grandin's exquisitely sensitive spirit it was one long trial and humiliation.

In several parishes they were welcomed, in others tolerated; in some the permission to preach and beg was refused. For people—even when they gave alms—occasionally grumbled at the incessant calls of missionaries, and their pastors felt alike their own parochial responsibilities and the disinclination of their people.

Father Lacombe's letters written during this winter's trip show plainly his difficulties—among them the disheartening fact that his oft-repeated story in broken English has grown thread-bare and uninteresting to himself—though the privations of his fellow-missionaries back in the western shacks do not lessen.

Writing in French from Philadelphia on March 22, 1888, to his friend Father Legal, he says he has just returned from the diocese of Baltimore with $1,500:

". . . But what work. *Mon tres cher!* I am always at the plough with letters, newspaper announcements, trips, and *then*—those sermons!

"Imagine me in the pulpit of one of these grand churches or cathedrals before an audience of priests or seminarists— and then saying to that multitude: 'My dear brethren, I am only a poor Indian missionary. The poor must have the gospel preached to them, therefore my bishop and myself, we come to make an appeal to your liberality,' and so on. I assure you, my body creaks, as I used to say out there. I would be discouraged and fail to know how to continue my address —if my imagination did not picture to me, you, my brother- missionary at your work. I take heart again and you seem to say: 'Go on; we are praying for you.' "

At the foot of this letter there is a little note for all the priests in the delicate handwriting of Bishop Grandin:

"I am truly desolate because of the illness of our dear Fa- ther Van Tighen. We have already experienced so many trials of all sorts that God might at least grant health to us all. Take courage however, my dear Father. If you suffer: if you have difficulties, remember that for my part I have known them too—and great ones. If it were not that our cause is God's also I would despair of it.

"I embrace you, and bless you all,
"Your affectionate brother,
"VITAL, O. M. I."

This characteristic note illustrates one source of the inspiration of the wonderful work done by the Oblate missionaries in the west—the exhortations and sympathy of their chiefs who appreciated just how heavy their burdens were, because they had first borne them all themselves.

Woonsocket, Pawtucket, and Providence are canvassed successfully, but Father Lacombe is beginning to feel the infirmities of age. He complains of the heat and of weakness in his limbs. . . . "These are terrible journeys for my strength, physical and mental."

One pleasant feature of the old missionary's tour was his meeting with Mother Katherine Drexel, of the Philadelphia Drexels, who had consecrated her life and fortune to the uplift of the Indian and negro. When they parted Father Lacombe was richer by several hundred dollars given by the nun to be devoted to hospital work among the Indians.

It was also while at Providence, R. I., this year that he was shown a beautiful private home and estate which had been donated by its owner as a Home for aged and orphans. As he looked, a vision sprang up before Father Lacombe, and remained with him for years till he saw its realization in the Lacombe Home.

X

WHEN Father Lacombe at last returned with
$6,000 to the western missions he found plenty of
cares awaiting him. Affairs at the Bow were *bien
tristes* for lack of money, he chronicled. But he had
the happiness of playing his old role of Lord Bounti-
ful.

He had no jurisdiction over the money collected.
He had, however, many presents for his friends—a
bell bought in Philadelphia for the mission at Banff—
an ostensorium for Father Van Tighen—a Way of
the Cross for Father Blais—a magic lantern with
New Testament pictures for Father Leduc and his
Indians; while for Father Legal his beggar friend
had secured a new saddle, a washing machine, four
volumes of the History of the Church, and an alarm
clock!—which luxuries are forwarded to the young
priest amid mutual expressions of delight.

Dividing his time and efforts this winter between
white and Indian missions in the south, Father Lacombe finds but one abiding source of humour in the
little brick Chateau and embryo orchard evolved from
next to nothing at Lethbridge by his ingenious
brother, Father Van Tighen. The orchard, which
first demonstrated the possibilities of horticulture in
Southern Alberta, and the Chateau were in time to

win a place in Southern Alberta records: this year they only afforded material for Father Lacombe to tease "that dear Father Van Tighen."

A visit to Edmonton in April, 1889, found him so worn-out that he collapsed physically and was ordered to bed for weeks, where he lay planning new movements in the interests of the southern tribes and writing long letters to his bishop begging him not to abandon this unsatisfactory field, as pressing needs elsewhere urged the bishop to do.

From Edmonton he went with Bishop Grandin to St. Boniface to attend the first Provincial Council of western Catholic clergy. This met in Winnipeg in July, 1889, and included a celebration of the seventy-first anniversary of the arrival of Bishop Provencher and Father Dumoulin. Where in 1818 there had been only two priests there were now one Archbishop, five Bishops, and one hundred and twenty-six priests together with numerous consecrated workers.

The Lieutenant-Governors of Manitoba and of the Northwest attended the first public session of the Council. Father Lacombe was named promoter of the convention, and it continued from July 14th to July 24th, with sessions public and private and solemn religious services.

That autumn, as Superintendent of the district his confreres assembled about him in Macleod for their annual retreat. He writes that they not only have a lay-brother to cook for them this year and attend to their wants, but this factotum is Brother Jean, a most capable man. The veteran chronicles with delight that at last they are going to make a retreat *en messieurs*—like gentlemen.

On October 12 Lord Stanley the Governor General visited Macleod and the carriage of Capt. Mc-Donnell, N. W. M. P. was sent on His Excellency's request to bring Father Lacombe to meet him. The missionary writes Father Legal that they conversed for an hour in French, Father Lacombe speaking to His Excellency very frankly about school matters and the inadequacy of certain Indian officials.

Apart from this the picture his letter contains of a western reception to Vice-royalty in the eighties is not captivating:

"Yesterday the Governor arrived. I was there with a few others. Little enthusiasm—the good people of Macleod were occupied with drinking. What a race of people! what rudeness! . . . But our mission-bell rang out, beside the pavilion.

"Last night at nine—was His Excellency's levee in the City Hall. Fiasco and failure! We were about a score of people, two priests and Reverend Mr. Hilton. . . . What a *triste* affair. But there were four ladies *deshabilees*—among them Mrs. ——, who as we passed out with the Governor commenced to leap about like a *danseuse*. His Excellency will have a grand idea of the people of Macleod."

In Christmas week Father Lacombe received a letter which was a fresh evidence of the regard of a man whose friendship has been marked by a series of graceful acts.   The letter enclosed a railway pass over the whole system of the Canadian Pacific.

"MONTREAL, December 22, 1889.

"Dear Father Lacombe:

"We are still following you wherever you go, with our rails and locomotives, and it is possible that you will hear our whistle at Macleod before the end of the coming year.

"I send you herewith a little charm against railway conductors, which you may find useful since you cannot get beyond their reach.

"With best wishes for your good health and long life,

"Believe me,
"Faithfully yours,
"W. C. VAN HORNE."

Twenty years after this Pass had been received Father Lacombe still fingered affectionately the letter that accompanied it, while he said with tender gravity that trembled with tears at the end:

"He wrote it himself. . . .   You see, why I love that man different from the others—*he* is himself different.   He has not only his genius, his brain, but he has a heart; that is more rare.   See, he wrote this letter himself; that man—and so busy.   But it was always so—he has been beautiful in the little things of Life. . . .   Ah, Omimi, I love that man —he is the brother of my heart."

The old priest's heart was both responsive and actively affectionate, yet he could be stern, too, when the occasion arose, and one record of it shows not alone his sternness but his unsurpassed perception of the Indian character and how to influence it for the best. This concerns five Indian Metis, three women and two men, who in contact with low whites had sunk as low as mankind can sink toward the animal state, and who had flouted the old priest's appeals to lead more decent lives.

On March 16 he concluded a mission at Calgary for all the Indians and Metis of the neighbourhood. He writes to Father Legal about the grand closing demonstration—the chanting of the *Te Deum,* the solemn baptizing of nine adult Crees who had been pagans, and the marriage of three couples. "It was all touching," he says; then adds:

"On the eve of the closing I believed it my duty to make a final striking *coup d'eclat*. I covered the altar with the funeral pall and to the sound of funeral knells tolling I denounced and excommunicated five public sinners—three women, two men—after which we recited the *Miserere*, greatly impressing and astounding the whole assembly."

It is doubtful if the indecent degraded lives of the five were in any way altered by these thunders of the Church, but the ceremonies certainly exercised a most wholesome influence on some of their brethren who were tempted to join them on the soiled primrose path of frontier Calgary's underworld.

In April of this year, 1890, Crowfoot lay down his sceptre of native power, named his brother Three

Bulls his successor, and met death with brave serenity befitting an Ancient.

His funeral was a striking compromise between the ways of the pagan and the Christian, for though Crowfoot had lived an avowed pagan he had died a professing Christian, and two days before his death he asked Father Doucet to baptize him and receive him into the fold of the Church.

Shortly before his death his people shot his favourite pony before the tepee in accordance with pagan rites, but at the last Father Doucet chanted the prayers for the dead by the open grave.

With Crowfoot the last of the great Indians of the plains passed into history.

In June as a deserved holiday Father Lacombe took Father Legal and Father Doucet to visit Sechelt, an Indian village north of Vancouver. The visit was made during the annual religious Congress of the Pacific Indians, where the tribes of Sechelt, Squamish, Sycannis, Lilloet, Chilcotin, Stickeen, Cariboo, Douglas, Stuart's Lake, and Fraser River met together accompanied by their missionaries.

Many of the Indians who had come out from the interior now looked upon steamboats and railways for the first time. Others of a newer generation came from Indian schools and brought brass bands with them.

The ninth or closing day of the Congress fell as planned on Corpus Christi and was marked by a procession. Its start was prefaced by the booming of cannons and it was accompanied along a flower-strewn way by alternate music of bands and chanting of Indian choirs. The procession came to a close with a Calvary-tableau on the hill overlooking the village.

At night a torchlight procession moved through the village streets like the current of a river in flames; and the intermingling of music and chanting of prayers in the quiet evening beside the Pacific was beyond words beautiful.

The missionaries of the plains returned home over the mountains with a fresh impulse to work for their less promising Blackfeet. Father Lacombe immediately directed his activities toward promoting French-Canadian colonies in the Saskatchewan valley.

Up and down the old province of Quebec, across the border into the Eastern States the stalwart veteran travelled preaching his doctrine of the new land, free farms and openings for young men. "On the road all the time," he reports early in September to his friend among the Bloods. "Yesterday I came up from below Quebec stopping only at the bishop's. I shall soon go again to Rimouski—*Ca c'est un commerce!*"

A week later he and Bishop Grandin are at Ottawa pressing their claims concerning Indian schools. Among the requests he urges upon the Minister of the Interior is the establishment of a hospital for Indians on the Blood Reserve. It is not a new request: he is merely renewing his petitions, as men sooner or

later learned this amiable, iron-willed old man would
do—until he obtained what he sought.

"Vous savez que je suis un homme a plans!" . . .
A man of plans, indeed; he might have said, a man of
accomplishments.

In October he wrote a brief rapturous note announcing to Father Legal that at last he has been able
though the charity of friends to buy two small organs
which he says stand as an evidence of his own audacity. "Of course, there is one for Your Reverence,
and one for Father Foisy; *mais, mon tres cher,* how I
have wanted for a long time to get one of these organs
for you!"

On each of his trips to Montreal in the eighties
Father Lacombe used to renew his pleasant friendship with Sir William Van Horne, Sir George Stephen and Sir Donald Smith, and dining one day at
the home of the last-named, with other magnates of
the C. P. R., he first met "Lord and Lady Aberdeen
arriving from Scotland."

This I note, because it marked the beginning of
another very pleasant acquaintance which was to
ripen into a warm friendship. For the Scotch peer
and his wife were immediately taken with a personality that combined intellectual and human interest
in the most picturesque fashion; while with Father
Lacombe their ready kindness and outspoken regard
won his responsive liking as readily as the sun drew
up dew from the heart of his own prairie-roses.

These visits to old friends in the east formed some

of the many bright hours of his work-a-day trips, but on the whole he was wearied—"overwhelmed with occupations," he says—and he confides to Father Legal his growing hope that on his return the bishop will let him build a house in the quiet foothills at Pincher Creek, to retire there as to a hermitage.

His memory and notebooks were as usual crowded with commissions for his fellow-priests and other friends—calls to be made on relatives; favours to be secured; lonely Metis children in Eastern schools to be called upon; pathetic petitions for necessities in the shabby missions. And like a big brother who goes out into the world he was only happy when he could return laden with gifts and affectionate messages for his brethren. . . . It is noteworthy that he never kept anything of all the gifts for himself!

On his return to the west he spent some time visiting the reserves. Writing to his bishop in December he ascribes the Blackfeet's tenacious paganism to their pride:

"Of an inveterate—I could say—an innate pride, they have no conception of the virtue of humility, nor any words in their tongue to express it. The Blackfoot will never say he is a sinner nor humble himself. On the contrary, from the chief and warriors—proud and superb in manner—down to the child beginning to shape a bow, the continuous refrain upon their personal goodness is the same. . . . But God withdraws Himself from the proud of heart and draws near the humble. . . ."

A further reason for their stand against Christianity, he finds, is their determined practice of polygamy. Even at this period the warriors maintained the right to their old-time prairie harems, and a girl's parents would sell her at the age of ten years to a grown man selecting her as a future wife. Crowfoot was an exception to the Blackfoot rule of polygamy: like the Head-Chief Sweet-Grass and unlike his lesser followers he was satisfied with one wife. And these two chiefs were noted for wisdom in their tribes.

For the past seven years Father Lacombe's letters have reflected his anxieties about various Indian school boys. Now in February of 1891 he has the most serious case of all to speak about—a young brave, Peter, who was accused of helping to steal horses at Medicine Hat. The boy cried so pitifully before he was taken off to gaol that Father Lacombe decided "I must go and do my possible with Judge Macleod" —and with everyone else in authority to secure clemency for the poor boy. . . .

For how was Peter to quite grasp the doctrine that what was glory in the days of the youth of Crowfoot and Sweet-Grass was crime in his?

Father Lacombe set out on his mission of mercy with such pleasure in the act of benevolence that the onlooker is set to wonder which is dearer to Father Lacombe—the wrong-doer who throws himself upon his mercy, or the charitable friend who opens sympathies and purse to meet the needs of his beloved missions? Either class has a strong hold upon his affections—but the balance of favour lies perhaps with the friendless sinner—no matter what his crime.

And for this reason the man of despair, divining the old priest's sympathy, always made a sanctuary of him.

In April Father Lacombe together with Father Legal drove from the Blood reserve into Montana to visit the southern Piegans near Two Medicine River. They ministered to these allies of the Blackfeet, visited the Agency and dined at the cafe of Joe Kipp of border-fame. On the return trip, losing the trail in a storm, they found shelter at night in the home of one of the numerous Mormon settlers then coming in to Southern Alberta.

In November, when he was again planning his retirement to the Hermitage, Father Lacombe went instead to Montreal on the bishop's request to represent St. Albert diocese at the fiftieth anniversary of the Oblates' arrival in Canada.

Father Lacombe's stay in the east, although a busy one, was not without social pleasure. Among clergy and laity his unusual personality and powers as a raconteur exercised their charm, and his company was still sought after by leading men in Montreal and Ottawa, who had seen the rich nature behind the humble exterior of the old plainsman.

At Ottawa he dined with Sir Adolphe Caron, with Sir John Thompson, and others of his friends among the *"gros bonnets."* [1] At Montreal he was enter-

---

[1] Big Hats—an Indian term for Chiefs.

tained by Sir William Van Horne, James Ross, and others prominent in Canadian finance and public life.

He was always sensitive to genuine social charm and of one evening and host he writes this charming tribute:

"Last Saturday I dined with my good friend Van Horne in company with several 'gros bonnets.' *The evening was a veritable triumph of refinement and amiability.*"

Whilst in Montreal he was presented with a very fine Italian painting [1] by the directors of the Canadian Pacific Railway. In the pleasing presentation which took place in the President's office, Father Lacombe recognized again the charming thought and temperament of his old friend.

On January 3rd, 1892, he writes from Montreal to Father Legal that he is "encumbered with business and commissions. Ah, I have need of a frame of iron," is the note of complaint with which he concludes the letter. He is evidently tired and his years are telling on him.

Some portion of his weariness may be due to the fact that he was greatly discouraged in his efforts to procure the hospital for southern Indians which had been practically promised to him a year earlier at Calgary by the Hon. Mr. Dewdney.

The prospects at Ottawa now were not promising and Father Lacombe appealed again and again to the Hon. Mr. Dewdney and the Hon. Mayne Daly—

[1] This painting still hangs over the high altar of St. Mary's, Calgary.

the latter one of the few politicians whom Father Lacombe credited with a serious sense of responsibility
toward the child-races of the plains, and a practical
sympathy with their needs.

He urged upon the two the truth that privations
and lack of food had weakened the Indians and that
new diseases were coming among them from the
whites. He begged them to build a hospital on
the Blood Reserve as an experiment.

A letter written by him on February 8th to Father
Legal shows him utterly disheartened, for the Hon.
Mr. Dewdney had brought him to Premier Abbott
and he was told by the latter that the hospital would
have to wait another year or two . . . there simply were no funds for it.

At the announcement Father Lacombe saw his air-
castles on the Blood Reserve shattered at his feet;
dazed with disappointment he looked from one to another of the *"gros bonnets"* . . . then broke out
with the eloquence of his despair.

The eloquence and disappointment combined so
moved the politicians that on March 9th Father Lacombe could write jubilantly to his western corre-
spondent:

"Dear Father:

"Thank God with me! Yesterday I had an interview with
Dewdney, who was very amiable. His first words to me were:
'Father, your Hospital is granted; I have got the money for
you.' My heart beat hard: I was so surprised and so
glad. . . ."

He then goes into details about the grant, urging
Father Legal to hasten to make a plan for the building: for the young Breton had added the architect's
craft to his other accomplishments since he arrived in
Alberta. . . . He continues:

"Now, my dear Father and friend of many days, we must
move heaven and earth to make a success of our famous enterprise. 'If you are successful,' said Mr. Dewdney to me,
'I assure you we will make similar establishments on other Reserves.' It is also intended that the hospital shall be con-
structed beside your house. I am weeping for joy of it; I
am so happy. '*Quid retribuam Domino?*' Quick, make me
a nice plan."

This was all for which he had waited; a few days
later he set off for the west with twenty-six cases of
baggage and supplies he had purchased or received
as gifts for the missions of the diocese.

XI

The east being still unaware of the resources of western Canada, it was the policy of the C. P. R. to invite leading men to visit the west as their guests. The directors realized that every visitor seeing would believe and return an apostle of the New West.

Consequently on May 16 a party of ecclesiastics left Montreal in two special cars, placed by the president at Father Lacombe's disposal. At St. Boniface Archbishop Tache joined the party, which then included the Archbishop of Ottawa, Father Lacombe, Bishop Lafleche who had been Tache's companion in the forties at Isle a la Crosse, Bishop Grouard of the Athabasca-Mackenzie district, Bishop Macdonald of Alexandria, Bishop Brondel of Helena, Montana, Bishop Lorrain of Pembroke, the Rector of Ottawa University, fourteen priests, Judge Routher of Quebec and M. des Cases.

At St. Boniface, Regina, Prince Albert, where Archbishop Tache blessed the corner-stone of a new Cathedral, and at Calgary their reception was "a succession of fêtes." Calgary extended a civic reception and a public dinner to the visitors, the music being provided by an Indian band from the school where eight years earlier Father Lacombe had brought his group of young savages to be trained.

From Calgary the route led to Edmonton, and St. Albert, and thence to British Columbia where at St. Mary's, the Canadian Oberammergau, they saw the Passion Play religiously enacted by Indians.

This was the most picturesque incident of their trip. On their arrival they found seven tribes of Indians encamped in a beautiful plain beside the Fraser. Greeted with a cannon's booming and the roar of musketry from hundreds of Indians lined up to welcome them, the entrance of the ecclesiastics in the valley was one of semi-royal splendour.

The Passion was protrayed in eight tableaux by Indians garbed as Jews and Romans. Throughout the tableaux the Indian multitude kept up a mournful chanting, but at the last scene a solemn hush fell on the valley . . .   then one by one the chiefs of the tribes rose and called out in a loud voice:

"The Christ is dead—the Christ is dead!"

That evening the seven tribes again assembled on the hill in an immense tent, where the Bishop of New Westminster officiated at a solemn benediction and the evening air was melodious with the chanting of hundreds of Indians; while on the plain beneath as darkness fell, the camp-fire before each ghostly white skin lodge made human spots of warmth and colour in the moonlit valley, which was itself a divine etching in black and silver.

By the middle of June the "Car of Israel," as the private coach had been named, returned to St. Boniface, and Father Lacombe's famous personally-conducted tour was at an end.

In July our Hermit went to his hermitage, expressing a firm intention to remain there. On September 16th he writes:

"To avoid being tempted to make voyages I have sent my horses to Mr. Gravel. That is what they call 'burning one's ships'!"

And so having banished Badger—the successor of his good ponies, Buckskin and Buckshot—he felt himself bound to stay at home and rest, to compose his mind and meditate on Eternity as he desired to do in preparation for the end.

The first interruption to his days of contemplation came in December. He writes to Father Legal that Bishop Grandin had to go east on business and needs him: and he feels he must go. He does not add—what was probably true—that the solitude of his hermitage had begun to pall upon him.

In the east he began a search for volunteer-nurses for the Indian Hospital now nearing completion. He found that the Superiors of convents were unwilling to let their nuns go for hospital work among Indians with such a reputation for bloodthirstiness and dislike for the tenets of Christianity.

Telling the story of his efforts decades after he said of the Superior-General of the Grey Nuns:

"Perhaps that good Mother could not spare her nuns, or—as people said—she was afraid to send her

young Sisters among the wild Bloods; for a Hospital
you know, was not the same as a school for young
children.   But anyway, me—I was vexed, and I say
—'*Tres bien,* for fifty years we Oblates and you Grey
Nuns have work side by side in the west to see which
can do the most good.   Now you would stop here—
Then Good-bye,' I said, and I went away not pleased
—me!

"At St. Hyacinthe, at Ottawa, at Quebec I went
to the convents, and it was always the same: the Superiors refused.   I was losing all my courage.

"Then at Nicolet, where I went to see the Bishop
on some other affairs, I told him of my disappointment—it was at last becoming my despair.

"Next day the Superior of that Nicolet Convent
sent word to me that if any of her Sisters would volunteer themselves for the Hospital, she was willing to
let them go.   .   .   .   Ah, that was joy for me—I
cannot tell you how great.   .   .   .   Four Sisters
came; more would have come if I had need of more—
ah, *ces cheres Princesses!*"

"I have told these nuns I am going to ennoble them
and call them Princesses of Charity," he wrote in his
enthusiasm to Father Legal, and east and west the
old man sang the praises of his dear Princesses, as the
Nicolet nuns were for several years known in church-
circles of the west.

While in the east he also secured from his friends
at the Canadian Pacific offices a tri-weekly mail-serv-
ice for Macleod instead of the weekly arrangement

planned by the road, and he tells as a choice bit of
news to his friend that the C. P. R. will shortly build
a line up into the Crow's Nest Pass.

He dines with his old friend, Edouard Fabre—now
Archbishop of Montreal—on February 28, the anniversary of the birth of each; and he chronicles the
delight they felt in recalling the good old days. But
his mind is more heartily in touch with the needs of
the present, and the same letter that notes the re-
union with Edouard Fabre announces happily that
the Superiors of eight more colleges and four convents
have each agreed to take a bright pupil from the western reserves and educate them free of charge.

.   .   .   .

Before returning to the west Father Lacombe par-
ticipated in an interesting occasion, which was at the
time recorded in *The Empire* of Toronto in the following despatch of January 22nd from Ottawa:

"It was an historic scene which was enacted yesterday in
the Privy Council Chamber here—historic because for the
first time in the history of the Dominion an appeal was being heard by the Governor-in-Council under the provisions
of Section 93 of the Confederation Act. Following the precedent set by the sub-committee of the Privy Council which
heard the preliminary argument, the proceedings yesterday
were open to the public. Every leading newspaper in the
Dominion had its representative present, while about a dozen
gentlemen represented the great Canadian public. Among
the more notable outsiders present were Rev. Father Lacombe,
the famous N. W. missionary. .   .   ."

This morsel of parliamentary correspondence is indicative of the new phase of public life that had opened before Father Lacombe. The Canadian Government was confronting a grave constitutional question which for years was to engage the keenest wits of Canada's publicists, and through the long-drawn-out battle it entailed the two commanding figures always were the statesman-prelate of St. Boniface and his indomitable lieutenant, our old veteran of the plains.

The question had been precipitated into the political arena by the ambitions of certain politicians in Manitoba, assisted by Dalton McCarthy who was still burning with resentment at the passage of the Jesuit Estates' Bill and the failure of Sir John Macdonald to appoint him Minister of Justice. The case was kept open no less by the working of political intrigue than by the resolute convictions and principles roused in the opposing masses. Canada divided on the question; political reputations were made and unmade in the *"grand lutte,"* as Father Lacombe was wont to term it; one government was thrown out of power and another elevated by reason of it—and in more ways than one the Manitoba School question impressed itself deeply upon the political history of Canada.

The agitation had begun in 1889, when the new Greenway administration resolved to abolish Separate Schools in Manitoba, and carried legislation to this effect. This was not only a subversion of a system that had existed for seventy years—or since the stately Provencher at St. Boniface opened the first schools of the Canadian West: it was also in direct contravention of the rights in educational matters assured to the Catholic minority by the Manitoba Act of 1870.

The Manitoba minority held the universal claim of their co-religionists to direct the schools maintained by their own taxes, to select text-books for use therein, and to provide moral training based upon religious instruction. These claims are not ordinarily objectionable to politicians of any creed, if the majority of voters in a community hold these views. When, however, separate-school rate-payers are in the minority —by the laws of opportunism that control the average politicians—the claims of the separate-school advocate are most reprehensible.

Manitoba politicians seized upon defects in the training and qualifications of separate-school teachers to condemn the whole system. Archbishop Tache and his school-boards growing aware of the defects, had resolved to improve conditions, but their opportunity was now gone.

Leading his people in an agitation for their rights the Archbishop cited not only the Manitoba Act, but the British North America Act—the Constitution of the Dominion—as providing protection for the minority and guaranteeing separate-school rights. His party instanced the generous treatment of the Protestant minority in Quebec: they appealed to a sense of common justice for the inalienable right of the re-

spectable parent to educate his child wheresoever he
would if he were himself willing to pay for it.

But as nothing they said made any impression upon
the provincial authorities Tache's party carried their
grievance to Ottawa.   They brought test-cases in the
courts and these were finally carried to the Privy
Council where the aggrieved party lost.

The Haultain administration of the Northwest
Territories, taking a leaf out of Manitoba's book, in
turn deprived the minority of their old school rights.
The work was done with a finer hand than in Manitoba, the leader being a man of much political finesse
and accomplishment; the results were similar.

Petitions for relief now poured in from the west
to the Ottawa Government, but with Sir John Macdonald dead and his party groping for such another
tactician and leader, the time was unpropitious for
decision: particularly as the Manitoba Government
was now shielding itself behind a new cry—Provincial Rights.

Echoes of the discussion rose on all sides and the
question, regarded by Ottawa's politicians as their
sorest affliction, gradually assumed national propor-
tions.   On one side were the Catholics of the west
led by the Archbishop of St. Boniface and his minister plenipotentiary, supported by all the Catholics of
Eastern Canada.   On the other hand were the Manitoba Government and a majority of western Prot-
estants backed by the entire element in Canada which
aproximates to the non-Conformists in England.

It was with small hope of any immediate settlement that Father Lacombe returned home in 1893, confident he would soon have to come east again and take further steps in the campaign.

On his return he received a charmingly playful letter from his old friend at St. Boniface, whose redoubtable spirit could still be gay, although he describes himself as an "infirm old man," and the sufferings from his disease have become so grave that he knows himself to be in the Valley of Shadows.

The letter was in reply to one Father Lacombe had written announcing his resumption of the life of a Hermit, with his unanswerable argument of '*On est Ermite ou on ne l'est pas*' (One is a Hermit or one is not)—the inference being that he was a Hermit because he desired to be and said he was, *tout simplement.* Whether or not the exigencies of his work drove him to unceasing travels, that fact was not to be permitted to upset his claim.

The aged Archbishop meets his friend's views playfully, but with an undercurrent of seriousness that suggests his own next cloister will be the tomb. The letter, which is replete with a delicious humour, suffers in the translation.

The Archbishop first professes his desire to be a hermit, too; then says:

"In the depths of solitude and silence I salute you by the watchword of your new Institution, 'Brother, one is a Hermit or one is not.' So since we may no longer mix ourselves in the things of this world I return Mr. Reed's letter to you.

I am even going to make my adieux to Monseigneur Durieu, who will not forego his existence on the agitated sea of the world. In the fear that his example might mislead me, the Inspirer of our isolation yesterday enveloped all visible Nature in a white shroud, an image of that which we will take at the gateway of our cloister, to indicate that nothing profane or soiled should enter within that Sanctuary, or that at least if one enters there with stains one must live without spot (*tache*) to become a dove (*colombe*). This last word, is it not merely an evolution from *lacombe?*

"Yes, brother, one is a Hermit or one is not, and as we are hermits, let us separate to unite again in the Lord.

"I commit you to God, Brother, till we meet again,

"BROTHER ALEXANDER OF THE

"OBSERVANCE OF PINCHER CREEK."

On May 14th, Father Lacombe writes from his new Hermitage. Now for the first time appears on his letters the rubber stamp—*"Ermitage de St. Michel";* he is determined to give his hermitage an air of permanency. He writes to Father Legal:

"*Me voila*—again a Hermit. I wish that those wags who will not take my position seriously could see into my Hermitage for a little while to-day—Sunday. Alone on the top of my hill with my dog and my cat again, I say to myself, 'It is so one is a Hermit!' I go into church to visit my one neighbour, who is also my kind Saviour, and I repeat the prayers and the office of hermits. Ah, wags, you who say there are no hermits now! *Erudemini   .   .   .   filii hominum.*"

About the same time he writes that he is expecting

a visit from his friend Sir William Van Horne, who
had lately written repeating his protests against the
proposed retirement of Father Lacombe:

"When it is given to one like you to kindle the love and
reverence of everybody you meet, is it right that you should
bury yourself in a Hermitage?   Surely not."

Sir William need not have feared that the delightful old plainsman would be lost to his friends.   He
was a Hermit: assuredly—had he not proclaimed the
fact throughout the Dominion?   But his friends were
not to lose him; for he was a Hermit—who would not
stay at home.

He finds the modern Hermit cannot live in a grotto
on figs and water.   Like many another missionary-
priest he learns again the cares of housekeeping, for
there is no lay-brother to spare for this mission, and
when a niece who was with him leaves to return east
he has the greatest difficulty in getting someone to
come in from time to time to keep his house orderly.
He grumbles: "This business of doing the cooking
does not agree with me."

Perhaps the cooking or the quiet or the loneliness
palled upon him, for when in June he received a telegram from his old Alma Mater at L'Assomption—
"Père Lacombe required for our feast without fail"
—he goes without demur, to the joys of the open
road and the jeers of his younger brethren.

After the College feast he went to Ottawa and
arranged with Mr. Daly to formally open the hos-

pital that summer, then on to Nicolet where he saw "those dear Princesses" bid a tremulous farewell to their quiet convent and sister nuns. A few days later he followed them to the west.

The autumn finds him quietly settled at the Hermitage—rested and content although very poor. He has to meet some of his debts by selling his horse and the heavy waggon at the mission.

XII

EARLY in the New Year of 1894 he was called to St. Boniface. The Archbishop, with sufficient trouble for one human frame in the grave disease he was battling, had set himself to meet a fresh crisis in the School Question as determinedly as forty years before he had reversed his Superior's order to abandon the western missions.

Physically unable to carry on any negotiations at Ottawa now, he turned all active work over to Father Lacombe, and in the fulfilment of this mission laid on him by his ailing friend—statesmen, prelates and laity were to come equally under the influence of the persuasive old man who knew but one cry, "Give us back our rights in our Schools!"

Since the repeated efforts of the Archbishop and his party to secure remedial measures had been unavailing the Archbishop's next step was to secure the formal co-operation of all his brother-prelates in Canada, and it was for this delicate mission that he had again called upon his old Hermit.

Father Lacombe brought the Archbishop's latest and most notable Memorial on the School Question to Montreal and had it published there. On April

345

1st he writes to Father Legal that the Bishops have all agreed to unite with Tache in demanding the restoration of their school rights.   He continues:

"Imagine, I leave to-morrow evening for St. Boniface with the Bishop of Valleyfield and secretary.   I have seen all the Bishops of Quebec, and with Bishop Grandin have prevailed upon Their Lordships to make our cause their own.   *Donc*, they all desire, and will regard as their doyen the Archbishop of St. Boniface.   It has been decided that Bishop Emard will be charged with this important mission to go in the name of his colleagues and carry their kindest wishes to Archbishop Tache and convey their sympathy with him, asking him what should be done *uno consensu;* to decide too upon a plan of campaign and some form of agitation to compel, by public demand, the authorities to render justice to us.   I have just come from Ottawa with Bishop Grandin.   We met there the Bishop of Montreal and Bishop Emard.   *C'est serieux.*   The Memoir, of which I have had thousands of copies printed in French and English is making a sensation.   It is a thunderbolt to the Government.

"McIntosh and Haultain are at Ottawa.   The frightened Ministry would wish to make them give way, but they will not, seeing that they have already been supported against us."

The petition now forwarded to Ottawa was signed by thirty-one prelates and was a wide and statesmanlike appeal for justice.   The document was presented by Father Lacombe in person.

From the serious tone of the resultant Order in Council it would seem to have impressed the Government more than any previous effort of the Catholic party: but whatever the plans and policy of the governing party this year they were upset by the tragically sudden death of the Prime Minister—Sir John Thompson—in December at Windsor Castle. Rumours of definite remedial action began to take shape however.

Occasional pleasures marked Father Lacombe's stay in the East, but it was for the most part fatiguing, and he sighed for his hermitage. He writes Father Legal on May 20th from St. Boniface:

"Dear Friend,—How I have hastened my return. How tired and worried I am with this *commerce!* Twenty-four hours before leaving Montreal I received a telegraph from Archbishop Tache and the Superior-General asking me not to leave before I received their letters. *Et puis*, all the same I came away."

He did not go directly to his Hermitage then however.

At St. Boniface he was asked to accompany the Superior-General who had come from France on a tour of the western missions, and he complied with pleasure, for he was always finely susceptible to the company of persons dowered in heart and intellect. These he found united in the commanding person of Father Soullier, their Superior-General.

While at Kamloops on June 21, Father Lacombe received word of the serious form Archbishop Tache's illness had taken, and of the operation performed in the hope of saving his life. . . . The following day he was informed of the Archbishop's death.

His sense of loss and grief was acute, for while
Archbishop Tache was widely accounted a great man
and a good one—to his colleagues who knew him best
the Archbishop was their Well-Beloved, their little
General.

Time has given him his rank as one of the noblest
figures in Canadian history: a man commanding respect alike from the man of the world and the man
of the sanctuary.

.   .   .   .

"Here I am so lonesome—*ennuyè bien gros.*
What an undertaking to have come here! But let
us stop—this is not to recite to you my Jeremiads,
but to talk about that man who was drowned with
his horses crossing the Kootenay—a lay-brother here,
French-Canadian, fears it may be his brother who
was coming from Montana to select a farm in Alberta. . . ."

It is our delightfully human old missionary who
in August, 1894, writes this plaint from Edmonton
where he has been called as pastor of St. Joachim's
Church. His heart is not in the task or the place.
"What a post for my white hairs!" . . . "It is
the hotel of the diocese," he says of his new residence
—with a continual stream of callers, lay and clerical,
going to and from St. Albert or the northern missions. There are no Indians under his care, and his
heart is crying out for the obdurate Blackfeet on
the wide southern plains and his Hermitage in the
foothills.

Edmonton, notwithstanding Father Lacombe's grumbling, was now a town of some life and aspiration. The extension of the railway from Calgary had put new energy into the frontier settlement. By the construction of this line the old stage route was thrown into disuse and the park-country of the north opened to settlement. As in the past Father Lacombe's information had largely assisted [1] the engineers selecting the route for the road and on its completion Van Horne sent a request to him for appropriate names for the new villages springing up along the line. Wetaskiwin, Ponoka, Otaskawan were among the names he gave, while others like Lacombe, Leduc and Hobbema were chosen by Sir William, who as a connoisseur in men and art at one stroke placed on the map of the west the names of two pioneers and an artist whose works he admired.

Despite his grumbling Father Lacombe soon grew accustomed to modern Edmonton. By Christmas he had put down some roots in his new abode. He was having a good rectory built; a hospital to be maintained by the Grey Nuns was under way, and

[1] ". . . The Company was indebted to him for very much useful information concerning the western prairies and the various mountain passes and his information was more exact and valuable than that of anybody else. He not only knew the country intimately but he had a wonderful faculty for describing it so that one could see it vividly. I remember well his description later on of the country between Calgary and Edmonton when the railway there was contemplated. This description left no exploratory work for the engineers to do—they knew just where the line should be laid."—Letter from Sir William Van Horne to the author, March 9, 1910.

he begins to be absorbed in new interests. There are no complaints or longings for the south. He has again made a place for himself in this Edmonton, which he knew before it was an Edmonton, but which with its strange faces he sorrowfully felt had small welcome for the old pioneer when he first returned.

In Christmas week he writes to Father Legal that he is now living in his new "palace." The Government has given him a telephone; the City has placed an electric light before his door. He surveys life with equanimity. Another of the Old Guard, he notes, has retired. After half a century of devoted work and subsistence on dried meat and fish and a meagre menu generally his old Superior of Lac Ste. Anne is enjoying the rest and physical comforts of St. Albert. Father Lacombe's nimble mind seizes on the facts and thus sums them up deliciously for Father Legal—

"Père Remas is in absolute retirement at St. Albert's, *like a rat in a cheese.*"

To Father Lacombe staying "for penance" at Edmonton "the great Question of the hour," as he now calls it, is to redeem the poorer class of Metis before it is too late. To this end he initiates a new work in which he will go and seek them in the highways and byways of the west. His voice must reach the dilapidated shacks on the outskirts of towns and villages and call thence those becoming morally, physically and financially, the lame, the halt and the weaklings of the west.

Then, he plans to turn to the discouraged and un-skilled half-breeds on poor farms, where they are endeavouring to stifle the blood's call for the gun and trap in order that they may accustom their hands to the ploughshare and make a decent living for the always numerous progeny.

From the one place and the other their old shep-herd, who had known and loved the Metis in their Golden Age, would now gather them into some fer-tile corner of the west, remote from the influence of white men, their liquor and their scorn. Instruc-tion in farming and the elementary trades will be given his Metis there, implements be provided for them: he will create a Metis Utopia!

This plan had been taking shape in his mind for some time, and during the past two years, he had repeatedly urged the Government at Ottawa to grant sufficient land for the purpose. The tre-mendous earnestness of the old missionary had its effect. Lord and Lady Aberdeen, who were now the vice-regal representatives in Canada and whose guest he was on each visit to the east, were early won to his belief in the plan. Sir Mackenzie Bowell listening one day to his ardent advocacy, ex-claimed:

"Your plan is an act of Christianity for you: for us it would be an act of patriotism."

Now in 1895 Father Lacombe resolved to make a supreme effort to realize his scheme. He wrote to Bishop Grandin:

"We, the old missionaries must not forget what we have done for the Metis and what they have done for us. For their fine attachment and devotion gives them a right to our affections still, notwithstanding the demoralization of a great number. Let me expend what physical force and energy remains to me in labouring for this undertaking with which God has inspired me, and in which I have faith. It seems to me that Providence has preserved to me, at my advanced age, such measure of health as I have simply that I may undertake and carry through this work which to others may appear impossible and absurd."

Bishop Grandin was doubtful of the result, but he could not withhold his consent to that plea, qualifying it, however, with a warning:

"Go, and may God bless your zeal, but remember if to-day is a Palm Sunday, there will soon be a Good Friday."

The warning fell on deaf ears: nothing could dampen Father Lacombe's ardour.

In February, 1895, he went east to St. Boniface for the consecration of Archbishop Langevin, the successor of Archbishop Tache, and from there to Ottawa. Here he received such encouragement in his plan that he felt justified in instructing two capable brethren, Father Therien and Father Morin, to go and look for a site for his colony in the vicinity of his old mission of St. Paul de Cris, north of the North Saskatchewan.

A letter to the Hon. A. C. La Riviere, M. P., written by Father Lacombe whilst journeying east, indicates how strongly he was preoccupied with his plans to uplift the Metis:

"ON THE SHORES OF LAKE SUPERIOR
"ON THE RAILWAY,
"19th February, 1895.

"*Very dear old friend:*

"Seated in a royal palace car of the Pacific, meditating on the things of the past—of the *Great* Past, and dreaming of what the future may have in store for us I am assailed by a thousand thoughts which flutter through my head like a flight of birds.

"I think of my benefactors so numerous and so generous, and I pray for them. I think especially of that King of the Canadian Pacific, Van Horne, my brother by adoption, who has done so much for our country and for our missionaries.

"But above all the souvenirs, happy and sad, of *le bon vieux temps*, above all my pre-occupation with the future, hovers one thought which little by little is absorbing my mind entirely. Now I wish to make of the realization of this idea —of this dream, as some may perhaps maliciously call it— the business of the remainder of my poor life as a missionary.

"The Latins said that they feared the man who read but one book. *Timeo hominem unius libri.* *Moi*, I have but one plan, one supreme plan and that is to secure to one unhappy race a place of peace and of sweet prosperity. . . ."

He refers then to letters enclosed, addressed to himself by some Metis—"naïve letters full of confidence," asking him to help them get a bit of land to farm. These he says, are but some of many letters received from Metis in Montana and the Canadian west; while a prominent westerner has just written asking him to look after other Metis who are in a very bad way.

Father Lacombe concluded his letter by telling Mr. La Riviere that there were at least 8,000 Metis in the west, most of them poor, many of them demoralized. They were undoubtedly in a bad way, but, their venerable advocate insisted that traders, missionaries, and the white race generally owed them a real debt for their diplomatic services with the Indians in the opening days of the white man's era. They were kind and grandly hospitable then—would the Government not be hospitable to these poor unfortunates now?

It was in this way Father Lacombe approached anyone and everyone who could possibly influence the Canadian Government to grant his request.

When he arrived in Ottawa he found the School Question in a fresh ferment. Archbishop Tache was dead, but the war he had planned went on. At last the Government understood that the Catholics of all Canada were supporting the western minority in their demand for a restoration of their schools, and realized the need of action.

Father Lacombe wrote in March to Father Legal:

"How big and hot this school question becomes. We have reached a most critical moment. Truly it is little reassuring. Our adversaries, obstinate enemies armed with falsehood, calumny and ruse, are achieving the impossible to obscure the question and gain their cause—which is that of Satan. What is going to happen in the face of such opposition? Is the Government going to resign? Will they hold a session? Or will they make an appeal to the electorate?"

Again:

"The School Question of Manitoba will not be settled for a good length of time. It is true that an Order-in-Council is going to be adopted, sent to the legislature of Manitoba and doubtless will be respected there.

"But when will this Remedial Ordinance be proclaimed law, if the parliament is dissolved and an appeal is made to the public? I have talked so much to-day that I am tired to death. . . ."

The Remedial Order was passed by the Council on March 21st, but to become effective it had still to make its way through Parliament.

Father Lacombe returned west in April, but the summer found him again in Ottawa together with the Mayor of Edmonton delegated to secure a bridge across the Saskatchewan at Edmonton. The railway terminated in the meadows across the river and as the directors would not incur the expense of a bridge to go into Edmonton, and the village grown up from the old trading-post would not move over the river to the railway, matters between the two stood at an *impasse*. An uncertain ferry solved the problem fairly at some seasons, but these circumstances naturally hampered the growth of Edmonton: while its towns-folk maintained a rebellious attitude toward the Government and railway company.

Various demands sent by them to Ottawa for relief were disregarded, for Edmonton's pioneers, a splendid group of Old-Timers, were more versed in Indian-trading and horse-racing than in diplomacy. Notably in 1893 they had defied a departmental order to move the Government Land Office across the river and after an exciting comic-opera insurrection with a Home-Guard, guns and Mounted Police in evidence—they brought the Ottawa Government to terms. All of which was soothing to local pride, but disastrous to the hope of Government grants.

Now in 1895 the Town Fathers conceived the idea that their one hope lay in this irresistible old missionary-diplomat, who had a few years before secured a grant from the Government for a bridge at Calgary. Father Lacombe acquiesced readily, and with the Mayor endeavoured not only to get the bridge, but also to have the Calgary and Edmonton line continued across the river.

In the discharge of his mission Father Lacombe interviewed the new Premier, Sir Mackenzie Bowell, Foster, Daly, Ouimet, Sir Charles Tupper, Sir William Van Horne, and William Whyte; and in relation to the Calgary and Edmonton he approached the leading stockholders in Toronto and Winnipeg.

He was readily granted the bridge. However, one member of the Government who had no personal cause for dislike of the Edmontonians of that day but who had an unqualified distaste for their methods

of doing parliamentary business, confided to Father
Lacombe that they were uncouth and buffoons.

The old priest kept the ministerial comment to
himself then, though it is likely that Edmonton with
its generous quota of western independence would
have cared little if it had heard the remark. The
bridge was soon built, and up to 1912 this monument
to Father Lacombe's diplomacy has had the distinction of serving Edmonton's needs alone.

During this visit east Father Lacombe also secured
a Government grant of four townships of land for
the Metis colony, and he returned home shortly after
with an enthusiasm and light-heartedness that
laughed at his sixty-eight years.

But his work for the Metis colony had only begun: he had still to secure funds for its operation.
By letters and personal visits on every trip he made
to the east for years thereafter the old missionary
was obliged to beg for money to help his Metis with
their buildings and purchase of farm implements.

The work was all the more difficult that people
generally believed the plan destined to fail.

Many of his brethren laughed at the plan. To
them it was hopeless to make the half-breed leave
the squalid splendor of the city's fringe for the
prosaic work on open fields at St. Paul de Metis.
Some papers, opposition organs, naturally attacked
the project as a misappropriation of Government
lands and assistance and occasionally referred bit-
terly to Father Lacombe.

It would be useless to say that he did not feel all this acutely—particularly the laughter of those of his friends who did not believe in the scheme, though they vowed they loved the old missionary for his great heart and mistaken zeal. He felt the hurt, but he was not in any way deterred. He believed . . . that was sufficient.

His next step was to issue a circular letter printed in French, English and Cree calling the poorer Metis to take shelter in his new colony. His letter in its solicitude for the welfare of the half-breeds reveals with what poignancy the old priest's mind dwelt on what might be called the tragedy of civilizing the Indian: the gradual degradation of this child-race— brought out of paganism by Christianity as taught —on coming into contact with Christianity as practised by the majority.

XIII

THE journey to Eastern Canada from which Father Lacombe returned in August was the second he had made within six months, yet once more at home his feet are "burning" to take him away again.

Each month finds him in a different quarter of Alberta, and at the New Year, 1896, he is in Ottawa again a minister plenipotentiary from the western Bishops to act in the school question. The moment was opportune, for general elections were approaching—and governments are proverbially impressionable before general elections.

He writes on January 9th:

"Very dear Father:

"Where are we now? To what point are we drifting? If you could look in on the trouble, the anxiety, and all that is passing at this moment in the city of Ottawa you would be astonished. The Conservative Government is falling to pieces. The question of the Manitoba Schools is more and more uncertain. Each day brings new fears.

"The newspapers have already told you of the embarrassment which exists. The Bowell Government is greatly weakened by the defection of several ministers and by the unfavourable results of bye-elections. . . .

"Sir Mackenzie Bowell, my friend, whom I regard as sincere and who is going to fall in defending us, is no longer

359

supported. Things are going badly. Laurier—what will he do when he arrives in power? For this is very probable, unless a re-organization takes place with the formation of a new cabinet by Tupper as leader and premier.

"For my part, I have no confidence in this arrangement. Since the Conservative party has come to this point and as our Catholic people show themselves so indifferent and so incapable—*C'est egal*—it is as well that the Liberals should come at once to take their place.

"How tired I am with all this bustle! All the same, notwithstanding my occupations and pre-occupations I do not forget you. I have seen about the schools. . . .

"This is very regrettable, but what would you have me do? The state of politics here does us an injury. My plans are all upset. This throws us back a year at least. . . . The day before yesterday I dined with Sir Mackenzie Bowell. Truly he is greatly disgusted with the state of affairs. I think that he will perhaps resign to-day.

"Attention. . . . *La*, the trouble will commence again —I tell you—greater than ever. I sigh for my Hermitage. Is it possible that those who pretend to be my friends plan only to separate me from it!"

A letter he wrote about this time to Wilfrid Laurier, the French-Canadian leader of the Opposition brought a lively squall about his sturdy self; but he was equal to meeting it. This letter which had been sent as a private communication to Laurier had been—possibly in the exigencies of politics—published in full and with unkind comment by *La Presse*, an active organ of the Liberal party in Quebec at that time.

The letter to Laurier reads:

"MONTREAL, January 20, 1896
"*Hon. Wilfrid Laurier, M.P., Ottawa:*

"MY DEAR SIR: At this critical moment for the School Question of Manitoba, permit an old missionary, to-day the representative of the Bishops of our country in this cause which absorbs the thoughts of everyone—permit me, I ask, to make an appeal to your faith, to your patriotism and to your sense of justice to beg you to comply with our request. It is in the name of our Bishops, of the Hierarchy and of Canadian Catholics that we demand of your party, of which you are the worthy leader, to aid us in settling this famous question, and to do this by voting with us for the Remedial Bill along with the Government.

"We do not ask you to vote for the Government, but for the Bill which will restore our rights, in the form in which it will be presented in a few days in the House. I consider, or rather we all consider, that this act of courage, of goodwill and of sincerity on your part and of those who follow your policy, will be greatly in the interests of your party, especially at the time of the general elections.

"I must add that we could not accept your proposition of a Commission for any consideration, and we shall do everything to oppose it. If, though may Heaven prevent this, you do not feel it your duty to meet our just demand and that the Government which desires to give us the promised legislation should be beaten and overturned, the while it stands true to the end of the fight, I must inform you with regret that the whole episcopate—as one man—united with the clergy will rise to support those who have fallen in defending us.

"I trust you may pardon my frankness, which makes me speak in this way.

"Although I am not an intimate friend of yours, I may say that we have always been on good terms. I have always regarded you as a gentleman, an honourable citizen and a clever man, qualified to be at the head of a political party. I trust that Providence may sustain your courage and your energy for the good of our country.

"I remain respectfully and very sincerely,

"Honourable Sir,

"Your devoted and humble servant,

"A. LACOMBE, O. M. I.

"P. S. Some members of your party reproach me for holding aloof from you and ignoring you. You have too much judgment not to understand my position. Having no political party myself I address myself to those who have been placed by the people at the head of affairs. If one day the voice of the nation calls you to the direction of public affairs, I shall be loyal to you and have confidence in you—as I am to-day to those who are opposing you.

"If you desire to see me and to have any further explanations I shall be at your service whenever it pleases you at the University of Ottawa or at your private office, provided that you inform me of the hour selected by you.

"I shall be at Ottawa on the 23rd to remain there for several days.

"A. L., O. M. I."

A despatch sent out from Ottawa to several Opposition journals on February 21, claimed that the significance of Father Lacombe's letter to Laurier was that "this old, respected and confiding and deceived missionary . . . has been used as an intermediary between the Dominion Government and the Quebec hierarchy." . . . The letter, it states, is a bold attempt on the part of the clerical forces to intimidate and coerce the leader of the Liberal party, whom they "threaten to destroy if he does not come to the support of the position taken by certain bishops who have mismanaged and bedevilled this subject from the start."

This despatch, designed like scores of others of this period to make political capital out of events, purports to be well-disposed to Father Lacombe. It is less flattering than direct attacks however in making the old "confiding and deceived missionary" out to be a simpleton and a tool. The writer ignores, or is ignorant of the fact, that the management of the School campaign from the start lay in the hands of the stateman-Archbishop of St. Boniface and his lieutenant and counsellor, Father Lacombe. And while an outcast, foot-sore and shiftless, could readily impose on the heart of the latter—no politician, lay or clerical, could ever deceive his mind.

Le Journal, an active organ of the Government party now as in duty bound in the political campaign published an editorial rebuking *La Presse* and those who inspired its comment, and proceeded to interpret Father Lacombe's letter in another way than the unpleasant one of *La Presse.* Whereupon Father Lacombe publicly voiced his thanks to the editor of the Journal, and this went to swell the tide of journalistic literature rising about the School Question and everyone engaged in the contest:

"I thank you for the interest which you take in me.   It is well; you explain the letter as it should be explained.   .   .   . Thank you.   I shall see you soon and I shall then give you certain information that will make those who have made an ill-use of this letter blush.

"Truly I regret that *La Presse* has forgotten itself in such a manner.   It harms itself more than me.   People will recognize that its zeal is a sham and this will only have the effect of damaging its arguments against 'the letter.'   .   .   .

"Since my friend, Mr. Laurier, is not more scrupulous than this, to take advantage of intimate communications sent him in the interests of the country's peace, to violate my confidence and exploit my views for his own benefit, by means of journals which live upon sensations: that is his affair.

"Those who cry out against an old missionary, who has every right and a definite commission to aid in the solution of this burning question of the schools, let them reflect a little and give me credit for my good intentions toward the Liberal chief to whom I only wish to do good.

"If *La Presse* had been a witness of my intimate interviews recently with a man whom I consider as a noble citizen and worthy of being the head of a party, this sheet would have expressed its zeal in another manner—How can people know how to write so well, yet to act in such a disgraceful manner!

"For your part, continue to defend our cause with courage. Say to those who read your articles and who will carry the word on to all my compatriots—that we will go right to the end.   We have decided to assist those who to-day have the power in their hands in order that justice may be done to us. Those who wish to make political capital out of this question, I disown them.   A solemn moment has arrived.

"To-day after five years of suffering on the part of an oppressed minority, which I am commissioned to defend, I make an appeal to all friends of Justice no matter to what party they belong, and I beg them in the name of patriotism and honour to fall into line on our side. Is it not simply this that I have done with Mr. Laurier and his supporters?

"Why then does *La Presse* in its zeal imply to me such false motives?

"It is not now the time to reply to that journal when it questions my standing with the Hierarchy. For the present let us only try to settle this question of the Manitoba Schools, and to this end let all intelligent minds lend their co-operation in what is an act of justice and patriotism.

"When this question is to be decided then may the nation recollect itself and prepare loyally and honourably to unite upon the field of combat, where once again people will give freely and conscientiously their votes for the party which should govern the country.

"As an old missionary accustomed to live among the savage tribes or ministering as a priest to the new settlers I am far from any desire to claim the skill of politicians. To my great regret, circumstances have thrown me into this atmosphere so foreign to my habits. Only obedience and duty can sustain me in the midst of these contradictions which I am encountering. . . ."

The attacks made by various papers upon Father Lacombe finally roused the *Montreal Witness,* a paper of much editorial weight in the nineties and one neither Conservative nor Catholic, to enter the lists and there break a lance for the old missionary— whose figure despite its inherent sturdiness presented a pathetic aspect as this storm of abuse broke around him in public and private.

Many of the Liberal party, who were raising the storm, probably did honestly believe that Father Lacombe or the Hierarchy behind him, was using the School Question as an instrument to aid the Conservative party in the approaching elections. In this, however, they did him an injustice. His one political dogma through life has been to uphold the party in power, to assist it in its administration—just so long as in his belief it was acting justly and in the interests of the people—as he saw the interests of the people. There was an official opposition to hackle and criticise the administration: his duty as a non-partisan was to uphold it.

When it was no longer able to serve the people or fit to govern it—then Red or Blue; Grit or Tory—he wanted to see its departure from office hastened and the new brooms set in motion. . . . and he would cry right heartily—"*Le Roi est mort: vive le Roi!*"

Nor was this mere opportunism in the old missionary. It was something nearer a high ideal of patriotism.

In 1896 he desired with all the ardour of his vigorous nature that the Conservatives should be returned to power, but simply because of their existing pledges to grant remedial legislation with regard to the School Question.

The tribute of the *Montreal Witness* of Febru-

ary 26th, 1896, first narrates the various services
which Father Lacombe had rendered the country as
an effective police-chaplain during the construction
of the first Canadian transcontinental road, and the
esteem in which he was held by prominent and discerning men in Eastern Canada.   It continues:

"Father Lacombe has done able and effectual missionary
work amongst the Indians, whose fruit is seen in the good
order which prevails amongst them, and the degree of civilization to which large numbers of them have attained.   Apart
from this aspect of his work, to which he has devoted himself
with much zeal, he has never been indifferent to the political
outlook.   He has always watched the trend of public affairs
with much interest, and it is undoubted that he has more than
once influenced legislation in directions which subserved the
interests of his Church as a whole.   He has always wielded
power at Ottawa.   Having laboured successfully to improve
Indians and keep them quiet, it has probably been felt that
the Government owed him some return.   At all events he has
always had the ear of those in power, nor have any of his
requests been denied.

"He is an able, far-seeing man, of keen intellect, and he
pursues his object, whatever it may be, with tireless but un-
obtrusive persistency.

"The Good Father has a store of reminiscences, which, if
printed, would make thrilling reading.   He has spent forty
years among the Indians, turning his back upon civilization,
and seen life in the wild in curious places.   When he comes
back to the asphalt and the corner policeman and finds himself
at the table of a friend, the genial missionary makes demands
upon the memory and tells story after story of pioneer life,

of Indian cunning and stoicism, and diplomacy triumphing
over force . . . of humor and pathos which is found in
all relations and associations of life.   Ordinarily he is reticent
and must be well assured that he can trust to honour before he
relaxes, but if the demand be made upon him in a happy moment the old missionary becomes a vivid dramatist, who en-
chants the hearers with the varied incidents of a fruitful experience."

On March 14th, Father Lacombe writes from
Montreal to Father Legal:

"I have just arrived, very tired, from Ottawa, where I have
a trying combat to sustain.   Who would credit it?   Here
am I, hurled into politics, exposed to many attacks of lies
and falsifying. . . .   Our Question of the schools is far
from being decided.   Our adversaries are making an infernal
opposition, especially the Liberals of Quebec who are hypo-
critically representing themselves as more Catholic than we
are.   It is unbelievable what people will attempt to get to
power."

This letter, like others of 1896, written to one of a
small group of very intimate friends, is significant
of Father Lacombe's real attitude on politics.   It
was a rather unusual outlook for one who had come
so much in contact with politicians.   For while he was
somewhat of a politician, he was nothing of a par-
tisan, but frankly the representative of the Indians,
the Metis and the Catholics of Western Canada.

He regarded the Government solely as the public
servant of the country rather than the opponents of

the "glorious Reform Party that had given Canada
Constitutional Government," or the upholders of the
equally "glorious Conservative Party that with a pro-
tective Tariff had made Canada."

Notwithstanding his attitude he found himself
literally embroiled in the last heated struggles of a
Government which was now—in a desperate hope to
save itself—willing to grant in their Remedial Bill
what the Catholics of Canada had demanded for five
years unavailingly. Several of the political leaders
had all the time professed their belief in the justice of
the minority's claims, although they did nothing to
secure them. . . . "Governments," as Sir John
Macdonald once remarked, "would always prefer to
do right if by doing so they could retain their seats
on the right side of the Treasury."

The proposed Remedial Bill was the direct if be-
lated result of the campaign instituted by the late
Archbishop. The Catholics of Canada had formed
themselves into a defensive fighting phalanx, the attack upon their schools having effected this, as it always has elsewhere and is quite certain to do at any
time.

They had effectual argument in living thousands
of Canadians educated in Separate Schools and who
were as broad-minded and as loyal citizens as any of
their countrymen and equally well-equipped to fill
their positions in life.

The party was enthusiastically led in this instance
by their bishops. Most of these prelates conformed

ordinarily to the understanding that a clergyman
should not in his public capacity use his clerical prestige to sway man to his private opinion on political
matters, however wise or legitimate his opinion as an
individual might be. In this instance, however,
where the conscience and religious life of a whole people were affected, they took sides squarely on the
question. They acted with as avowed a purpose as
in more recent years the non-Conformist clergymen
of Great Britain have come out in chapels and even
upon the hustings to combat the Education Act of
the Unionist party.

The Canadian prelates sent pastoral letters to the
parishes under their jurisdiction, calling on their people to support the Government which had promised
remedial legislation.

But the courage to apply even this remedy had
been achieved too late by the Conservatives. The
people of Quebec had lost faith in the sincerity of the
Government's intentions. Several very wise heads
in the clerical party believed the Remedial Bill was,
as one said, only a *"trompe d' oeil."*

Moreover, long before this Bill came in on the
eve of an appeal to the country, the opposition, led
by Wilfrid Laurier, the brilliant young French-
Canadian leader, had imbued the laity of Quebec and
many of the clergy with the belief that the Liberals
would make a more satisfactory restoration of the
Catholic Schools to the Western minority.

The choice then lay between the opposition's promises and the stop-gap policy of a dying Government —between Laurier and Tupper.

Quebec *en masse* called for Laurier, and a "solid Quebec" sways the balance of power this way or that. The end came on June 23, 1896. The Government went down in a most crushing defeat: Quebec, once roused, had done its work thoroughly. Ministers of the Crown saw themselves defeated there by mere striplings of politicians. Even the Liberals were astonished at the extent of their victory and the Conservatives had no words to describe it.

It was this School Question which had overthrown the Conservative Government after a reign of eighteen years, that brought the Liberal party back into power with its opportunity to be "more Catholic than the Bishops." In opposition it had shown the aspiring politicians' fatal facility for making promises. Once in power, however, with an equal facility for post-campaign inertia common to all governments, it gave only an unsatisfactory settlement, and left the Catholics more or less unpropitiated until [1] 1904.

[1] Then in the Autonomy Act, it again constitutionally pledged Canada to uphold the minority's educational rights in the new provinces of Alberta and Saskatchewan. This somewhat cleared the political atmosphere on the famous school question.

XIV

SHORTLY before Father Lacombe's departure from Ottawa a pleasant note from Lord Aberdeen invited him again to luncheon at Rideau Hall. This, with similar occasions that winter at the homes of other friends, marked for Father Lacombe the oasis in his journey through what he calls "an arid and burning wilderness of unpleasing politics."

In June he was "freed from this Edmonton." His old comrade Father Leduc was installed there "to the satisfaction of everyone and especially of me," Father Lacombe writes to his friend in a bright letter from Macleod as he stops over-night on his way to his Hermitage. He is travelling there "in a big rough farm-waggon like any ordinary man! Lo, what it means to be a Hermit." But he assures the other he has no regret for his "palace" at Edmonton or the fine horses and carriage he had there.

Was ever a Hermit more abruptly or more persistently thrown back into the world from his retreat? . . . On August 4th he is again in Macleod, called to Calgary by the serious illness of Bishop Grandin. The Bishop lies in the Calgary hospital pending the doctor's decision as to the need of going to Montreal. If he must go, Father Lacombe must take him. Poor Hermit! "I was already

372

seated in the solitude of my Hermitage and the programme of my repose was traced, when this unlucky telegram came. Am I then condemned to be always in motion?" he asks.

Two weeks later he is in Montreal with the bishop at the hospital.

On May 13, 1897, his friend, Father Legal, was appointed coadjutor to Bishop Grandin with right of succession.

The announcement was a source of genuine pleasure to Father Lacombe who had been expecting such an eventuality for years. He promptly sent the young bishop the mitre and breviary that had been given him as souvenirs of his dead friend Archbishop Tache, and in a letter of this date assures him he will continue to be "a faithful friend, a devoted missionary, to aid you in my humble position to carry the burden which they have placed on you." Thus simply this venerable counsellor of bishops slipped into his place as adviser and trusted friend of the new bishop.

All summer and autumn he spent at his Hermitage with occasional visits to Macleod and Calgary. From the latter place he writes on December 1st this pathetic little note:

"Just a word to tell you that it is very cold—and still colder. My kidney-trouble seems a little better, but to offset that I have a frenzied cold in my head which torments me cruelly—Look you, *I am old.*"

He was then but two months away from his

seventy-second birthday, and like most of the Oblates
who had so generously worn themselves out in the
painful and exacting mission work of the west, he
had not escaped bodily ills.

For close on to twenty years he had suffered from
disorders of his kidneys and bladder, and at times
he was seriously and painfully ill because of these
ailments. Yet he was still obliged to do his share
of parochial work. The influx of new settlers into
the west calling for new parishes, together with the
needs of the Indian missions and schools, made it
almost impossible for the Bishop of St. Albert to
release any man from his post.

Added to his failing health is a rather constant
care self-imposed by his work for the Metis at his
colony. He had secured as resident superintendent
Father Therien, a priest of admirable executive ability and tact, but the latter had his hands well-filled
with the administration of the colony and efforts to
locate the unsettled and unlikely-to-settle Metis: he
could give little time to help secure a revenue.

The burden of financing consequently fell upon
Father Lacombe alone.

His friends had been very generous to his appeals
for funds, but there was necessarily a great deal of
money required by a plan that comprised a chapel, a
residence, a boarding school, a flour and saw mill,
implements, cattle and horses for the Metis and other
assistance to them from time to time.

The colony had now been formed three years and

in view of the aid already given the Government
sent an official to make a full report upon the conditions of the colony, its finances, and administra-
tions: likewise with regard to the proposed school for
which Father Lacombe was then seeking assistance.
Lord Aberdeen commented in writing upon the Report when submitted to him:

"It is with much pleasure that I signed this Report, and I
take this opportunity of offering cordial good wishes for the
success of the scheme which has been devised with so much
warm-hearted earnestness and practical sagacity by my friend,
Father Lacombe."

Mr. Ruttan's report is very favourable throughout. "It is wonderful," he states in one place, "what
has been done with so little money."

Encouraged by Lord Aberdeen to seek further assistance in the east Father Lacombe left Calgary
toward the end of 1898, and early in the following
year he reports to his friend at St. Albert generous
gifts from Lord Strathcona, James Ross and others.
Apart from these he found little practical sympathy
for the Metis, and his entire general collections
amounted to only $1,000.

On this visit to Ottawa Father Lacombe had met
Lady Minto, the wife of the new Governor-General,
and although he formed no deep friendship with this
vice-regal pair as he had with his whole-hearted
friends, the Aberdeens, their relations would seem to
have been of a pleasant nature, for Lady Minto in

April conveys to him a portrait of Queen Victoria sent to Father Lacombe by the Queen with a letter from her daughter.

This gracious remembrance was deeply pleasing to the loyal old missionary, who had frequently spoken to his Indians of the virtues and power of the great Queen Mother across the seas.   It brought him, too, the renewal of a charming acquaintance with the Abbe de Bie, then Abbot of Bornheim Abbey in Belgium, but in the early seventies secretary of Monsignor Smeulders, the Papal Legate to Canada.

This pleasant letter, written in French like almost all of Father Lacombe's correspondence, reads:

"ABBAYE DE BORNHEIM, May 11, 1899.
"*Rev. Father and Friend:*

"*Voila,* my dear Reverend Father, what a fit of jealousy seizes me!   I have just read in a Brussels daily: 'The Rev. Father Lacombe, the valiant missionary of the northwest, at present in Montreal working in the interests of his beloved missions has received from Queen Victoria the portrait of Her Majesty sent by herself and accompanied by a letter written by the Princess Beatrice, in which she says: "The Queen is deeply interested in what has been told her about Father Lacombe and has agreed with pleasure to your suggestion to send him her portrait.   .   .   ." ' "

" '*Tiens!*' I said to myself, 'I am very glad that the Queen of England feels such an interest in Father Lacombe and sends him her portrait, but how can she feel as much interest in him as you, who lived some time with him in Montreal— you who have received from him so many marks of friendship and fraternal affection?'

"My project was quickly made—knowing you to be in Montreal, I hasten to write you a little letter accompanying it, too, with my portrait as your gracious Sovereign has done. Without doubt this will be much less honour for you (and if all those who are interested in you should send you their portraits you would have enough to decorate all the palaces of the Saskatchewan), but at least I hope that it will not be disagreeable to hear a word again from your friend, the little secretary of the late Monsignor Smeulders, the Apostolic Delegate to Canada.

"D. Amedee de Bie."

   .   .   .   .

The movement of the gold-seekers north from Edmonton in 1898—or, as it is known in western history, the year of the Klondyke rush—had not only brought Edmonton into the eyes of the continent and given it a first impulse toward becoming a great inland city—but it had brought the whole north country before the consideration of the Government.

Since a find of minerals was liable at any time to send a rush of other and more permanent settlers there, it became necessary for the Government to get some control of the Crees, Chipewyans and Beavers in the Athabasca and Peace River countries. It was consequently decided to send a party of Commissioners in there to bring these tribes into treaty relations with the Government.

The committee of the Privy Council appointed by His Excellency to consider this matter reported on May 3rd, 1899, that the Superintendent-General of

Indian Affairs had reason to believe there would be trouble in negotiating the Treaty with the Indians of Athabasca district and dealing with the claims of the half-breeds, as the Indians were suspicious of white men entering their country and the Metis likely to be dissatisfied with the measure of recognition given to their claims. The Committee moreover were handicapped by the meagre knowledge that the Department could furnish them concerning these Indians. . . .

These considerations led the Committee to the belief:

"That it would be desirable if the Commissioners could have the assistance and counsel of the Very Reverend Father Lacombe. Father Lacombe has been so long in the country as a missionary, knows the Indians and half-breeds so intimately and possesses their confidence in so marked a degree that he would be able to render most valuable and effective assistance to the Commissioners in their difficult mission."

In view of this Report the Hon. Mr. Sifton, Minister of the Interior, called upon the old missionary and requested him to give his services to the Government in this connection, to urge the Indians and half-breeds to make the Treaty peaceably. Although decidedly pleased at the compliment conveyed by the offer, Father Lacombe refused to go.

"It is too much for me," he said to the Minister, "I am too old to travel hundreds of miles in little boats, and I will only bother your people to take care of me if I fall sick. Try to find somebody else."

"No, we want you," Mr. Sifton persisted. "You will have everything at your disposal to make the trip comfortable."

The Prime Minister also added his persuasions.

"Bien," Father Lacombe said finally, "Telegraph to Bishop Grandin. If he orders me to go, I will go."

When the proposed Treaty was under discussion in the House of Commons in June of this year the Minister of the Interior said:

"Along with this Commission we have asked the Reverend Father Lacombe to go, not as a member of the Commission, but in an advisory capacity. Everyone who has lived in the northwest for the last fifteen or twenty years, Protestant and Catholic, knows well that there is no man in the northwest looked upon by the Indians with the same reverence and affection as Father Lacombe." [1]

"Hear! Hear!" interjected Nicholas Flood Davin, the brilliant, genial member from Regina, calling out from his seat on the Opposition benches.

On May 11, Father Lacombe wrote from Montreal to Bishop Legal—"I have decided to accept the offer of going on that Commission. Pray for your old missionary. It is finished. There is no more repose for me. May the good Saviour have pity on me!" Again he writes, "This is doubtless the last service I will render our Congregation and my country—As God wills!"

[1] Debates, H. of C., 1899, Vol. 1, p. 5694.

The party left Edmonton on May 29th, driving
in heavy stage-waggons and escorted by eleven
Mounted Police, among whom was Fitzgerald of
heroic memory.   At Athabasca Landing, then a tiny
hamlet dotting the water-front, the party crossed the
border-land into the wilderness.   From here to the
settlement on Lesser Slave Lake they travelled in
open scows, tenting by night.

Father Lacombe and the physician of the party
shared one tent, the younger man always finely solic-
itous for the comfort and health of his venerable companion.   As the journey lengthened, however,
Father Lacombe to his extreme delight found that
his health was improving: he felt himself renewing
the days of his prime, and again proclaimed the woods
an anodyne.

He had brought a light portable chapel with him,
which was easily converted into an altar, and some
mornings he celebrated Mass in his tent with Commissioner McKenna as his acolyte and the half-breed
trackers as a congregation.

From Bishop Grouard of Fort Chipewyan, who
was returning from Europe and had joined the party
at the Landing, Ex-Governor Laird, President of
the Commission, learned that June 13th would be the
fiftieth anniversary of Father Lacombe's priesthood.
The entire party, like a group of boys before Christmas, thereupon planned a celebration to surprise their
old travelling companion.   They succeeded:

"It was on the eve of my feast that they did celebrate it," he recalls. "That dear old man, the Governor, he was at the bottom of it, I know. . . . Well, that night at a fine open place where the Saulteau river meets the Little Slave—a fine place with the green forests on each side—the Governor called out the word to camp. It was early; I was surprised that we camp so early, for we were in a hurry to meet the Indians as we promise.

"While the rest—they pitched camp, I walked off with my breviary. When I came back I see everything in fine order—and a flag-pole up with a flag flying. But I did not guess anything then.

"I was sitting in my tent in a little while, looking out on the river—Oh, that was fine—*pœtique* —to look on! . . . And suddenly the Governor he came to my tent and ask to come in. . . ."

The whole party came behind Mr. Laird with an address and a poem inscribed on birch bark, and after the speeches a banquet was spread on the grass.

"Next morning the bishop and I said Mass, that good old bishop serving mine. The door of the tent was wide open, and many knelt on the grass outside. After Mass we pitched our tents and started for the Lake. . . . Ah, that was a pleasant day —fifty years from the day the old Bishop Bourget ordained me for the missions of the west."

Reaching Lesser Slave Lake settlement [1] on June

[1] Now named Grouard in honour of one of the most delightful of ecclesiastics, the venerable Bishop of Athabasca.

19th, they found the Indians awaiting them in hundreds of tepees on the fine open meadow-lands.

These Indians, among the most advanced in the north, entered into the Treaty willingly enough after much parleying by the Chiefs Moostoos and Kenooshayoo with Mr. Laird and Father Lacombe. The concluding speech was made by the old missionary who, notwithstanding his little contact with the Northern Crees, was known to several of these Indians personally and to all of them by fame. On the following day the documents were signed and the annuity-payments began.

The Metis had to be dealt with next and this proved a more difficult task. Their chief speaker declared that he and his people did not want the Government's money in exchange for their land: they wanted to be left undisturbed in their own country. This with much more in a disaffected strain was only a preliminary to their objection to non-negotiable script being paid them as the Government proposed.

The intention this year was to make half-breed scrip non-transferable, to save the unwary half-breed from speculators. This was a condition that Father Lacombe together with other friends of the Metis had been particularly anxious should be attached, and he now made an ardent and impressive speech to the half-breeds urging them to safeguard their own and their children's interests by accepting it. He recalled with indignation the way in which the half-breeds of the plains had been parted from their scrip lands by greedy and often unscrupulous speculators.

Here again the half-breeds clamoured for the right to do as they pleased with their scrip—to sell it or not as they chose. They insisted upon this point being ceded; their alternative was a refusal to enter into any negotiations with the Government. The motley gathering of white traders and scrip-hunters who had camped on their trail were perhaps not without influence upon the half-breed leaders in maintaining this attitude.

That night a Council was held by the officials of the Treaty party and Father Lacombe, when it was regretfully decided that the scrip should be distributed in the old way with no conditions attached. It was essential that there should be no failure to negotiate with this insurgent group of Metis or they would grow disaffected and rouse other Indians against the Treaty.

In the House of Commons in 1900 fault being found with the Government for this action, Sir Wilfrid Laurier informed the House that when Commissioner Laird and Father Lacombe found the half-breeds would not take the new non-negotiable scrip they had been obliged to issue the old form. "There is no man," he added, "who has taken a stronger view than Father Lacombe against the excesses resulting from issuing scrip or who saw less benefit in its results to the half-breed. But in view of the de-

termined attitude of the half-breeds . . ." no
other course was open to them.

With the treaty-making past the party pushed on
to the north.   Some days later Father Lacombe
wrote to his friend from the banks of the Peace saying he had wanted to tell him about their journey
on the ninety miles of Peace River Trail, but concluded he had no words to describe it.   The road
was obstructed by stumps, by swamps, by creeks
swollen with the rains—and "all this in the middle of
a forest so black and high that we scarcely knew there
was a sun.   The rain went with us during the first
five days.   Clouds of mosquitoes and flies followed us,
fighting for more blood. . . ."

These last were what he called the little amiabil-
ities of the journey.   But he rather enjoyed the experience on the whole, for—

"All these difficulties of the voyage bring me back to my
old days—the superb airs, this battle with the elements, makes
me forget that I carry with me seventy-two years, and per-
suade me that I am not made for the luxuries of fine civilization."

On the sixth day the party emerged from the forest-trail to the superb open landscape of Peace River
Crossing, and in its tranquil beauty forgot their
trials.   Here again, and later at old Fort Dunvegan the scenes of Lesser Slave Lake were repeated.

At the Crossing as at the Lake Father Lacombe
saw a prosperous mission—a farm, a church and a

large school where thirty years before he had seen only a beautiful wilderness. In a letter written to Bishop Legal he assures him—that while the latter is probably supplicating Heaven for the *voyageur,* he may be easy in his mind about the old man, as he would not exchange his journey for all the feasts of the greatest *gros bonnets* he knows. His proper sphere is still, he claims, at the end of his days to be with the Indians and half-breeds. . . . "It is so my destiny is written."

From the Crossing to Fort Vermilion they continued their journey in open scows, drifting easily down stream by day and night. It was pleasant travelling, but at night Father Lacombe lay awake "to watch the mountains, the trees, the river. To me they were like phantoms."

From Fort Vermilion the party floated pleasantly down in open scows between banks that had witnessed hot scenes of rivalry in the old days of opposing fur-companies. After several days the entrance to Lake Athabasca was reached. The boatmen planned to camp here for the night, as the wind was very high; but across the neck of the lake the travellers could see the white sides of Fort Chipewyan gleaming like gypsum walls in the moonlight, and on the shore a hugh bonfire had been lit to greet them.

It beckoned warmly, and Commissioners and half-breeds alike said—"We will go!"

A small fire was lit in the prow of the leading scow, and all were pulled out from the still silver current of the Quatres-Fourches, leaping ahead to hospitable old Chipewyan.

"It was witching that night, when we reached the mission at eleven o'clock," Father Lacombe wrote to his friend.

As the boats beached at the mission landing-place the entire population of the mission-colony was grouped about a large bonfire on the shore, while the banks behind overflowed with hundreds of the Christian Indians of the Chipewyan tribe. They had assembled for the Treaty, but for the moment were intent only on welcoming home Bishop Grouard, the gentle prelate who had grown white in their service.

XV

Father Lacombe found Chipewyan rich in associations of Mackenzie and Simpson and Franklin and many another of the north's great explorers and traders. This Fort had been made the Athabasca headquarters in the days of warfare and loot among the rival fur-companies, and was consequently over a century old.

The Master of the Post extended to the travellers the traditional welcome of the Gentlemen Adventurers. There was an atmosphere of the Past clinging to the place: clerks moved leisurely about their duties; train-dogs swarmed within the quadrangle; the bell for rations swung near the main gate. But the bastions, the guns and sentinel tower were gone; the great gates no longer clanged shut at night— and no sentry kept watch from the tower or paced a gallery within the palisade.

When free from his duties with the treaty party Father Lacombe spent his time at the Mission, eagerly absorbing tales of his brethren—Grouard and Faraud. The mission had been established by Tache in 1848 and the field had proved as full of privations as of interest. But since the days of

387

Alexander Mackenzie the very austerity of the rocky place seemed to have endeared it to men who were strong-hearted enough to live there.

The treaty party now proceeded up the Athabasca to Fort McMurray by the Company's steamer Grahame, which was crowded with returning gold-seekers. All along their route the Commissioners had met small parties of these disconsolate mortals homeward bound: they heard of others who had set out over "the Trail of Death"—the overland route from Edmonton through the Swan Hills—and who would never return.

Here on the Grahame they felt overwhelmed with the tales of disaster from men who had pushed past the Mounted Police pickets the previous year, certain that they were on the rosy way to Fortune.

On the Fort McMurray meadows at the base of a spruce-covered mount the Indian bands, mixed Cree and Chipewyan, were encamped. These were also brought into harmonious conformity with Canadian institutions by means of the usual ceremony and payments.

The tents of the Commissioners were pitched on the meadows beside the trading-post. One night a furious storm of wind and rain came on: the wind picked Father Lacombe's tent up from its fastenings and left him exposed to the downpour. Hastily collecting his blankets and effects he ran for shelter to another tent, and notwithstanding his age felt no ill-effects from the drenching.

From McMurray the party spent several days travelling in open scows drawn through the rapids by trackmen, and early in September they arrived in Edmonton.

Treaty No. 8 had become a matter of history.

Father Lacombe announced his return in a letter of September 8th. He was well—not even fatigued; and he comments gaily:

"They cannot kill me—neither bishops nor Governments."

Shortly after his return to civilization Father Lacombe received a letter from the north that brought him again into relations with the Indians of the North Country.

Father Falher wrote reminding him that three Indians, accused of murder and taken out from Lesser Slave Lake shortly after the arrival of the treaty party there, were now in prison at Edmonton or Fort Saskatchewan.

They had been snatched up out of their tepees and woods to be deposited between the bars and timbers of a Mounted Police guard-room hundreds of miles away. They had scarcely understood there was a white man's law, until they found themselves like animals in a cage, dumbly wondering at the cause of their own misery.

The northern priest recalled the circumstances of the case and begged Father Lacombe in the name of all the Crees of that district to secure some leniency for these men by explaining to the whites the old be-

lief of the Crees concerning the *Witigo*. The circumstances were unusual.

The Pheasant, a Lesser Slave Lake Indian, had
suddenly lost his reason and run amuck in the camp
threatening to kill and eat whoever crossed his path.
This had happened before—and the Crees held the
old tribal belief that this man was possessed of a can-
nibal spirit which prompted him to destroy his own
kind. They first tried traditional remedies, by im-
mersing him in boiling water and in other ways endeavouring to melt the icy spirit possessing him—
but the *Witigo* persisted in his madness and his
threats.

Then solemnly as for an execution they prepared
to kill The Pheasant. One struck him with his axe;
as The Pheasant dashed away another fell on him,
then another—and when dead they cut him open to let
the Evil Spirit escape. This done they returned
calmly to their daily life, the tribe feeling free to
breathe again with the man-killer dead.

Father Falher reminded Father Lacombe of his
own knowledge of similar cases before the Crees were
Christianized. He noted further that the first axe-
stroke was inflicted on The Pheasant by a man who
had only been converted from paganism two years
earlier. The letter was eloquent in its very simplic-
ity:

"I address myself to you, my dear Father, because I
know that you love our Indians. . . . For my part I
love them only the more when I see them in trouble.

"I would have you go and visit them that you may console them a little, and even defend them if possible, pleading the extenuating circumstances of the case. You especially who understand the Indian and his superstitions can easily explain this to the whites, who would not otherwise be able to understand the case they are going to judge."

Father Lacombe made the visits as requested to the unfortunate Crees, consoled them in their cells, took up their case with the authorities, and had the satisfaction of seeing all three released after their trial. They returned very gladly to their homes and since then have been exemplary Indians, carefully avoiding collision with the Police and the white man's laws.

The fiftieth anniversary of his priesthood had been celebrated on the banks of the Little Slave River, but his friends would not let that suffice. Consequently on September 25 St. Albert was *en fete* in honour of its founder. Bishop Grandin and his coadjutor had planned a celebration worthy of the old missionary.

Indians and half-breeds came long distances to camp about the Cathedral and assist at this triumph of their old friend. Priests gathered from every portion of the diocese; Archbishop Langevin and Bishop Dontenwill, the brilliant young incumbent of New Westminster, had come to honour the jubilarian.

There was a solemn religious service, followed by a banquet and on the concluding night a shower of fireworks was employed to delight the Indian visitors.

The memorable feature of the celebration was a toast proposed to the Man-of-the-Beautiful-Mind, the Man-of-the-Good-Heart—Albert Lacombe—by his old comrade-in-arms, the Bishop of St. Albert.

It was during this address that Father Lacombe received the name by which he is now known to his friends on two continents—the *Datur-omnibus.*

The Bishop, who was as visibly happy in the celebration as his guest of honour, rose to propose the toast:

"When I was at Rome," he said, "in 1869 we met there a vehicle on which was written these words: *Datur-omnibus.* I enquired the meaning of the inscription, and was told that this carriage wended its way from end to end of Rome wherever trouble was; and if anyone, innocent or guilty, was pursued or in danger he could take refuge there.

"The driver was instructed to take the refugee to some safe place, where he might await in peace the decision upon his case. This was a custom years ago, when the Pope was King of Rome.

"*Eh, bien,* let me apply the phrase to our dear Father Lacombe—*Datur-omnibus!* It is thirty-eight years since he came here accompanying the lamented Archbishop Tache. The latter marvelling at the beauty of the site decided to establish a mission on this hill and dedicated it to the patron-saint of Father Lacombe.

"And he, who is still with us, set himself to this new task laying the foundations of the mission which has flourished so remarkably, and is now even an episcopal see.

"He has not only worked for this diocese, but for the whole ecclesiastical province of St. Boniface. Had anyone need of an intermediary—one to deal with the Government or the Canadian Pacific Company, or a man for any other important mission—they asked me for Father Lacombe. . . .

"More than once I have heard this comment, 'How is it that Father Lacombe is not a Bishop?'

"This thing, my friends seems to me very easy to understand. Apart from the fact that those who are deserving of the office cannot all be bishops—or we would all be bishops here—it must not be forgotten that the Creator forms special men for special missions. The Bishop is charged with the administration of one portion of the Church—or, if you wish, a particular Church to which he must devote himself entirely.

"But Father Lacombe has been in some sense the universal man—*Datur-omnibus*. If he had been a bishop he could not have been this; he could not for instance have performed for the Government the service which it requested of him quite recently in going to facilitate the proceedings of a treaty which it desired to make with the Metis and Indians of the Peace and Athabasca Rivers—without mentioning the numerous other missions which he has accomplished during his fifty years of priesthood in Manitoba, in the Northwest and, I may say, in all Canada.

"God, who directs all with wisdom, has willed that he should be free, that he should lend himself to all and for all. *Datur-omnibus!*"

The remainder of the year 1899 was spent by Father Lacombe in Southern Alberta, with brief visits to Edmonton and Hobbema. He was invited to the latter point by the Indians themselves to settle difficulties concerning the schools. A few days earlier he had been summoned by telegraph to the Piegan Reserve, where the dissatisfied Indians were raising a disturbance about the size of their rations.

He feels himself the shuttle-cock of circumstances, and he rebels against it to Bishop Legal:

"If this continues, when shall I ever have repose or tranquillity? And they want me to write my *Memoirs!* . . . Don't you consider this a farce?"

Nevertheless his sense of obedience, which as certainly as his genuine piety underlay the little vanities of his words and the activities of his latter days— urged him to attempt the Memoirs. On November 12, in the little rambling rectory at Calgary which had grown room by room around the original log-cabin, we find him arranging one apartment "with light and quiet," in which to write his Memoirs.

He plans these in the form of letters to his benefactors M. and Mdme. Forest; but because of his advancing years, no less than the fear that it was then too late to acquire the writer's *metier*, he was very unwilling to undertake the work. He was also reluctant to turn himself away from humanity and

its irresistible appeals, and bury himself in a room
with dead paper and ink—

On December 4th, he writes:

"At last I have begun to write my Memoirs. That appears absurd to me. But, 'One obeys or one does not obey'
. . . Then I obey. That in itself is something."

He sets himself to work now with what will he
can call up, and the result of the next two months
and stray moments in the next year or two resulted in
filling five or six notebooks with a mass of formal
discursive writing. This contained a brief and incomplete outline of his life up to 1864, and is blended
with numerous lengthy reflections of a pious
nature.

With the terror of producing a book always hanging over him he dropped the charmingly natural
style of his letters. Here and there his broken narrative lightens to a fine bit of descriptive writing—
and these portions have been quoted in the earlier
part of this work.

Father Lacombe did not give undivided attention
to his uncongenial task, however; his letters to Bishop
Legal now are filled with plans and suggestions concerning diocesan affairs and the half-breed colony at
St. Paul. The attempt at concentration upon his
early days and labours apparently only spurred him
to renewed activity upon what still remains to be
done.

"I perceive," he declares with unconscious naïvete,

"that in writing these Memoirs I find a grand opportunity of forming new plans."

But he is not left alone with his memories. His friends in Eastern Canada availed themselves of the Christmas season to send him presents for his Jubilee year: presents, which like everything else detachable that his long life had brought him, were speedily distributed among the different missions.

"In Prussia," he writes to his friend, "there are Bishops who are princes because of their episcopal position. In our northwest there are Curés who are princes, because of the kind favor of circumstances."

He might have said—Curés who are princes because of their unique and royal personality.

A year earlier Father Lacombe had written of his position as adviser to the treaty commission: "It will be the last service I shall render my Order or my country. As God wills."

He could now add a postscript to that; another mission was beckoning to him.

This had to do with the newest Canadians, the inrushing tide of European peasant settlers drawn by the free farms of the west. Of these the Ruthenians probably outnumbered any other nationality. They were a good thrifty class of Slavs, whose industry on northwest homesteads recommended them as future citizens.

Practically all of these were Greek Catholics in full adherence to Rome and the Pontiff there, although in the form of their ceremonials they followed the Ruthenian rite and their services were conducted in their own language. They consequently found themselves in a country without spiritual directors of their own language and rite, suddenly transplanted from the surveillance of a too-paternal feudal Government to a new land of few restraints—to freedom in such large measure that it was intoxicating and apt to be unwisely used. The transplanted Slavs were now more than ever in need of moral guidance.

Prosletysing forces at work in their ranks were producing a religious indifference and scepticism which Father Lacombe and his confreres viewed with indignation and alarm. It was felt that an appeal for Ruthenian Catholic priests and funds to support them must be made to Rome and to Austria. Father Lacombe in accordance with his mission of *Datur-omnibus* was selected as the most suitable ambassador.

So the opening of the Twentieth century finds the aged hermit of the foothills still pursuing meditations chosen a decade earlier to fit him for the next world—but weighing them as he waited in ante-chambers of the Papal and Austrian courts, and amid a whirl of journeying that brought him from France to Italy—to Germany, Austria, Belgium and back again to France.

He sailed from Halifax on March 29, and on Easter Monday was at Viarmes where three Curés spent the evening with him and, he said, made him talk so much that he was utterly fatigued and had

an attack of indigestion from it.   This is the only
indication in any of his letters of how great a tax was
made upon his nervous force by the hours of causerie
which his European acquaintances demanded.

In one of his Paris letters there is a living breath
from the tomb of Tarte, that brilliant likeable but
whimsical political genius, who bequeathed to the Canadian world of politics the "Business is business"
maxim—as well as the frank epigram—"Elections
are not won by prayers alone."

On April 29th Father Lacombe dined at the
residence of the Austrian Commissioner with the Hon.
Mr. Tarte, who was then Canada's representative at
the Paris Exposition.   Tarte was on the point of
leaving for London to attend a banquet to be presided over by the Prince of Wales, and which had
been arranged in connection with the Colonial con-
tingents supplied for the Boer War.

"Poor Tarte," his fellow-Canadian comments in one letter, "how is he going to draw himself out of the embarrassing
position, since he must speak—he who was so opposed in Canada to the sending of the troops.   He only said when I made
these remarks to him: 'Wait, I am going to play with those
Englishmen.' "

"I feel rather indisposed," he jots in his diary at
Rome on June 15.   "The extreme heat has begun
—but *bon courage!*—for the old man!"

Only once during the entire trip does the note-
book record a restful day: *"Je me repose,"* is all
he writes that day.

Cardinal Satolli and his colleagues, Rampolla Ledochowski and Orelia, were in turn besieged by the venerable Canadian pilgrim anxious to forward with them his plea for the Ruthenian Catholics in Canada.

In July he was back in Paris and Brittany. Whilst in Paris he was actively at work helping the young Canadian colony there to secure a chapel. Thence his itinerary led him to Anvers and Brussels on matters pertaining to Belgium emigration to Canada—to Cologne, Hunfeld and Munich—everywhere delivering lectures to colleges of students or priests, always seeking new recruits for the missions, new funds for their upkeep.

His letters of this period contain numerous snatches of Latin, owing to the fact that this was his one means of conversing with many of his hosts in Austria and Germany. His other lingual accomplishments—his French and Cree, Saulteau and Blackfoot, and what he calls his "good English of the Nor'-West"—avail him nothing.

One letter tells its own story of little economies. His journey—pending a decision from Rome upon the Austrian enterprise—had been unexpectedly prolonged, and his funds are limited. He writes to Bishop Legal:

"To make the most of my purse I travel third class and I eat crusts. The third class cars are not as uncomfortable as they were some years ago. . . . Do not be afraid for my travelling expenses. That is my affair. I shall manage, as always in the past, so that neither you nor any one of the others will have anything to pay until my return to St. Albert."

He evidently finds the means to travel further, for his next letter under date of September 9th, is from a Franciscan monastery at Vienna:

"What are you thinking as you look on the address of this letter? How much I have to tell you, and through you to our venerable Bishop and missionaries. Truly I do not know where to begin—I have been busy with so many things. But now, the old missionary in Austria! . . . It is very true that I devour distances, as you say. . . . I intend to see the Emperor and the Premier. What audacity on my part! . . . I speak Latin like a tutor, when they do not understand me otherwise. . . ."

After a lengthy postscript concerning his plans of work and travel he concludes archly—

"*Enfin*, is this not enough for to-day? I kiss your hand —that is the fashion here. What a country! What people! A. L."

He has at last reached the Austrian government, and is endeavouring to have their co-operation in his mission to Europe. He had several interviews with the Premier, M. Golowkowski, whom he described as "a handsome amiable man who spoke French, and in whose office I feel perfectly at home."

He assures Bishop Legal that since he has come in direct communication with the Government—"I am as much at ease with them as I am with my own

at Ottawa." . . . "The ministers and deputies,"
he writes, "all speak French.

"The Minister of Foreign Affairs, a Pole, has been very
amiable and interests himself greatly in our question of Ruthenians and Galicians."

He now decided to make a personal visit to the
Province of Galicia from which the Ruthenians had
emigrated. The Austrian Government, which
through its ambassador at Rome had been interested
in Father Lacombe and his mission, defrayed the
expenses of his journey; likewise those of the Mother
Provincial of the Franciscan Nuns and a companion-
sister.

The former, a brilliant and zealous woman and a
member of one of the leading families of Austria,
had promised Father Lacombe to secure in Galicia
several nuns for orphanages in Canada. She was
also to act as his interpreter and, to some degree by
her family influence, as his advocate.

He departed for Lemberg, armed with letters to
the Galician government and Bishop Szeptickyi of
Stanislaus, the latter a warm personal friend of the
Pope. At Leopoli, Stanislaus, Pryzenyls he was always the guest of his brethren, the Ruthenian ecclesiastics, and most cordially welcomed by them.

He made the best possible use of his time and opportunities, and returned from his mission successful in
everything he sought.

XVI

On his return to Vienna Father Lacombe received a command to the Court. The impressively large packet containing the invitation was addressed to the

REV. ALBERTUS LACOMBE,
Vicar-General of Canada.

In it His Majesty the Emperor summoned the old missionary to an audience on the following morning.

Father Lacombe was then the guest of the Countess Melanie Zichy (née Princesse Metternich). His hostess thoughtfully prepared him for possible disappointment in his audience.

"You will see in our Emperor a man of sorrows," she told him. "It is written in his face. He never laughs and rarely talks. The mile-stones of his life have been made of grief—the last was the assassination of his wife, the Empress."

The next morning, when the carriage came around to convey him to the Imperial Palace the Countess with filial tenderness looked the old missionary over with anxious eyes to see that he was fittingly garbed to meet the Emperor. The scrutiny was satisfactory. Even then at seventy-four the habitual and rather notable neatness of the old priest had not deserted him.

But a thought suddenly and very naturally flashed to the mind of a lady of the court. . . . "This old Canadian priest is distinguished in his Canada. —Where are his decorations?" She voiced her solicitude.

The old priest smiled. . . . In Canada who had ever thought of conferring orders or decorations upon an old missionary?

Then flashing suddenly from gay to wistful—as was his wont—he pulled the wooden and brass cross of the Oblate Order from his sash. It was the crucifix with which he had times innumerable blessed his Indian proteges. It was the same he had upheld to invoke peace that memorable dawn between the warring Crees and Blackfeet:

"Hah!" he said smiling gravely, "with this I have been decorated for fifty years. It is my only decoration."

The Countess smiled through tears. Then—

"Go," she said reverently—tenderly. "You could not have a higher."

He arrived at the Palace. His quick eyes took in all its magnificence and transmitted vivid impressions to his open mind. It was more superb than anything he had ever seen before—rich with a splendour that he felt should only be lavished upon a House of God. It was magnificent—this palace of an unhappy line of Kings.

"The guards, the gilded chambers!" he exclaims in his diary—and stops there.

Through many rich corridors and between stately functionaries he passed to reach the audience-room, entering this alone.

He found the Emperor there—a stately old man with light brown hair silvering, with a mouth and beard like the men of the House of Hapsburg and with indescribably sad eyes. The figure of the man fixed then on Father Lacombe's sensitive mind so excited his sympathies that in speaking of it afterward his voice always gravened:

"The Countess told me he was a man of sorrows —I understood that when I saw him."

The little old Canadian priest, whose one decoration was his worn crucifix, bowed his silvered head and bent shoulders before the Emperor; then told him of his mission in seeking aid for his Ruthenian brethren, funds to build chapels and priests to minister in them to retain these people in their Ancient Faith. He answered the Hapsburg's questions about the welfare of his former subjects, about the Government and the Church hierarchy to which they were now allied.

But the splendour, the coldness and formality of the interview numbed the man of the Plains. The Countess had done well to prepare him.

Throughout the audience the Emperor remained standing; always grave and cold and courteous. The rich and original personality of the Canadian that had so charmed his Ministers was without interest to him. Had not most things lost their concern for him?

Their discourse never unbent to the charming causerie others enjoyed in contact with Father Lacombe. The Emperor was not seeking thrills of human interest: his Old Man of the Sea forbade that.

The conversation died of inanition: Father Lacombe bowed himself from the audience-chamber, struck to his soul with pity for the man within— glad in every fibre of his warm old heart that he was not the Emperor of Austria.

His last days on the continent were busily occupied. At the Neuf-Chateau, Luxembourg, he addressed a large assemblage; in Paris he bought a magic lantern with slides illustrating the Bible history and catechism. Numerous small commissions were performed for his brethren, and by the middle of October he arrived in London in the midst of a fog, which he describes as night at midday.

Here he was entertained by Lord Mountstephen; and the quondam pastor of St. Mary's, Calgary, with the ex-President of the C. P. R., smiled to recall the drama of their exchange of office that day by the Bow when both were younger. The Comte de Bassano and his wife brought their interesting old friend again to their home for their own and his enjoyment.

On October 29th he witnessed the arrival of the soldiers from Africa. A splendid procession he felt

it was, though he was not a little amused to find the
staid English "losing their heads on this occasion!"
But back of the glory, the drums, the bonfires and
acclamations, the eyes of the old man were wet with
pity at "the disorder of hell in the streets, and the
shame and sadness of the sight of drunken women
and their companions."

A pleasant note of invitation from Lady Aberdeen, whom he still addressed as *"ma grande
cousine"* or "my sister," brought him to meet the
former Governor-General and his wife at their town-
house on Grosvenor Street on October 27th.

With their customary sympathy this genial pair
heard the old man's plaints of his sadly-interrupted
Hermitage, and in half-jest—whole-earnest—offered
him the hospitality of their Scotch estate, where he
might find a little nook sufficiently retired from the
world to end his days in a manner quite *convenable*
and to his ideal.

But while his soul still inhabited his restless, energetic house of fire and clay he knew there could
be no place of abode for him but the wide West.

.   .   .   .

January, 1901, found him back at St. Mary's busy
with routine parochial duties and especial care for
the Metis who hung about the poorer quarters of
the town.

"Me voila encore lancè dans une foule d'affaires!"

he writes on the 21st to Bishop Legal, and one catches in this a note of triumph that he is still capable of being a man of affairs. All is not a bed of roses for him, however: alcoholism and its consequences have brought too many of his Metis to the town-gaol and into evil ways generally.

"Pauvre Metis!" he writes in the same letter. "How it hurts me to see them so demoralized. . . . But I will move heaven and earth to redeem them."

In another letter this month there is a quaint flavour of the old days of toil and hardships he had known—of the log huts and earthen floors and parchment windows. . . . He complains that a new and energetic Curé of one town parish is painting the exterior of his outbuildings!

His old heart is indignant at the extravagance, when the diocese has so many poor missions where men need even the necessaries of life. Father Lacombe was still only twenty years away from the mud-chinked hut at Macleod.

The diocesan strong-box gaped in emptiness; Father Lacombe in his anxieties turned again to good friends in the East. From one he received this reply:

"MONTREAL, 19th May, 1901.

"Dear Father Lacombe:

"I have been running about everywhere and have not until now had an opportunity to reply to your letters of the 19th and 26th April. I am sorry to learn that you are in debt.

I suppose it worries you because you are not used to it as I am. I am nearly always in debt. It is the creditors who should be unhappy, not you. However since you are not used to it, I send you a small cheque towards helping you out.   .   .   ."

With this charming note the genial President of the Canadian Pacific had enclosed a handsome cheque.

This spring Father Lacombe wrote to Bishop Grandin about Bishop Legal's desire that he should take charge of Macleod and a couple of outlying missions.—"The wishes of my Superiors have always been orders to me," the imperious old man writes —oblivious of how often he has dictated the wishes of his Superiors. He adds a slight grumble that just as he had felt himself "seated at my fireside— I find it necessary to make my bundle again."

He ends by accepting the responsibility, for indeed there is no other priest free to take it. But on May 27, again a wanderer from his fireside, Father Lacombe writes airily from New Westminster, pooh-poohing the idea of Archbishop Langevin that he must now be bound for Australia—seeking a new continent to conquer as a beggar for his beloved missions.

On his return to Calgary Father Lacombe decided to accept the invitation of his old friend, Archbishop Ireland, to attend the golden jubilee of the diocese of St. Paul. Father Lacombe had associations with St. Paul for more than fifty years: he had known

Bishop Loras and the gentle Ravoux. He had occupied the latter's coffin-bed and spent the first month of his priestly ministry there. He felt he must attend the Jubilee.

Meanwhile the financial affairs of the diocese, which had been going from bad to worse, had now reached a crisis of tenuity. Father Leduc, the diocesan bursar, investigating conditions, finds that with the best possible management all the means at their disposal for the next twelve months can only meet the needs of two.

Father Lacombe, becoming aware of this, concluded that nothing remained but for him to take up the unenviable role of beggar and go east with his hands outstretched again.

In August he is in Montreal with Father Therien, the supervisor of his Metis colony. He writes that he is preparing a grand campaign. Even if he comes as a beggar he does not intend to appear without the eclat he now craves more with each year that comes to burden him. Perhaps his failing vigour requires the eclat as a stimulant. He has at least begun to show his age very clearly in his shrinking muscles and tired steps. He no longer has the shoulders of an ox or the old unflagging energy.

The campaign opened with an appeal published in the French papers throughout Quebec. In this he recalled the fine unselfish part Quebec had played in the earliest days of the western missions. He quoted Pope Leo's words to himself the previous year,

when in an audience he deplored the diminution of
the mission-funds from France; and the Pope had
said—

"Let New France support these missions."

Finally Father Lacombe quoted his own stimulant
—the farewell words of his old protector in 1849:

"If God is with you, who can be against you?"

So again the old missionary had thrown his soul
into his work.   The immediate results of his appeal
were sufficiently gratifying, and he writes com-
placently to Bishop Legal:

"You will see in the newspapers of to-day my grand *coup*,
my appeal—*C'est serieux*. . . . Ex-Governor Royal has
just been here.   He declared to me that he had not believed
I could make a genuine *coup d'etat*.   Excuse his naïvete: but
it is the kind Saviour and your prayers that have given me
this strength and ability."

Like a capable generalissimo, he adapts himself to
modern and urban conditions in his campaign.   He
cannot attract or hold the attention of people here,
as he did on the Plains, by riding out around the
camps on a cayuse, holding aloft his Red Cross flag
and chanting the Indian crier's—*"Oyez!   Oyez!"*

Instead he selects a daily paper, which in return
for securing news of his work at first hand promises
to keep his campaign before the public in an efficient
manner.   It evidently was *La Presse,* for when his
work was half through he writes: *"Le Journal* is my
organ at present, as I have parted company with

La Presse. They had become too exacting, always wanting the *prime* of my news."

His force of two he soon found inadequate, and he urges Bishop Legal to join him. His work will be greatly strengthened by this relief corps, he states.—*"Allons, Monseigneur de Pogla!"* he entreats.

"C'est serieux; still it must be done," he writes later. "There must be no more flinching. But prepare yourself—it is a very hard trade." And therewith he assigns his Bishop to an assault upon the large cities, while he and Father Therien, and possibly Father Royer, sweep through the country.

In letter after letter he continues his persuasions, but fruitlessly. The coadjutor could work like a navvy at home; he could live half-nourished on the fare of his poorest Indian missions and cheerfully share his last dried meat with a starving Indian—but he could not easily make up his mind to beg; there were too many humiliations in the trade.

Father Lacombe sends him $650. It is his earliest harvest, and he hopes the sight of it will be an inducement to *"Monseigneur de Pogla."*

One Sunday he personally distributed his printed appeal to a congregation in church, and then writes —"Am I not audacious? But they pardon me because of my white hair"; and again—"Everywhere I am received *almost* like a Bishop, *in partibus infidelium.* It is fabulous."

By November 20th he and his assistants have transmitted $2000 to Father Leduc "to begin to fill up the Gulf of St. Albert."

In October Father Lacombe was joined by Bishop Legal, and he would have been happy then but for the miserable attacks of a Quebec journalist. The latter brought forward the charge that Father Lacombe and the other western missionaries administered their finances badly, and that the money being so laboriously collected from Quebec parishes would be wasted in useless works for undeserving half-breeds already beyond reclamation. He also questioned Father Lacombe's authority to beg.

The attacks upon Father Lacombe and his work only ceased after November 27, when Bishop Legal called in person upon the journalist and with other arguments presented him with Bishop Grandin's letter to the bishops of Quebec, stating that the collections made by Father Lacombe on his authority were to be appropriated to the general needs of St. Albert diocese.

To Bishop Grandin his old comrade wrote:

"Thank you again in behalf of us all for the beautiful letter, in which you defend us so fraternally against crooked minds like this — —. You tell me I must treat him gently. No. . . . I will not spare him, and I do this in the interest of our good cause. He is a creature who must necessarily be exposed. He is filled with pride and self-love, notwithstanding his fallacious pretext of being the defender of the Truth. Let him not attack me any more, this rascal. I am watching for him."

Which goes to show that the great-hearted *Datur-omnibus* could still cherish a very human resentment on occasions and deliver a deserved reprimand as energetically as ever an old chief of the Plains lashed with his scorn an insolent young brave.

Early in February, 1902, Bishop Legal was re-called to St. Albert by the serious illness of Bishop Grandin. On February 13th Father Lacombe wrote him:

"I take no recreation with my brethren. . . . Tell him if he still lives, my venerable friend and Bishop, how my heart is grieved because I am not with him. He knows how I cherish him and will cherish him to the end. But notwithstanding your invitations the greatest proof of my devotion will be to stay here, working for the good of the diocese of St. Albert. At least that is what I think in my heart of an old missionary.

"But—ah, my God, how sad I feel! Dear Bishop Grandin! Is he then going? . . . Tell him a farewell from me till I see him again, in the Fatherland. Embrace him for me, I pray you."

For a time then he was sadly confused and troubled by two letters which reached him from the two bishops. The younger man in well-meant kindness urges him to come and see his friend again before the end. The other, dictated by Bishop Grandin to his nephew, advises Father Lacombe not to leave his present mission—and the bishop sent a last adieu to his old comrade.

"Truly, between you—you tear my heart. . . ."

Father Lacombe writes; but out of the chaos comes the determination to match the sacrifice of his old friend. He writes:

"I do not believe I should go to St. Albert. I shall stay to the end." Again he writes: "The thought of my suffering friend, praying for me, comes to encourage me when I ascend a pulpit to beg."

He now sends $2000 more to Father Leduc, to be divided as follows: one-quarter for the Metis colony; one-quarter for the diocesan seminary and one-half for the needs of all missions throughout the diocese.

With Bishop Legal back in the west Father Lacombe finally had to "make the assault" upon the Ancient Capital himself. An impressionist letter picturing his first Sunday there is somewhat incoherent, but delightfully naïve:

"*Donc*, it was at the Basilica that the old Chief made his entree in the midst of a fine assemblage of clergy, students from the Great and Small Seminaries and the University. In the crowded congregation I noticed Sir Hector Langevin, M. de la Bruyere, and doubtless my friend [1] . . . was there."

"'*Petierunt panem et non erat qui frageret eis!*'

"'Dear friends of our young diocese of St. Albert, I come before you with the permission of your Archbishop and as the ambassador of my Bishops. I have been told that in your city you do not like long sermons: that if I wish to be agree-

---

[1] The Quebec Journal, from whose attacks he had suffered.

able and make a good collection, I must be brief. *C'est cela.*
I am going to be brief.'

"Everybody in the church smiled. It was with this first
blast that I opened fire in the old Basilica, the mother of
churches in New France—'To arms, my friends, open your
purses. Furnish ammunition to sustain us against the attacks of adversaries. If the feet of the evangelizers are
beautiful, *et cetera*—how beautiful are the hands of our benefactors, who place in ours the mite of the Propagation of
Faith, with the good wishes of our friends in Canada. . . .'

"They smiled no longer. They wept with emotion. Abbe
Marais said to me at dinner: 'You opened the cataracts of
the eyes and the heart.'

"Pardon, my Lords, this recital of the doings of your old
Chief—result, $434."

One day this spring there came to Bishop Legal
from his mendicant-friend an amusing outburst of
indignation over the seeming extravagances of the
newer generation of missionaries. The Bishop had
written him asking special assistance for one of these,
who had been assigned to a city parish and who felt
he should approximate eastern conditions in the upkeep of the rectory and church.

Father Lacombe is evidently of another way of
thinking:

". . . This dear Father . . .!" he writes to the
Bishop. "It is unbelievable there could be a being so short-
sighted. Listen—I am going to write him a letter. Imagine
—to go and buy an altar and put up a shed for his cow, when
we have still so much to pay on the church!'

"But no, I assure you, I shall not send him a cent.   How droll he is!   Now how will he collect enough to pay off this debt?   He is naïve and fool enough to believe that I should settle it.   The poor man!

"Truly, here is something to shock my Reverend Father Superior."

Yet when he had given expression to his feelings by raising small tempests like this—and the bishop or somebody would remind him that times had changed in the west; that mud-floored houses, dried meat menus and rough board altars must be considered out-of-date, at least in Edmonton, Calgary and Lethbridge, he would relent.   Then he would generously help the young priest engaged in making his poor parish buildings adequate.

His old territory of Alberta had already entered upon the remarkable period of development ushered in by the new century.   Motor-cars were beginning to disturb the quiet of the Indian trails along the Bow and the Old Man's River.   Elevators were everywhere rising on the level horizon.   The Age of Progress was insolently thrusting itself upon the perceptions of the old Chief of the foothills; but he yet blandly refused to recognize it.

XVII

WHILE the mendicant missionary made his way from parish to parish of Quebec his old comrade-in-arms was climbing the last stretch of the Trail, serenely waiting for the close of a life which many undemonstrative westerners have accounted exalted in its simple goodness and thought for Humanity.

He was nearing the gates of the Fatherland, but found the last steps of the trail very painful, as the worn-out diseased body clung to its spirit. When he could not conceal his agony from friends at his bedside he would smile and quote LeMaistre:

"If the warrior thanks the general who sends him to the assault, why should we not as well thank God who makes us suffer?"

As a young priest with a lifetime of achievement before him he had faced death bravely in that awful winter night on Great Slave Lake. He welcomed it now with smiles.

It was a solemnly beautiful drama of Death that was enacted in the bare sleeping-room of St. Albert's bishop. . . . The end came at sunrise on June 3rd, when as the sun rose, mysteriously overcoming the

mists and shadows of morning twilight, the priestly
soul passed on to a new ministry—went in from the
shadowy vestibule of Eternity to the incomparable
realities.

Those last three weeks of Bishop Grandin's life
diffused about St. Albert a new strange benediction,
inexpressibly touching to the men who came and went.
The secret of this perhaps was revealed in the
Bishop's sole remark to the students kneeling at his
bedside:

"My children, when one loves God dearly one has
no fear of death. To have loved and served God
well—behold that is all that remains to a man, when
the End comes!"

* * *

Whilst he had been vigorously pursuing the campaign for funds, Father Lacombe was not without
consolation from another quarter. As a result of his
visit to Austria, Father Zoldach, the secretary of the
Ruthenian Bishop of Stanislaus, had come to Canada
to investigate conditions.

On his return he sent out four Ruthenian priests
to Manitoba. This summer he informed Father
Lacombe that several missionaries would be sent to
Alberta.

Moreover his new collections were particularly
satisfactory. Before February 23, 1902 he had together with his aides amassed $12,754; while the Hon.

Rodolphe Forget had contributed in addition to this $5000 for a church in the Metis colony.

By the close of the campaign, which took place in October 1902 at St. Sauveur' in Quebec, Father Lacombe had poured $21,000 into the empty coffers of St. Albert.

He had begged, exhorted, prayed and wept— though these waves of emotion were the jest of his younger brethren—and this $21,000 was his satisfying harvest. Looking on the result he forgot all it had cost him.

Before the New Year of 1903 he was again established in Calgary, surveying the southern district thoroughly after his prolonged absence. He was not always pleased.

A critical, almost a carping disapprobation of the methods and manner of the newcomer is practically inevitable on the part of the old-timer, and has marked the early progress of every portion of the west. Our pioneer Oblate, human as any other old-timer, did not escape this, and while he was adjusting himself to new conditions his heart flamed up in apostolic zeal more than once because of the ways of the young priests fresh from seminaries of the east.

His particular grudge against them was one he held against all the pale-face newcomers—an indifference or lack of sympathy for the Metis, who still clung to the skirts of the towns. He was himself splendidly loyal to this sad remnant of a people; and the more pitiful their condition the more passionate an advocate he became—the more assidously he sought them out and gave of his charity, spiritual and material.

During this winter Father Louis Lebret, one of the old Guard, died at the Grey Nuns' hospital in Calgary after forty-four years of service in the west. Every day and many times a day before the end came his old friend trudged over from the Rectory, leaving aside his memoirs and Metis audiences to bring comfort to the dying soldier of Christ. When he died Father Lacombe's arms were about him.

In a letter to the Superior-General he writes:

"Father Lebret, wherever he passed, went his way doing good. . . . He was the type of the true priest, a man of God. . . . Three days before his death I gave him the Viaticum of the wayfarer into other worlds. . . . Seated in his arm-chair, retaining all the clearness of his intelligence . . . he received the last great Sacrament of the dying.

"Having anointed him I said to him: 'My brother and dear associate in these missions, show us how an Oblate should die.'

"He responded to all the prayers and having received the last indulgences it was then—after his thanksgiving for the Holy Viaticum received that morning—he begged us to take seats near him. He said to us:

" 'I have come to that solemn moment of life when I must take leave for another world. I have finished the course; and my God, I come to Thee: into Thy hands I commend my Spirit!'

" 'Father Lacombe, be my messenger to our Father-General,

whom I salute for the last time and from whom I ask pardon for my faults and failings. From you, my other Superiors, I ask forgiveness; and from you, my brothers in religion—I beg you to pardon me and pray for me.'

"Then taking up the Cross he had worn so long as an Oblate, with his rosary in his hands and his scapular on his breast, he renewed his vows. How beautiful it was to witness such a scene! How happy I was to be an old Oblate and a brother of this apostle of our missions!

" 'Go,' I said to him then, 'my dear brother, depart for the true Fatherland. Go and ask our God to give me such a death as this.'

"Yes, truly blessed are they who die in the Lord."

During this winter—1903—Father Lacombe's worries over the financial condition of his colony deepened. The outlook was not promising and it was not easy for even his robust heart to throw off such depression at seventy-seven. Most of his letters now are tinged with the growing fear of failure.

Writing on February 14th to Father Therien, the administrator of the colony, he confesses that he is "heartsick of this problem." Having expended the $5000 collected in Quebec for the Colony they are still $1100 in debt. Must they sell the cattle, close the school and tell the colony they can do no more for them? he asks pitifully.

"And people will say then:

" 'We spoke wisely in declaring Father Lacombe's plans were only Utopian.' And I, hanging my head, will have to say: *'Bonum est quia humiliasti me. . . .'* "

His troubles jaundiced his vision. He can think of little else. A letter of March 13th to Bishop Legal opens with the growl—"It is dog-cold here"; and it runs to an apologetic conclusion through several unrelieved pages of details about his troublesome colony.

But relief is approaching. A number of letters to Eastern friends have resulted in a fresh harvest for the master-beggar. The most important is probably one from Lord Mountstephen, enclosing a cheque for $2000:

"17 CARLETON HOUSE TERRACE, S. W., March 4th, 1903. "*My dear Father Lacombe:*

"I duly received your letter of 21st of January. I had not forgotten you and the old days of which you remind me. The photograph you gave me stands on my table and never out of my sight.

"I think your efforts to train the young half-breeds to industrial habits so that they may be able to gain their own living, is an excellent thing to do and a truly religious work. . . ."

As a result of this kindly communication and accompanying gift a letter written by Father Lacombe on March 19th, St. Joseph's Day, stands out in warm relief from all his other correspondence of this period. It glows with all his old bonhomie and enthusiasm. It is replete with the imagination of a child who still wanders in fairy-gardens—only that here the old priest's fancies play about his beloved advocate-saint

and image him wraith-like invading a London draw-
ing-room to befriend an old suppliant at Calgary.

Truly some of the conquerors of the West have
been "men with the hearts of Vikings and the simple
faith of a child."

> "CALGARY, March 19th,
> "Feast of St. Joseph.

" 'Sowing in tears we reap in joy.'

"Yesterday I went into our private chapel before the most
Holy Sacrament, with St. Joseph and St. Anthony of Padua
as witnesses, to pour out the excess of my heart. You know
that I weep easily and that the fountains of my eyes flow
often in abundance. *Tempus flendi et tempus ridendi!*

"Many times during my long life I have wept with grief,
in hardships, contradictions and embarrassments; as likewise
I have shed tears in moments of joy and satisfaction. *Voyez-
vous,* I have lachrymal fluid for all occasions.

"*Donc,* after this preamble, this is to say that yesterday—
St. Joseph's Eve,—this great saint accompanied by the Saint
of Padua brought me this cheque for $2,000, which he had
snatched from Lord Mountstephen in the city of London.

"To-day with my whole heart I am giving thanks to Heaven
and earth. . . ."

He then consigns the money to the Bishop to be
expended for the Metis colony, and he continues with
a return of his old optimism:

"It is for this undoubtedly that the Good Saviour prolongs
my days, to aid in the completion of this redemption which
appears impossible to all the world but ourselves. . . .

"P. S. I pray you, return to me this dear letter from my
noble friend, Mountstephen."

Early in April Father Lacombe, in reply to a laughing comment about his foot-loose wanderings, writes gaily to the Bishop:

"Will you tell the Fathers at St. Albert that I have been closed up here since last autumn and my feet 'do not burn' more than usual?   Band of humbugs that they are!"

Now the time arrives when he can prove to his scoffing friends his inclinations as a Hermit.   In April a vicarial council was held at St. Albert and it was there decided that Father Lacombe might now retire to his Hermitage.   He hailed the decision with joy, and arranged to leave Calgary on May 5th.

He had watched the log-mission grow to a prosperous parish.   He had helped to establish an excellent order of teaching-nuns—the Faithful Companions—and the Grey Nuns' Hospital.   He felt he had earned a release from further work in Calgary.

Years ago a gold watch had been presented to him by the Mayor in the name of the citizens of Calgary. Now complimentary addresses and tributes of respect were paid to the retiring rector in such numbers that he seems to have grown suddenly aware that this demonstrative affectionate Calgary might be a more desirable residence than he had imagined. . . . Still it was for him—*"Hourrah pour le Hermitage quand meme!"*

Many of his comrades had retired or were dead. He felt that at his age it was proper, pious and *convenable* that he too should go into retirement to prepare his mind for another world. So he went. What he did not reckon with was his own habit of being continually and ardently seized with ideas for the advancement of the missions, and the necessity of travelling to carry out his ideas.

On May 7th he writes the bishop from Pincher a letter full of content and gladness. He is at liberty again, and rejoices even in the use of his toy—the rubber stamp of the Hermitage—which has lain idle since it was dropped so unexpectedly a decade earlier to take his place at Ottawa as Archbishop Taché's lieutenant. He writes:

"My Lord and Venerated Friend:

"*Enfin! tandem!* at last! I have arrived at this dear Hermitage—the goal of my desires for a long time, as you know.

"Yesterday morning at six o'clock I went up the hill. I knelt there in the silence of the dawn at the feet of the statue of my dear St. Michael—*Quis ut Deus?*—to say my great *Te Deum.* I gave the *Benedicamus Domino* [1] to Father Blanchet and to dear Brother Ryan.

"You know this was a solemn moment for your old pioneer! I went up to the Altar in the pretty church, where the morning sun came in through those splendid windows dazzling me. And then in the organ was the voice of St. Michael revealing himself to welcome me . . . !"

He regrets the tumble-down condition of his old Hermitage, but declines the bishop's offer to have it repaired, as the building is not worth it. Not un-

[1] The morning salutation.

til they can pay the $3000 already owing here will he build a house, he says.

A fortnight later however finds him busy on plans for a new Hermitage, as "my good friend Pat Burns tells me to give him the bill." He had accepted the kind offer of Calgary's first millionaire gladly—as readily and as free of embarrassment as he would divest himself of his own possessions for a poorer man.

One would look now for a few months repose for the hermit in his Hermitage—a breathing-spell at least until his feet begin to burn again. . . . But Nature itself conspires to rout him out from the quiet of the foothills.

Shortly after his return the terrible disaster of the Frank slide occurred, and Father Lacombe immediately departed for Frank. The misery of others was intolerable to him, unless he could at once spend himself in bringing relief: which he did for several days in the desolate mining-district.

But he has been disturbed from his Hermitage, and once on the road with his modest bundles—from sheer force of habit he keeps there. He visits Calgary and Macleod; from the latter point he writes imploring the bishop to transmit a special pastoral letter to their poor friends the Metis who are only sinking lower and lower. The Metis are always "on his back"—and in his heart.

From this time, June 7th, his letters show a quick passage of the hermit from Macleod to Cranbrook to St. Eugene, Nelson and even New Westminster. Upon his return to the Hermitage he devotes a week to his annual retreat of prayer and meditation, and shortly after writes:

"So the dear Father Vegreville is dead. . . . Ha, the old ones are going! It is for this I made my retreat. One must be ready for all possibilities."

In September he made a trip down the Saskatchewan on a raft and later by democrat from Edmonton to his colony. *"Coute que coute,"* he writes the Bishop, he must not neglect his Metis. In December he visited several southern points as superintendent of the district of Calgary; but a letter from Lethbridge on Christmas begs the bishop to release him even from this in future. His request was granted.

His visit to St. Paul de Metis had not been reassuring. He finds he is obliged to pack his hermit's sack again and set out for the east to find new assistance for the colony. At St. Paul, where he was the guest of Archbishop Ireland and of James J. Hill, the latter slipped into the old priest's hand on leaving a cheque for $5000 to forward the work for his beloved Metis. In New York and Montreal Thomas Ryan and Sir Thomas Shaughnessy added still other thousands to his Metis funds, and the old man's mind grew easy again.

A trip to the Holy Land was now being planned for the old missionary by Archbishop Langevin. Outwardly he witheld his consent to the trip. For although his feet were "burning" for this new and fascinating voyage—was it altogether *convenable* for the hermit of seventy-eight who had so often proclaimed his retirement to prepare for Eternity?

Finally he consented, and set out for Europe with one eye fixed with desire on the Holy Land—and the other turned with apologetic regret to the deserted Hermitage and the blank pages of the unwritten memoirs.

XVIII

ACCOMPANIED by Archbishop Langevin and Father Corneiller of Ottawa, Father Lacombe sailed from New York late in April. His friends, hearing of his proposed tour, had subscribed the expenses of the journey—as he quite expected they would when he consented to go. Wild horses could not draw him from his fixed policy of spending nothing upon himself that could possibly be diverted to the western missions.

At Marseilles the Canadians joined a pilgrimage of French Catholics sailing for the Holy Land. During a series of lectures given on board the ship Archbishop Langevin suggested to the director that his venerable companion be asked to lecture upon the Indians and his experiences.

The evening of the lecture came, and the audience was astounded when *"le vieux Papa,"* as they had named the old priest from Canada, took his place before them. Why was he chosen among so many brilliant men to deliver a lecture?

The pilgrimage was made up of a highly cultured class of French laity and clergy, members of the old *noblesse* and some profound scholars.

The audience's speculation concerning the lecturer scarcely outlasted his introductory remarks. Then he revealed himself; the crisp dramatic sentences, the indescribably picturesque and individual French with its infusion of English and Cree, the vivid eyes of the old priest captured them. And soon he was in most perfect rapport with his audience. His magnetic personality reached out and drew them to him . . . before long he was playing on them as on a harp.

They were laughing with him at tales of John Rowand's day; weeping with him over the miseries of the abandoned squaw; thrilling at the battle of Three Ponds and the tribute of Sweet-Grass to Pope Pius IX in their winter-camp on the plains.

Up to this he had been an obscure old missionary: now, again as in Montreal and Ottawa in the nineties, he was a Lion; and while he had not chafed at his obscurity he received the new homage of his companions with naïve delight. Day by day his warm nature opened up in the sunshine of their appreciation, at once finely sympathetic and intellectual; he feasted them with stories of the plains-life; his facile humour and flashes of scorn revealed the fire of the man's spirit; his sense of the dramatic attuned to their own led them from noisy Indian-camps to the quiet Hermitage among the foothills.

He called himself the Old Chief, the old Indian—and the French pilgrims, alert even on a pilgrimage for the novel and picturesque, felt that they had come upon an *edition de luxe* of a frontier type.

His first lecture was such a success that Father

Lacombe was urged to give another. He chose his own subject this time and to the consternation of his Canadian companions, he talked upon the famous book of Abbe Loisy, then recently published.

He undertook valiantly to demolish the arguments of the book, and at the same time delivered a reprimand to those of a younger generation on board who could find anything to praise in it. . . . In a very few moments the old missionary was floundering shoulders-high in a stream of theological argument for which nothing in his active plains-life had prepared him.

He had played many roles in Canada, but he had never been regarded by his brethren as a scholar. Yet here he was in righteous indignation and picturesque dialect matching himself against Loisy and his subtleties—with a galaxy of French culture looking on!

It was to laugh, as the French phrase has it. But his audience was too keenly disappointed at missing his own matchless stories; in addition they were rapidly becoming bored . . . when Archbishop Langevin hazarded a suggestion to his old friend to talk Indians.

With an almost impatient submission and an explanation that "the bishop did not understand the necessity of probing this matter"—the old missionary paddled back out of the troubled waters of Modernism into the picturesque streams of Indian life. But his heart was battling Loisy and his tongue refused

its office. . . . The lecture shortly ended as a
failure.

From Jerusalem he writes on May 18th to Bishop
Legal:

"Jerusalem! Yes, Jerusalem—the Holy City—where we
arrived last night. . . . Is it possible that I, a poor old
Indian, am to-day in the country where our Saviour died?
Is it possible that this morning at three o'clock I offered the
Holy Sacrifice in the magnificent basilica of the Holy
Sepulchre on the tomb of the Great Arisen! It is a favour
which was spontaneously accorded to the old chief of the
Northwest. . . ."

His stay in the Holy Land was one long succession of spiritual delights, of which he says he never
could give adequate interpretation in his letters or
conversation.

While in Jerusalem his love of novelty brought him
into an amusing and embarrassing situation. One
day donning the gown and head-dress of a priest of
the Greek rite a rumour spread among the pilgrims
that the venerable Father Lacombe had adopted the
eastern rite in order to devote himself to his Ruthenian brethren in Canada. The garments were
merely a gift to him from the White Fathers, who had
persuaded him to try them on, and enjoying the
novelty of his latest role he had kept them on.

The old missionary only smiled mysteriously when
confronted with the rumour. Wearing his Greek
vestments to church that evening, however, he was

overwhelmed when the director of the pilgrimage called upon the congregation to pray for this devoted old Canadian priest who "notwithstanding his great years had adopted the rite of another branch of the Church—out of love for his Ruthenian brethren."

The congregation of priests and laity prayed fervently: the Archbishop and his embarrassed compatriot exchanged glances—teasing, amusement and astonishment in the one, and perplexity and mortification in the other. . . . Promptly on the conclusion of the service the old plainsman in his Greek attire hurried off to the hotel, studiously avoiding his new friends and their congratulations on his devotedness.

The Greek vestments did not again see the light of day on that journey.

On the return trip to Rome the captain of the *Etoile* gave a banquet on the anniversary of Father Lacombe's ordination, and the old missionary in an amusing after-dinner speech retrieved the failure of his address on the Abbe Loisy and Modernism.

At Rome he received a warm welcome from the new Pontiff, Pius X. They met first at a public audience where the Pope moved slowly between two lines of pilgrims speaking a kindly word of greeting to all. When he came to Father Lacombe he stopped, at Archbishop Langevin's instance, and the old missionary was introduced.

The two men, humble and good and great, looked into each other's eyes with mutual recognition of the fine soul of the other. It did not matter that their

positions were as wide apart as the color of their robes
—the snow white of the Pontiff, and somewhat rusty
black of the Missionary.

The heroic son of the French-Canadian habitant
knelt for the blessing of the great son of the Italian
peasant, and as he rose the Holy Father added smiling, "Well done—well done! *Ad Multos annos!"*

On June 27th, the Canadians left for London by
way of Vienna, where the Emperor again received
Father Lacombe. His Majesty was on the point
of departure from Vienna, and the audience had to
be very brief. When admitted the Archbishop spent
some minutes in an exchange of courtesies, affably
paying his respects to Austria's overlord, Father
Lacombe meanwhile chafing impatiently at the
loss of precious moments and the dimming chances
of a petition carefully framed for the Emperor's
ears.

He suddenly interrupted, with an impatient gesture
toward his Archbishop:

"But the time is short; and—*M'sieu l'Empereur*—
what we want is some money for those Ruthenian
missions we have in our country!"

The Emperor turned smiling to the old *"saint
audace"* assuring him of a gift; and as this was forwarded to him next day, Father Lacombe could
never be brought to see or regret his breach of
etiquette.

On the railway journey in Germany, some hours
out of Frankfort, Father Lacombe had the mis-

fortune to lose the cross that for fifty-five years he had worn on his person as a member of the Oblate Order. At Liege in Belgium he attended the General Chapter of his Order, and shortly afterward sailed for home.

By November he was again in his Hermitage. But he was summoned from it on the 15th of January, 1905, by a disaster so sudden and cruel that it required all the hope and strength and faith of his old heart to rally under it.

The big convent industrial school at the Metis colony, built by the alms of his friends and sheltering one hundred and twenty children, was burned to the ground the night before. Practically nothing was saved from the flames. One poor child was burned and the sisters, who had repeatedly risked their own lives in bringing the children out of the convent, had several narrow escapes.

Hurrying north he writes to Bishop Legal who was then in Montreal:

"I am en route to Edmonton to meet Father Therien. God's will be done, we say—but what are we going to do? The children will have to be dispersed—and the Sisters, where are they? My God, how sad it is! Again what are we going to do? The only resources I have—$1,500—are already lent for five years to these poor Sisters of Pincher Creek, or rather to their community. . . . I am nearly sure that you will want to send me to Ottawa. But I am not going there. If Father ——— (whose feet burn), and Father ——— wish to go, it is their affair. . . ."

He immediately wrote an impassioned appeal for
help in the form of an open letter and published it
in *La Patrie* of Montreal, which was owned by his
friend, the Hon. Mr. Tarte.

From somewhere he secured $100 which he for-
warded to Father Therien, the Superintendent of the
colony, to help him start a house for the Sisters.   He
feels unable to make a fresh campaign in the East
for funds: he is worsted—there is no light ahead.
He writes to the bishop:

"My Lord, I will not again take up my beggar's staff.
That is finished. If money does not come otherwise, our
work must fail."

And he adds a postscript:

"What will the Government do?   Will they withdraw from
their contract with our corporation?   At least I hope they
will leave to the half-breeds already established the right of
occupying their land and homesteads."

.   .   .   .

If it be true that one trouble mitigates another by
a process of counter-irritation, then Father Lacombe was fortunate on going to Ottawa in 1905, to
find new cause for worry. The Autonomy Bill,
providing for the creation of the new provinces of
Alberta and Saskatchewan, was then being discussed
in the Commons, and the clauses relative to school
matters had started an embittered discussion within
and outside the House. In their Bill the Government had yielded a tardy justice to the demands of

the Western Catholics and their brethren in the East, making provision for a system of Separate Schools in the new provinces.

Sir Wilfred Laurier, who had brought the Liberal party into power in 1896 by promises held out to the Catholic school party felt that this was an acceptable occasion to redeem his pledges to some extent, and in the war that waged then about the frail, handsome figure of the first Canadian of his day he showed to greater advantage than ever before.

Toward the end of March Father Lacombe returned to his Hermitage: then he passed the summer in parochial work at Pincher and Medicine Hat, for the mission-field was widening and was already beyond the number and force of the younger missionaries.

His work brought him again in contact with the half-breeds who lived around the towns so that in October when he made his way back to his Hermitage from the Hat and received disappointing news from his colony it is not surprising he should write this heartbroken letter to the one friend who with himself believed in the work for the Metis:

"Nobody to-day can understand my trouble, my grief, my disappointment—I have only God for witness of my devoted desire to save this population. I will go down into the grave with this sorrow in my heart repeating '*Bonum est quia humiliasti me.*' My poor Metis! I see them to-day in the prisons, demoralized, about the cities begging for the leavings of the whites to nourish them and clothe their nakedness.

And what is most sad is that, humiliated and debased by the whites, some do not venture to come to the divine services but remain drinking in their tents.

"I can only weep in secret over this deplorable state—not even before my brethren, who have no longer any sympathy for these disheartened Christians.   At least you, the first pastor, aid me to save these unfortunates."

The handwriting in his letters now noticeably increases in size and unevenness, even as the letters grow shorter.   All this betrays the fatigue of age.   His years are printing themselves still more plainly on his weakening form, but with his habit of eating little —scarcely more than one meal a day—he contrives to be always in fair health.

In January 1907, he made a brief visit to Edmonton and St. Albert district.   At Beaumont, a small French-Canadian settlement in which he had established the mission twelve years earlier he officiated one Sunday of his visit.   People flocked from all over the countryside to hear the *"fameux Père Lacombe,"* who said to them during his address:

"We are told that in the earliest days of the Church an old white-haired man, bent with age and particularly tried by the labors of a long and painful apostolate, being no longer able to walk by himself had himself carried by his disciples into the midst of an assemblage of the faithful and there he did not cease to repeat:

" 'My little children, love one another.'

"This old man was the apostle St. John.   *Eh, bien,*

to-day you have before you another old man. Having had the happiness of founding this good parish, he has wished to visit once more a place filled with memories for him, and to come to give you some advice which I am sure his white hairs will make you hear with respect: I will say to you nothing else than that which St. John said; like him I shall repeat to you,—'Love one another.' "

Even yet the old missionary could thrill his audiences when he chose; and he did so that night as he closed a lengthy address on the West with this clarion call—

"Advance the work of colonization! Do not rest idle in the shade. Do not go elsewhere to seek the benefits you have here and can enjoy with more advantages. The future is yours, if you will seize the present. Courage and tenacity—these form the secret of success!"

It was while he made this sojourn in the north that, meeting me, he renewed a request first made in 1904: would I not relieve him of the work upon his Memoirs? This time I agreed, arranging to spend some months near the Hermitage to secure his reminiscences.

By February 28th, which was his eightieth birthday the old Chief—as he was wont to call himself now—was in Montreal. Archbishop Bruchesi, placing the Palace at his disposal, suggested that he give a birthday banquet to his friends. Father Lacombe was charmed with the novel idea, deeply touched too at the "delicacy of thought and the courtesy of this dear Archbishop," and straightway issued numerous invitations.

In April he wrote his bishop with some *malice prepense* in the idea of turning the tables upon his teasing brethren:

"*Donc*, soon we shall commence the *fameux Memoirs*, but I have a new plan concerning them! It is very interesting for you and others of my friends to push me unceasingly to undertake this work which is far from making me smile.

"But will it not be permitted me for my part to ask all our Ancients to write their Memoirs also, uniting them with mine to make one entire book out of them? I propose this and ask you to have the following missionaries write their Memoirs:

"1st. Bishop Legal, who apart from his title and position has had a long experience among the Indians in the foundation of this diocese. This would make a fine complement to the Life of Bishop Grandin.

"2nd. The venerable Father Lestanc. How many things would this venerable missionary have to tell of his remembrances of whites and Indians, and his voyages with the half-breeds into the prairies!

"3rd. Dear Father Tissier—who could relate his sojourn at the Peace River and his work among us.

"4th. Dear Father Leduc—who has also reminiscences *en masse*. With his good memory, what interesting things would he not recall! It seems to me that he is one of Ours who has achievements and deeds to record.

"5th. The Rev. Father Grandin with his position of Vicar, would he not be counted among the Ancients? He had his

experiences also among the savages, half-breeds and whites.
Being the nephew of our first Bishop and a capable missionary, we should invite him to write his Memoirs.

"6th. The benign Père Doucet—is he not one of the most
ancient? Notwithstanding his humility and his reluctance to
talk, he should be compelled to write his Memoirs. How
many things could he not tell us about the Indians, Metis and
the rest? . . .

"*Donc*, My Lord, such is my new plan! It is very fine
for you to start me upon this job, but let each one take a
part in the work, which should be of especial interest to all
these Ancients."

Spending the most of the remainder of 1907 at
the Hermitage he writes solemnly on New Year's
eve to his bishop. The letter is that of an old man,
full of years and wisdom. He assumes again the
role of first Counsellor as in the days of Bishop Tache,
concluding the letter with a word of advice to the
bishop to give latitude to young priests, especially
when they possess a certain aptitude and capacity for
their duties.

"With politeness and charity," he says, "put the
old aside, for they will have enough good sense to
understand their position."

XIX

THE year 1908, which was mainly spent in his Hermitage, brought the old "Chief of the Foothills" to the parting of the Ways.

He was eighty-one. He had lived to see the last traces of the frontier regime lost in the progress of modern cities—to see old trails trod by himself and his *"fameux Alexis"* buried beneath asphalt. But up to this, in his colony of St. Paul, he had held himself staunchly identified with his now-humble friends —the Metis—in contradistinction to the "proud palefaces who overrun *our* lands."

He was now to witness the breaking of this last tie.

The superintendent of the colony had realized for some time that it was no longer possible to continue that settlement on the basis planned by Father Lacombe. Of those who had been brought there and surrounded with every advantage many had willed to turn their backs on the quiet country life, to drift again to the lights, the cheap pleasures and vice of the city purlieus they had known.

Several others had moved out of the colony to ordinary homesteads. Those who remained—about eighty families in all—were well-established on farms and on the way of making an independent live-

442

lihood.   Father Therien urged that the plan of community life should be broken, and the Metis put on the status of any other homesteader in the West.

In consideration of the money expended in that region by the Oblate order and their friends he suggested that a certain portion of land be deeded to the controlling syndicate, while the remainder should be thrown open to homesteaders in the usual way.

The plan immediately recommended itself to Bishop Legal and Archbishop Langevin, two members of the syndicate who had begun to consider this expensive philanthropic work something of a white elephant.   Father Lacombe was the last to be won to it, but he was confronted by the continually failing finances and his own enfeebled forces.

As cogent as either of these reasons was the indisputable fact that many of the Metis he had hoped to "redeem" would not submit to the redemption, when they found themselves confronted with the routine of farmwork.

On March 28th Father Lacombe wrote to Bishop Legal that if all the members of the syndicate favoured the plan and the Government consisted to it—"then I submit to it."   This was his renunciation of the one big undertaking of his life in which he felt he had not succeeded.

In the spring of 1909 the alteration of the Colony was effected by the Government, and St. Paul de Metis as a protected colony ceased to exist.

Father Lacombe, deprived of one scheme of benevolence, immediately sought another. He was now inspired to throw all his energies into a Plan, which had been in his mind in a vague way for years. . . . Very occasionally he had spoken of it, wistfully and timidly almost, as "my dream of an old missionary." He resolved to realize this now —and so provide a refuge for the orphans and homeless aged of Alberta.

Progress had made its own of the old hunting-ground of his Indians, and in its spectacular march the weak—as elsewhere—were thrust to the wall. Father Lacombe's heart called out to him to help these.

Everyone else in the West was intent upon the opportunities and necessities of development. Governments were absorbed in constructive legislation and public works. Young missionaries expended their energies in forming new missions for the in-pouring immigrants. Individuals were busy making fortunes or places for themselves.

They had no time to seek those in danger of falling by the way: this mission remained for the Man-of-the-Good-Heart.

As soon as Father Lacombe realized that this was to be his next undertaking his mind became a glowing smelting-pot of plans about the Home. There must be found money to build and maintain the institution, a competent staff to conduct the Home, a suitable site in some pretty country place, where the children could learn to work the land—and a stream by which the old people would have a pleasant seat under the trees to dream or pray their last days away.

Strangely enough, in view of his own busy old age and inability to be tranquil—Father Lacombe never lost his belief in the tranquil old age as the Ideal.

He now approached Mr. Burns of Calgary, and after a couple of interviews the delicious old diplomat came away the possessor of 200 acres of good farm-land with the stream and trees and in the exact locality he desired. Then he mapped out a progress through the province to beg again—more audacious, more imperious and more wheedling than ever, because he felt so little time remained to him.

Upon the initiation of His Excellency Lord Grey a celebration of Quebec's tercentenary had been arranged to take place during the following summer. Elaborate preparations were being carried out for a pageant of the Old Regime, and Father Lacombe as an historic figure, known from end to end of Quebec, was invited to take some part in the festivities.

He writes the bishop on June 15th:

"*Donc*, I am not going to Quebec. There are many other things more important for the old Chief of the Mountains than to go and bow myself before the crosses and mitres of the centenarians. Excuse me, I forget myself—bless me!"

The more important matters which occupy him are the plans for his Home—"*cette oeuvre ineffable*"—and the giving out of reminiscences for his memoirs.

His plan of campaign for the Home is not yet complete—but when it is, he dictates serenely to his ecclesiastical superior,

"You will publish a pastoral letter to announce our work."

It will be recalled that Father Lacombe was one of the founders of the Indian school system in Canada. A voluminous correspondence with the Indian Department, which remains in his possession, indicates to what a large extent the department was guided by him in its earliest administration of the schools.

He was naturally interested this year when a question arose concerning the need of improving the system. He was frank in his expression of opinion:

"With my experience of those schools on which so much thought and money has been expended I can only say that they have not been the success we hoped for. We taught some boys and girls who were bright as white children. . . . But that was only the beginning—the real problem came when they left school.

"To go back to their homes—not white, and not Indians any longer! Many were failures. . . . Oh, it is very sad to think about all that—when you remember all the love and work and sacrifice we put into these schools. . . .

"I am too old now. I am useless for that," the octogenarian continued with painful emphasis of his own failing powers. "But if I were a young man

again" and his voice rose to fresh strength as his indomitable spirit fired him—"*that* would be my mission
—just to make a success of our Indian schools."

In November he accompanied Bishop Legal to
Chicago, where thousands of laymen and ecclesiastical
dignitaries attended the first Catholic missionary
congress of the New World. Here he went his way
content in an obscurity overcast by the forms of thousands of young, eager men marshalling their forces
of organization.

Apart from the large issues discussed there were
numerous side-lights which caught the still-harvest-
ing eyes of the veteran and revealed him no non-
progressive. When the newer missionaries described
to him a chapel-car which was kept moving along
western railroads among settlers living in isolated
groups without churches—he told them of the chapel-
tent built by himself forty years before.

His host, a Chicago millionaire, took the veteran
for many rides in his motor car—once gliding along
miles of smooth boulevards at the rate of twenty-five
miles an hour. At the end the party found Father
Lacombe serenely exultant, his eyes afire with pleasure, his sturdy old-timer's spirit unquenched by the
lightnings of the New Age. They awaited surprised
comment from him; instead he remarked to his host
with a twinkling eye—

"Why don't you go more fast? This is not fast
enough for me!" . . .

Had not his dogs—shaggy Pappilon and his mates

—skimmed over the hard snow at a rate that took one's breath away? And would Papillon's master confess to surprise at the speed of a Chicago automobile?—Not so long as the heart of an old-timer burned in him.

Father Lacombe in the retirement of his Hermitage had now no part or interest in the political world, into which he had once been thrust so prominently. But his former intercourse had given him decided convictions, as indicated in a conversation this autumn:

"I have never belonged to any party. As a citizen and patriot I would always support the party which rules the country for the time. It is stupid to do otherwise.

"The people have voted: the majority has said—'This party shall govern the country.' Then it is my duty to help that party govern in the wisest way. The work of opposition is for the opposing party in the House. But even they should not stir up the people wrongfully.

"I consider it criminal for a member of the opposition who, when he believes a certain measure good for the country, votes against it because it was introduced by the Government and its passage may strengthen the governing party with the people. . . . Criminal! Stupid!

"Such men, politicians—to whatever party they belong—I would see them thrown down like that!" he said, with a vigorous gesture of his closed fist toward the floor.

"They have no conscience—no patriotism. I would excuse such conduct only in the unformed school-boy, who believes he must follow his 'gang' in everything they do.

"Why should I oppose the party that governs, as long as it is doing right? Stupid! That is a strange way to be a patriot. . . . But when they do wrong—then let everyone unite and turn them out!

"When Sir John was governing the country I did all I could to help him. When Laurier came I did what I could to help him. But one day I said to Laurier: 'If you went out of power to-morrow, I would support the next Government.' He only laughed and said: 'I believe you would.'"

The time was now ripe for his new campaign, and he blithely opened the New Year—1909—with a series of collections for the building-fund of the Home. Throughout Alberta he passed, until he had exhausted the generosity of his friends there—when he journeyed on to Eastern Canada and renewed his efforts.

At Quebec in August he attended with hundreds of other ecclesiastics the first Plenary Council of the Church held in Canada. Here as at Chicago it was the old missionary's part to look on at the energy and scholarly ability of younger brethren.

On his return west he accompanied the bishop to St. Albert, and was there the centre of a festival in celebration of the sixtieth anniversary of his ordination. Linked with this was the celebration of the fiftieth anniversary of the Grey Nuns' arrival in the diocese.   For two days the little Cathedral town was *en fête.*

Under the trees in the gardens of the Indian School sweet-faced nuns of many Orders and in varied garb moved gently, the guests of their pioneer sisters—the Grey Nuns.

But over the hill on the grounds of the rambling old wooden Palace, the scene was more vividly interesting, if less picturesque.   For the Old Guard of the Indian missions were there in force mingling with scores of younger Oblates.

They were of the men who had touched upon the first score of years Father Lacombe spent in the West. Some had held their splendid physique almost unimpaired.   Others were shrunken and stooped and transparently frail: one and all were modest, unassertive and light-hearted as school-boys.

There was Father Tissier, gentle and shrewd, who still dated the past from the year Father Lacombe blessed his isolation on the Peace by a fraternal visit: Father Leduc, capable, great-hearted and drolly humorous, bearing still with him the marks of the plague of 1870, and Father Blanchet who had shared the dangers of that period with him.

Father Grandin was there, with leonine head and masses of silver hair—now the Provincial head of his Order in Alberta: Father Doucet, the gentle and meek—"God's lamb" and the beloved of his sturdier brother, Father Lacombe.

Father Lestanc was there too—stooped and deaf, but alert and genial still, his tongue sharp as of old to turn wit or satire, and his spirit as ready as on the night he opposed Donald Smith in old Fort Garry; Father Legoff, linguist and author, and in 1885 a prisoner of Big Bear. Finally there was the bishop himself, who had elected as an Oblate to know exile from Old France and had shared the mud-chinked hut on the Blood reserve with Father Lacombe.

A banquet was given at which the governor of the province, members of the Government, prominent men of the district and old-timers were guests.

Father Lacombe made an after-dinner speech there, revealing such exquisite humour and depths of diplomacy with bursts of naïvete that his audience for more than half an hour hung on his words and punctuated his phrases with delighted laughter. It was a notable speech for a man of eighty-two.

Here and there in the crowds on the sunny lawns those days moved quietly a slim, erect young-old man who bore a striking resemblance to Father Lacombe. It was Gaspard Lacombe, the foot-loose wanderer, anchored at last. But while the priest of eighty-two was still an eager, high-spirited boy in heart the lay-man of three-score was tired and more than a little wistful.

At a soiree in the Hall dusky small boys clad as Indians enacted in fascinating pantomime set to music the battle of 1865, when Father Lacombe had interposed between the Blackfeet and Crees.   In another scene girls symbolically represented the twelve foundations laid by the old man who looked on with childlike delight at their skilful representation.

Finally there drifted out from the wings a fairy-like troop of children who crowned the veteran with flowers.   Then discrowning himself the old priest made his way slowly, heavily through the strewn flowers to the stage.   There he delicately turned the tide of feeling from himself to the three nuns who had so bravely ventured in to Ste. Anne's forest-mission fifty years before: devoted women who had passed to their reward while he still lingered as a link with the Past.   .   .   .

After the soiree the darkness of the night on the hill was radiantly troubled with showers and swords and balls of pyrotechnic fire: and here the festival ended.

A few days later Father Lacombe went to Edmonton to greet Lord Strathcona who was then on a tour of the West.

The two old friends met on the lawn at Government House, where smartly-frocked westerners were assembling for the reception to the High Commissioner.

The great empire-builder went forward to meet the little man in the black cassock—also an empire-builder in his way.

"Ha, my old friend!" said Father Lacombe with caressing notes, "I am glad—glad to see you."

Deep pleasure lit up the face of each, as though consciousness of a kinship—in which none of the new-comers shared—had suddenly transmuted their mutual esteem and liking into a glowing affection.

Strathcona had been thrown from his carriage a few days before in British Columbia and had his right arm in a sling. The injured member now caught the attention of the Man-of-the-Good-Heart and he put out a quick hand of sympathy, suddenly mindful of the other's age and the fatigues of his journey.

He spoke his fears: but Strathcona brushed them aside as laughingly as he would have done on their trip to St. Paul forty years earlier: and the old priest murmured his admiration:

"Ha, that is like you, always—you never would complain!"

The two pioneers now withdrew to a bench beneath the trees, oblivious of the assembling guests. As they sat together, Strathcona's hand in the warm clasp of Père Lacombe, the two old men studied one another covertly for the marks of the years.

They rallied each other on their youthfulness, these two white-haired veterans who would not grow older: and they laughed at Strathcona's assurance that they were still boys.

Then as memories rose like exhalations from the Past shutting off themselves and the years they had known from the gathering ranks in gala attire, they dropped into tender reminiscence of the old-times

—*le bon vieux temps*—for which they stood alone that day.

Presently the conversation was lifted from the Past—the live Present had pressing claims upon these boys of more than four-score; and when the gentle transition was complete it was the new Home—that dream of an old man—of which they talked.

Father Lacombe was making a plea for a "little souvenir" for the Home and the poor it would shelter; but it is doubtful if the other heeded his words greatly. This man of many dreams and vast possessions felt the greater urgency of an appeal that was wordless —the well-spent years, the radiant humanity of the man in the cassock.

They had each gone into the wilderness striplings with staff and scrip and the mind to do great things. The one man was now a peer of the realm and a man of immense wealth; the other had little more than his staff and scrip, but with them he was a prince of hearts and good works.

His lightly worded plea for aid was scarcely uttered before the assurance came—and with this little matter past the two picked up the threads of old memories until the hour for the reception.

They took leave of each other now. , A long warm handclasp—a long steady look of farewell: "Goodbye; God bless you!" from Father Lacombe, and a wistful question unspoken between the two! Then the old priest swiftly lifted his friend's hand to his lips; and was gone.

The "little souvenir" came shortly after from Strathcona. It was a cheque for $10,000.

In 1910, having collected $30,000 for his Home Father Lacombe ordered its construction at a cost of about twice that sum. He then spent the summer at Midnapore pottering delightedly about the building, watching it grow brick by brick; while the workmen grew pleasantly familiar with the inquisitive paternal old form stooping over his stick.

He lived nearby in a small frame-building as bare as the shack at Macleod in the eighties. Nothing of all the funds he had begged remained to him—nothing of all the gifts that had been showered upon him: for giving has been his especial weakness.

But the old man needed none of these. He was still rich in his own personality. The primal elements of joyousness, fearlessness and grit that sustained him in his prime were still with him: though frequently obscured with the small vanities and curiosities of a child, or fitful bursts of annoyance.

These last only waited upon a comprehending gleam in another's eyes to be dissolved into smiles— deliciously-knowing, self-accusing smiles that fluttered roguishly across the fine old face. No estimate of Father Lacombe is adequate that does not emphasize the charm of this delightful responsiveness and accompanying humour. Even at eighty-four no transition of another's thought was too quick or subtle for his Gallic intuition—unless he chose for diplomatic reasons most blandly to ignore it.

In October of 1910 Father Lacombe went to Edmonton to meet his friend, His Excellency Count Andreas Szeptickyi, primate of the Ruthenian Catholics, who was then touring the Ruthenian missions in the west.

On November 9th the Lacombe Home was officially opened at Midnapore by Bishop Legal. It was not for nothing that the failing forces of the old man had been rallied: that a master-brain and a master-hand had laid his world again under tribute. Because of it this last beneficent dream of Father Lacombe had been realized.

But the Home was practically without revenue, and his poor could not live on his sympathy alone. The old man had to bestir himself again. He explained his needs to his friend, Mr. Burns, and the institution was thereafter bounteously supplied with good meat.

He went to St. Albert and commandeered from the bishop's farm a carload of potatoes. He descended on Lethbridge and returned with a couple of carloads of coal from a friend's colleries. From another source came the lordly gift of lumber to erect large outbuildings, and two railways conspired with the generous donors in transporting these gifts. The officials were not afraid of creating a dangerous precedent: there could never be another Père Lacombe nor such another irresistible beggar in the cause of humanity.

Before six months had passed over two-score of persons were gathered there under the mantle of his charity and he was dwelling in the Home with them. He is now content. His feet no longer burn to go on long journeys; but incessantly active still he wanders about his habitation and its precincts— searching among his new proteges for a cause in which he may benevolently meddle.

It is here, he says, with the poor of Alberta— with *his* poor—that he shall close his eyes in the last sleep.

And it is here, in this House of Fatherly Love, that the tangled trails of the west, which beckoned to the stripling in 1849, meet and find their end.

XX

THE EXIT

On December 12, 1916, the Trail reached the Great Divide—and Albert Lacombe passed into Eternity.

But before the end came his immortal spirit was straining on its human leash. His feet burned to set out on the journey home to his Master; and more than once he voiced the protest of an eagle spirit pinioned in an outworn body.

"It's too long—too long," he said with some of his old high impatience to Père Grandin visiting him. . . . and another day he exclaimed to his friend, Père Hetu:

"I am not well—no, not well. But in four days it will all be over."

It was as he said. Within four days he was released; the old Chieftain had penetrated the mists that shroud the Great Divide and pitched his tent in the beckoning, uncharted meadows of the Land Beyond.

He had begun the highest adventure, the fateful journey back to his Creator through the Unknown. But he was superlatively well-equipped for it—with the spirit of a pioneer and crusader and the unquestioning faith of a child.

It was December 8th, the feast of Mary Immaculate, that marked the beginning of the end. Mary is the name-patroness of the Oblate Order, and no liege-lady had ever been served more loyally or by a knight more chivalrous.... Did she come herself to pronounce his "Nunc Dimittis?"....

At ten o'clock on the night of the 11th his nurse feeling the end near called to his bedside his aged comrade Père Blanchet and the Sisters of the Home —his "daughters in Christ," "his Princesses of Charity," his "Pearls of the world," as he was wont to call them. They watched and prayed with him to the end, which came three hours later.

He was not able to talk to them during that time, though he gave signs of recognition. There was one long serene lingering glance at each before he finally closed his eyes. Death came in with gentle feet. There was no agony, no effort in the transition. He went happily to sleep in the Lord.

On the night of the 13th his body lay in state in the Cathedral at Calgary on a catafalque before the altar. His stole, biretta and rosary lay on top of the casket.

After the requiem mass, celebrated by Père Grandin with Archbishop Legal and Bishop McNally assisting, a significant procession passed down the streets of Calgary. There were Indians and Metis and Oblate comrades of the dead. There were men whose lives had been spent in the service of the two great Companies of the early West.

There were Old-timers and new-comers, with his friend Governor Brett representing at once the State and the Old-timers, while the Premier, the Hon. Arthur Sifton, and his colleagues had appointed the Hon. Wilfrid Gariepy to represent the Province.

There was a guard of honor of the storied red-coated horsemen of the west, a detachment of the Royal Northwest Mounted Police under Major Fitz

Horrigan, the commander of the post. It was the last tribute of this splendid force to a pioneer who had before their day been the Rider of the Plains par excellence.

A special train, assigned by his friend, Lord Shaughnessy, and colleagues of the Canadian Pacific Railway, awaited the cortege at the railway station. As was fitting—the four great forces that laid the foundation of civilization in western Canada had met about the bier of the dead pioneer.

At Edmonton the body lay in state again in St. Joachim's Church on the hill above the old Fort and landing-place at which he entered on his western pastorate sixty-four years before.

Then from Edmonton through sun-drenched airs his funeral cortege moved slowly along the old Trail from the Fort to St. Albert—across *the Bridge*—the first on the Plains—his bridge which had so angered Governor Dallas with its mute defiance of the Company's policy of exclusion—up the hillside where his first grain was stacked, and in to the church he built where Alexandre Tache had planted his staff in the wilderness.

It was Père Leduc, one of the Ancients, who preached here the final oration—from St. Paul's text: "I have fought the good fight; I have finished the course; I have kept the faith...." And seated in the sanctuary were the thinning ranks of his comrades who had kept the faith with him....Legal, Tissier, Merer, Grandin, Blanchet, Therien, Van Tighen, Naessens, Lemarchand, Jan, Hetu....

His body—the venerable shell of a crusading spirit—was borne by six comrades to a vault beneath the high-altar, and laid there near the body of his friend,

Bishop Grandin. His spirit had already passed through finer ethers to more spacious spheres.

He had not burdened his friends with the reading of testaments or arrangements of business for him. He had followed literally the Master's advice to leave all and divide his goods with the poor. He had done more—he had divided with his poor all that he could induce others to give.

In the end he possessed nothing—but his own soul. But he had left his country richer, endowed with inspiring memories of him! As the *voyageur,* joyous, vivid, fearless, dramatic in instinct, gesture and story ....one to whom it was given, as Sir William Van Horne wrote him, "to kindle the love and reverence of everybody he met!" as the born priest of simple goodness and childlike faith, cherishing Humanity alike in its frailty and its strength.

Memories of him too as the Beggar, *"le saint audace,"* with hands of munificence; as the Man, without a selfish fibre in his body, before whose unbounded kindliness and compelling charm artificial barriers of class, pride and income melted like April snows, for he held these had no right to exist.

His steady insistence on the right of all men to justice and square dealing and the wherewithal of living was not based on modern theories of reform, but on the ancient teachings of Christ. He had no knowledge of up-to-date economics; they were for the generations that followed him. He had no hope of a universal remedy for the conditions of his poorer brethren which so distressed him.

The Metis Colony, his one big effort to eliminate poverty in a distinct group, had failed. He hated but did not fear poverty. Like Tolstoi he felt that if some men must be poor then for love of them he must share their poverty. But unlike Tolstoi, he was with it all as joyous a knight-errant of Life as the hero of any blithe medieval romance.

Perhaps because he was moulded out of the heart of nature, and like nature hated incompleteness he could not be idle while needs confronted him, while injustice clamored or weakness called to him. Consciously multiplying his forces and efforts here, drawing on every reserve in him—he did in his lifetime the work of many men.

There has been no greater individual force than his in the moulding and making of western Canada. There has been no man so loved by the Indians or so revered by the whites. His life was an apotheosis of personal service in a period when individualism was rampant, and money or high position the popular measure of success for man.

Here—then, he lives a beautiful and inspiring memory.

There—Beyond, renewed in force, joyously questing new Grails of self-immolation and service, still working with an eager force and a high faith that love and truth and justice must prevail....he is—in Heaven as in Quebec—*le saint audace.*

INDEX

A

Abbott, Sir John, 331.
Aberdeen, Lord, 326, 351, 372, 375, 406.
Aberdeen, Lady, 326, 351, 406.
Alexandria, 333.
Alexis, "the famous," becomes guide of Father Lacombe, 50, 98, 108, 113, 141, 146, 196, 264; death of, 267.
Algonquin, 44.
Andre, Father, 115, 127, 161, 163, 184.
Angus, R. B., 274, 276.
Anvers, 399.
Athabasca, River, 168, 181, 364, 377.
Athabasca Lake, 385.
Athabasca Landing, 380.
Austria, 397.
Autonomy Bill, 436.
Autun, 220.
Avoca, Vale of, 129.

B

Baker, I. G., and Company, 170, 265.
Baltimore, 317.
Banff, 319.
Bannock, 105.
Bassano, Comte de, 218, 405.
Battleford, 261, 286, 287.
Battle, River, 197.
Baudin, Father, 231.
Bear Hills, 305.
Beaver district, H. B. C., 47, 261.
Beaver River, 206.
Beaver Hills, 104.
Beaver Indians, 377.
Beaumont, 438.
Bedson, Gov., 309.
Belcourt, Rev. George, visits Montreal, 9; in Pembina mission, 21, 24.
Belgium, 376, 399.

Belly River, 196, 270.
Benton, Fort, 168, 170, 195.
Berthier, 37.
Bie, Abbé de, 376.
Big Bear, Chief, 296, 309.
Big House, the, 43, 47.
Bitter-root Valley, 105.
Blackfeet, the—trading at Edmonton, 59-61; epidemic in camps of, 70-72; call for Father Lacombe, 80, 89; threaten Edmonton House, 101, 105, 115, 176; revenge-party formed, 178; dying with smallpox, 185; starvation among, 243; downfall begins, 267.
Blackfeet chieftains tour East, 310.
Blackfoot Crossing, 270, 298, 301, 302.
Blais, Father, 319.
Blanchet, Father, 61, 315, 459, 460.
Blanchet, Rev. Father, 183, 450, 460.
Bloods, the, 59, 196, 266, 267, 303, 331.
Boer War, the, 398.
Bornheim, 376.
Bourgine, Father, 183.
Bourgeau, M., botanist, 74.
Bourassa, Father, 39, 46, 64.
Bourget, Bishop, 8, 16, 156.
Bow River, 107, 200, 262, 277.
Bowell, Sir Mackenzie, 356, 359, 360.
Brazeau, the interpreter, 101, 172.
Brest, 220.
Brett, Governor, 459.
Bridge, first in Alberta built by Father Lacombe, 87; at Calgary, obtained by Father Lacombe, 355; at Edmonton, also obtained by Father Lacombe, 355.
British North America Act, 339.
British possessions, the, 171.
British Columbia, 204.
Brittany, 221, 399.
Bruchesi, Archbishop, 439.

463

in Winnipeg, 231; pleads Indian
cause at Ottawa, 244; voyage to
Europe, delegate to General Chapter,
246; becomes chaplain of first
trans-continental, 249; returns to
Far West missions, 261; aids in
keeping peace during Rebellion,
298-307; begs in East for missions,
316; secures first Indian hospital,
331; engages in School Question,
338-342; conducts School-Question
campaign for Archbishop Taché,
345, 354, 359, 372; originates plan
of Metis colony, 351; illness, 374;
adviser to Indian Treaty Commission, 378-390; attempts his Memoirs,
394; opens last campaign of begging,
409; retires to Hermitage, 424;
voyage to Palestine, 429-435, re-
linquishes enterprise of Metis colony,
443; plan a Home for aged and
orphans, 444, 458-462.

Lacombe, Albert, Sr., 5.
Lacombe, Gaspard, 103, 128, 451.
Lacombe, Joseph, 6.
Lacombe, Mdme. Agathe, 6, 174, 271.
Lacombe, Christine, 174, 262.
Lacombe Home, its founder begins to
plan, 444; building of, 455; open-
ing of, 456.
Lac la Biche, 49, 62; transportation
by, 168, 174, 181.
Lac Ste. Anne, established, 61; de-
scribed by Lord Southesk, 75, 76.
Lac Rouge, 20.
Ladder, (Echelle), of Father La-
combe, 203.
Laflèche, Bishop, 318.
Laird, Hon. David, 380, 382, 383.
Langdon, 298.
Langevin, Archbishop, 352, 391, 429.
Langevin, Sir Hector, 227, 228, 296,
414.
Larivière, Hon. A. C., 352, 354.
L'Assomption College, 8.
L'Assomption, 174, 271, 343.
Laurier, Sir Wilfrid, 360; corresponds
with Father Lacombe on school-
question, 361-362, 364, 370, 449.
Lebret, Rev. Louis, 420, 421.

Leduc, Father, arrives in West, 137,
163, 183, 319, 440, 450, 460.
Ledochowski, Cardinal, 399.
Lefloch, Father, 115.
Legoff, Rev. Father, 163, 451.
Legal, Bishop, 269; meets Father La-
combe, 306, 319, 323, 330; co-
adjutor bishop of St. Albert, 373;
aids Father Lacombe, 411, 447, 459,
460.
Lemarchand, 460.
Leopoli, 401.
Lesser Slave Lake, 66, 181, 381, 384.
Lestanc, Rev. Father, 440, 451.
Letaille, M., 216, 247.
Lethbridge, 319.
Le Verandrye, 2.
L'Heureux, Jean, 245, 287, 311.
Liège, 435.
Lilloet, 324.
Little Pine, 100.
Little Slave River, 66.
Livingstone, Sam, 128-129.
Loisy, Abbé, 431.
London, 217, 274.
Longue Point Asylum, 230.
Lorne, Marquis of, 257.
Lorraine, Bishop, 318.
Loras, Bishop, 17, 409.
Louisville, 263.
Lowell, 232.
Luxembourg, 405.
Luxton, W. F., 235, 237.

M

Macdonald, Donald, 180.
Macdonald, Joseph, 99.
MacDonnell, Captain, 321.
Macdonald, Sir John, conference with
Taché, 227-228; on Indian Schools,
286; quotes Father Lacombe, 299,
301, 340.
MacKenna, J. A. J., 380.
Mackenzie, Sir Alex., 388.
Mackenzie, Murdo, 124-125.
Mackenzie District, 137.
Mackintosh, Governor, 346.
Macleod, Fort, 266-268.
Macleod, 320, 336.

Warwick Bros. & Rutter, Limited
Printers and Bookbinders
Toronto

CPSIA information can be obtained at www.ICGtesting.com
Printed in the USA
239309LV00003B/132/A